Caring for Your Children

A Practical Guide

Martin Herbert

Basil Blackwell

© Martin Herbert 1985

First published 1985
Reprinted 1985

Basil Blackwell Ltd
108 Cowley Road, Oxford OX4 1JF, UK

Basil Blackwell Inc.
432 Park Avenue South, Suite 1505,
New York, NY 10016, USA

British Library Cataloguing in Publication Data

Herbert, Martin
    Caring for Your Children.
    1. Child rearing   2. Child psychology
    I. Title
    649'.1'019   HQ772
    ISBN 0-631-13824-2
    ISBN 0-631-14426-9 Pbk

Library of Congress Cataloging in Publication Data

Herbert, Martin.
    Caring for Your Children.
    Bibliography: p.
    Includes index.
    1. Child development.   2. Children — Conduct of life.
    I. Title.
    HQ772.H446   1985   649'.1   85—3887
    ISBN 0-631-13824-2
    ISBN 0-631-14426-9 (pbk.)

Typeset by Pioneer, East Sussex
Printed in Great Britain by Billing & Sons Ltd, Worcester

Contents

Introduction

Parents (and teachers) observe the development of the children in their care with a mixture of pleasure and bewilderment. Development, one is led to believe, is a progressive series of orderly, coherent changes, leading the child toward the goal of maturity. Well, that may be the grand design, but as many long-suffering parents and teachers know to their cost, their children's progress through life is often disorderly and incoherent, and the changes (when change is not being resisted) are not always in the direction of maturity! When this happens, such reactions are quite likely to be labelled as 'problems' and sometimes even thought of as abnormal.

This book, therefore, is about the development of children — from birth to the pre-adolescent years. It aims to provide parents and others with an understanding of the way children learn about life, and of the everyday (and more serious) difficulties they face as they grow up. Understanding sounds a rather passive intellectual enterprise; in these pages it is thought of as a more active endeavour involving the care-giver in the observation, recording and analysis of the problems — big and small — experienced by the child.

Many people complain that there are countless books available which suggest ways of understanding children, but they tend not to offer practical advice about what actually to *do* to remedy, or better still, prevent their problems. Or, if they do provide answers, they are couched in such general terms, that precise action is not possible. In an attempt to meet this criticism I have written a pragmatic 'nuts and bolts' sort of book, with suggestions about long-term strategies (guidelines on child-rearing) and also about the kind of tactics which might change worrying and unsatisfactory situations. The tactics are *not* based (in the main) upon prescriptions or general formulae, but upon the care-giver's own individual analysis of a child's behaviour and his or her particular circumstances. An attempt is made throughout to take account of the child's point of view!

I call this a 'problem-solving' approach, and it is based upon social learning theory. The perspective comes from my search through the psychological literature for helpful knowledge about child care (far too many references to detail here), but also from my many years of research and clinical practice in child and family guidance clinics, family and children's homes, and a wide range of ordinary and special schools.

I put forward the view that problem behaviour in children (sometimes called abnormal behaviour) is not very different from normal, ordinary behaviour in its development, its persistence and the ways in which it can be altered. Many problematic behaviours can be thought of as a consequence of a child's failure to learn successful ways of coping with his or her environment or as the result of applying inappropriate strategies for dealing with life. This is an optimistic book. It suggests that children can unlearn self-defeating behaviours; they can learn new, more advantageous ways of going about things; and that in all of this, parents and teachers are generally the best persons to help them achieve the necessary changes.

My aim has been to write primarily for parents, but also for practitioners, especially those in, or about to enter, professions such as teaching, school counselling, social work, medicine, nursing and health visiting, where they will inevitably come across children with problems. All parents are students — in the sense that they have to learn, usually in the school of hard knocks, about the ordinary and more extraordinary difficulties associated with childhood. But the book is written with a particular group of parents in mind — those who know that there are no simple answers to the complexities of human behaviour, and therefore do not expect easy solutions to the whys and wherefores of their children's problems.

Part I comprises a discussion of three important questions: the what, why and how of behaviour, problematic or otherwise. What is a problem behaviour? Why does problem behaviour occur? How, more precisely, did *my* child come to behave in *this* manner, and how can I do something about it?

Part II deals with children's early development and social training (socialization) and what can go wrong.

Part III concentrates on the older school-going child and some of the ordinary (e.g. sexual) difficulties and more unexpected problems (e.g. dyslexia) of this stage of development.

In Part IV, I offer some general advice about matters such as discipline, while providing a specific step-by-step programme for analysing and changing unwanted behaviour. The reservation that parents and professionals should bear in mind about all books and articles about children applies to this book: each child, every parent, and all families are unique, so no *generalized* advice can meet all cases, every circumstance, or a particular individual's special difficulty. There are *no* short-cuts to understanding children, and, despite the claims of some 'experts' no panaceas for dealing with behaviour problems — so this book has no cut-and-dried prescriptions for immediate application to problem youngsters. But, hopefully, it does offer a way of thinking about children's difficulties that should help readers in their task of rearing creative and contented children, or helping restricted and discontented ones.

PART I

What, why and how

The phrase 'Oh, she's a problem child!' is often heard as an exasperated complaint, explanation or excuse. It is worth remembering though, that children who have not, at some stage of their development, been the cause of quite serious concern to their parents (and, indeed, their teachers) belong to a very rare species. Problem children are, usually, normal children.

Teachers may take a somewhat more jaundiced view than the fond parents of the pupils passing through their hands. Nevertheless, the mixed blessings of pleasure and worry are also the lot of dedicated educators viewing their pupils' progress through school life. Their children — yes, perfectly normal youngsters — display year by year a bewildering variety of 'problems'. Teachers will probably have to cope with pupils who are shy or timid, those who show off and are aggressive, as well as others who are destructive and lie or steal.

Adults naturally become somewhat bemused when they are faced with a persistently difficult child whose behaviour they fail to understand. After all, she appears to be behaving in a manner that does not *seem* normal. But there lies the rub! What precisely is or is not normal? Children are frequently troubled and also troublesome; they (especially teenagers!) often act in ways that seem incomprehensible to their elders.

This book will address itself not only to some of the normal, everyday problems of run-of-the-mill children, but also the more serious problems (excluding extreme psychiatric disorders). We shall be asking what sort of signs or symptoms — telltale childish actions — should alert us to the presence of some abnormality that merits serious concern, be it at home or in the classroom. Are there particular parental attitudes and actions which will tend to enhance their child's movement toward maturity or, conversely, make their offspring more vulnerable to problem development? There is a complication: while parents and teachers are generally able to communicate, and thus share, their trials and tribulations, children are not always very good at expressing frustration, depression or uncertainty. They cannot always adopt an inward-looking, reflective approach to their problems; or they may not be adept at putting into words what ails them. But children do have a language that adults can learn to translate — the language of their behaviour. It is these behavioural manifestations of their problems that we shall try to decode. Some of them may represent a cry for help — warning signs of an unhappy child; others indicate a self-defeating attempt to solve some life-problem. Children might be better off if they wore an L-plate; to remind us that they *are* learners! Many of the problems of childhood are caused by a failure to learn skills and means of resolving difficulties — bedwetting, aggression, reading problems are but a few examples.

We need to know how to draw a distinction between the various problems — normal and not-so-normal — which beset children; a knowledge of 'normal' development and the crises of day-to-day life, will be of value in this task.

The search for the specific and crucial conditions in children's cumulative experience with their family and school is an ancient one. Here is a couplet which contains an ironic comment on child care:

> Come listen now to the good old days when children
>   strange to tell,
> Were seen not heard, led a simple life, in short,
>   were brought up well.

This is not, as might be thought, a present-day grand-mother bemoaning the passing of Victorian child-rearing practices. The lines are from Aristophanes, and date back to the fifth century BC. Mind you, this *is* a relatively contemporary statement. An inscription discovered and attributed to an Egyptian priest has him complaining — some 6,000 years ago — that 'our earth is degenerate; children no longer obey their parents.' Nothing much changes!

In part, the modern scientific enquiry into childhood arises out of a conviction about the powerful influence and the 'long reach' of early experience; a belief that good care and training of children during the impression-able years of life will function as a kind of vaccination — inoculating them against the future problems of ado-lescence and adulthood. As such, it has all the pathos of the researches of those early alchemists, seeking a formula to transform base metal into pure gold.

Fortunately, there is enough information available to formulate *general* guidelines (or strategies) to facilitate children's development. These can help parents to develop a deeper awareness of their child's needs, of the way in which their own attitudes and actions influence her well-being. This is the long view. But parents live in the here-and-now. They are certainly concerned about their child's future and how to do their best for her, but they also want to know how to manage her behaviour at *this* moment, and from day to day. Psychologists have developed well-tried methods for training youngsters in new skills and for bringing about change in unwanted behaviour.

In applying this knowledge to some child's puzzling and apparently self-defeating pattern of behaviour, we shall ask the following question: 'What problem is she trying to solve when she behaves in this manner?' Children are invariably trying to *solve* a problem rather than be one! Their 'solutions' are often misguided and crude because their conception of the problem is faulty or their skills leave much to be desired. The trick is to look sympathetically and empathetically at what the particular child is trying to do. Try to see things from *her* point of view.

This approach should help hard-pressed parents and teachers, and other professional workers, to develop a better understanding of the meaning of behaviour, and to devise constructive strategies for dealing with it. When we wish to understand something, we ask the questions: what, why and how? These are the questions which I shall deal with first.

1

What is problem behaviour?

The importance of being able to *understand* a child's behaviour will be apparent from this fragment of conversation overheard on a bus:

> . . . Oh dear yes! Poor Mrs Fletcher, she is so worried! You know why she's upset, don't you? She has a real problem on her hands. She doesn't know what's got into Kate; she says she just doesn't understand her any more. She says she never knows what she's going to be like from one day to the next. Sometimes she's as good as gold, then she's a little devil . . . and there's no rhyme or reason. No! And it's not only Mrs Fletcher you know . . . even the teachers at school can't do anything with the child; she just won't listen.

If we try to unravel the meaning in this neighbourly gossip we are able to perceive several of the most common elements which appear in a layman's 'diagnosis' of problematic behaviour. The label 'problem child' is most readily attached to a youngster whose actions are puzzling, if not unintelligible ('she doesn't understand her any more'); whose acts are unpredictable and inconsistent ('she never knows what she's going to be like from one day to the next'); or notably when her acts are uncontrollable ('even the teachers at school can't do anything with the child'). In the popular view of normality, behaviour should be understandable, consistent and controlled; in other words, it should conform to certain limits of meaning, predictability and self-discipline. If it doesn't it is 'abnormal', and the child who manifests it is thought to be a misfit. Parents tend to get anxious if such patterns persist.

Let us look at one example of a worried mother, Mrs Harris, and her four-year-old son, Robert. These are her own words:

By the time his sister Ann was born, Robert had got used to being the king-pin in the family. He liked all the attention that illness brought him, enjoyed the privileges of being an only child, and he was beginning to learn the art of getting his own way in a sly manner. He was intensely jealous of the new baby. Feeding times with Ann were a nightmare with Robert taking advantage of my immobility to throw tantrums, be disobedient, and to be aggressive towards me and Ann. He couldn't bear her to be held close, and was so spiteful I daren't leave him alone with her even for a few seconds. He threw things into her cot, pulled, poked and scratched. Occasionally he tried to tip the cot over.

As time went by, Robert developed into a small despot. He developed a general aggression, a high degree of wilfulness, and various other unacceptable behaviours. He whined, clung like a limpet, was insecure and anxious, and incessantly disobedient. In fact, Robert's so-called 'problem' behaviours — insecurity and tantrums, disobedience, aggressiveness, and so on — are displayed by *most* children. Indeed, a list of complaints brought to the typical Child and Family Guidance Centre would include a series of annoying or worrying manifestations ranging from rebelliousness, temper tantrums, attention-seeking, sleep disturbances and bed-wetting to shyness, fearfulness, feelings of inferiority and reluctance or refusal to go to school.

when is a child a problem child?

There is no clear distinction between the characteristics of problem children and other children. The differences are all relative; there are *no* absolute symptoms of psychological maladjustment in children. There are no high temperatures as in infections, no spots as in measles, and no recourse to the laboratory tests or X-rays which are so helpful in making a definitive medical diagnosis.

We are not, in fact, dealing with disease as doctors understand it. Emotional or behaviour problems, signs of psychological maladjustment are, by and large, simply exaggerations of, deficiencies in, or handicapping combinations of behaviour patterns that are common to all children. Typical examples might be aggressiveness, shyness and the awkward combination of poor concentration and under-achievement. So-called 'abnormal' behaviour in children is not very different from normal behaviour in the way it develops, the reasons it persists and the manner in which it can eventually be changed. It seems more profitable to ask how a child develops behaviour in general, rather than to restrict the question to how he develops problem behaviour as such.

We have said that there is no clear distinction between 'problem' children and 'normal' children. Yet laymen and professionals tend to treat normality and abnormality as clear-cut and easily definable concepts. Some see them as mutually exclusive, representing opposites like black and white, clean and dirty. In this view, normal children are clearly marked off from other, allegedly abnormal children. The abnormal children are thought to deviate, in some general sense, from the normal children. But in fact, the problem child is not all 'problem'. She is simply a child with some handicapping problems.

problem behaviour

Minor variations of behavioural problems can be identified in most essentially 'well-adjusted' children. A majority of children have tantrums (to take an example) at one time or another. Some, however, display incessant and extreme explosions of temper. In other words, normality and abnormality are viewed as the extremes of a continuum; normality merges almost imperceptibly into abnormality.

There are, broadly speaking, three classes of problematic behaviour:

that is *excessive* (e.g. screaming, hitting). These kinds of behaviour are called 'behavioural excesses' or 'surplus' behaviours.

Behaviour|< that is *'normal'* or 'appropriate' of itself but occurs in restricted or inappropriate contexts (e.g. compliant behaviour to delinquent gang values but not pro-social family norms).

that is absent from, or *poorly represented,* in the child's behavioural repertoire (e.g. incontinence, poor social skills, low self-esteem). These kinds of behaviour are called 'behavioural deficits'.

This rather daunting term refers to the fact that behaviour is not usually manifested on a random basis; the probability of a specific action occurring varies according to circumstances in the surrounding environment. Thus a child who is troublesome may display his unacceptable behaviour in his home, his school classroom, his playground, or perhaps on the streets of his neighbourhood. Furthermore, there may be refinements of such specific situations in which the problem behaviour occurs. For example, the child with severe temper tantrums solely at home, may show them only at bedtime and at mealtimes. He may be quite co-operative and pleasant at other times of the day when he is at home.

situation specificity

The best way to predict how a child is going to behave tomorrow is to observe how he behaves in the same situation today! It helps, in understanding children, to ask: 'Does he do X or say Y with everyone?' No? 'Can I think of anyone — a granny, teacher, friend — in whose presence he does not do X or say Y?' One may be able to learn what it is they do, or insist on from the child, that he presents his 'better side' to them.

As there are no cast-iron criteria for diagnosing abnormal behaviour in childhood, we need to be very cautious about judging children. This means being aware that we have biases and prejudices arising from our own upbringing, personality and training, which may make us somewhat arbitrary in our judgements. One example of our 'blind spots' is shown in the tendency to equate normality with untroublesome behaviour. Thus, the quiet, withdrawn 'well-behaved' child with emotional problems is easily overlooked in the classroom, and sometimes in the home setting as well. Teachers have responsibilities to many children; they have to cope with group situations and disciplinary problems, so it is not surprising that surveys of teachers' attitudes toward childhood behaviour problems show that they are most concerned with behaviour that is aggressive, actions which disrupt school routines, or which generally reflect a lack of interest in school activities.

Problem behaviour tends to be very annoying, but this does not necessarily mean that all behaviours which annoy and create problems for parents are to be equated with maladjustment. Parents vary in what they can tolerate in the way of 'bad' behaviour. The eminent child psychiatrist, Leo Kanner, observed that 'the high annoyance threshold of many fond and fondly resourceful parents keeps away from clinics . . . a multitude of early breath-holders, nail-biters, nose-pickers and casual masturbators who, largely because of this kind of parental attitude, develop into reasonably happy and well-adjusted adults.' It has been found that the reason behind the referral of children to a clinic is as closely related to the reactions of their parents (that is, whether they are anxious, easily upset and lacking in ability to cope with children) as to whether they actually have a problem. Similarly, teachers with only a few years of experience tend to view undesirable acts as being more serious than do those teachers with ten or more years of experience.

Ultimately, the judgement of children's psychological well-being must be made in individual terms, taking into account their unique personality, their particular circumstances and all the opportunities, disappointments and stresses associated with them. We have to ascertain where a child stands on the developmental 'timetable', whether her progress and status — mental and physical — are appropriate to her age, retarded or advanced. This involves asking a series of questions:

1 Is the child's behaviour appropriate to her age, intelligence and social situation? And does it have consequences that are favourable for her emotional and social well-being and, indeed, those around her?
2 Is the environment making reasonable demands of the child?
3 Is the environment satisfying the crucial needs of the child — that is to say, the needs that are vital at her particular stage of development?

Parents and teachers may make excessive or conflicting demands on the youngsters in their care; unhappy parents, for example, can make children the emotional battleground upon which to wage marital warfare. Society uses the family to act as its main agent in the social training (socialization) of the child, and it is precisely here that the child is most vulnerable. Generally, the process of socializing the infant and producing an

independent and constructive member of the community
is carried out well. But occasionally the basic unit of the
community — the family — is itself, to a greater or
lesser degree, abnormal. Thus, if the child's behaviour is
abnormal (unusual) or troublesome, and the answer to
questions 2 and 3 is 'no', then there is still a problem —
but rather more of a 'problem situation' than 'problem
child' as such. I shall return to a more detailed discussion
of these matters in chapter 13.

2

Why does problem behaviour occur?

'Why is my child's behaviour causing me so much worry?'
Questions beginning with 'why' in child psychology are
temptingly easy to answer with snap judgements. After
all, almost everyone likes to think of themselves as child
psychologists, and despite disclaimers, as experts on
human nature. We have all been children, so we can
claim to know at least something of what childhood is
about. Furthermore, it is never difficult to find reasons
for human behaviour. If Sandra shows an extreme fear
of going out to play with other children, we can speculate
about what it is in her make-up or environment that is
causing her difficulties. Our interpretation of her
problems may be based upon what happened to ourselves
as youngsters (or to our children) in similar situations. It
may be formed from books or articles we have read, or
from personal observations and theories about human
beings in general.

childhood   Adults have always entertained theories about the nature
of children and their development. One of the ancient
notions was called 'preformationism'; human tendencies
and attributes were thought to exist preformed at birth.
The 'homunculus' view of human development was an
elaboration of preformationism; this theory proposed
that the sperm contains a fully formed, miniature man or
woman, who simply develops, once conception has taken
place, in an incremental way, until maturity is reached.
This notion can be illustrated by contrasting the growth
of a butterfly with that of a leaf. Once a leaf has grown
from its origins as a seed, it never changes its basic shape
or organization while it grows larger; growth seems to
be continuous, with no transformations in form. By

contrast, the butterfly passes through several dramatically different forms — or stages — before it reaches its adult organization. The mature form of a maple leaf can be predicted easily from an early version, but it would be difficult to guess that the caterpillar and the butterfly are part of the life history of the same creature.

Psychologists have been concerned about which psychological systems grow continuously without marked transformations, and which pass through different stages in growing toward maturity. Jean Piaget, on the basis of his observations and questioning of his own and other children, described several successive stages in the development of cognitive/intellectual functions. He proposed that as a child grows older, his understanding of his environment changes qualitatively (in kind). His grasp of things does not depend merely on the cumulative effect of more and more experiences. The *nature* of his thinking changes; meanings alter. What a child tells himself about his experience — his understanding of it — influences his actions.

We shall see, when it comes to the child's understanding of issues like right and wrong, that these theories of development are not merely of academic interest.

the 'stories' we tell ourselves

We all carry in our minds what are called implicit personality theories, 'stories' we tell ourselves to explain — and anticipate — the way people behave. We construe the world in which we live, and our explanations are *causal* statements; someone acts the way she does because of X, Y or Z. The trouble is that there are so many causal stories available. Since we act on the basis of these stories, it makes life very complicated when we get hold of the wrong one.

One of those stories (figuratively speaking) is that the difficult youngster is like a small volcano 'erupting' unpredictably with bad behaviour. This 'story' implies that the eruption is caused by subterranean events — things going on within the child. This is why the term 'problem child' is an oversimplification. It makes it sound as though the problem belongs to the child alone. In fact it is misleading to consider a child's difficulties without also looking at his home and school circumstances, and the effect they have had on him. It may be the 'problem situation' which needs attention, rather than the 'problem child'. Problems arise from a child's interaction with other people, at home, at school and in the playground. He has to learn to cope with these various environments. Such adjustments are challenging and can often be the cause of distress.

the nature of problems

In chapter 1 I suggested that abnormal behaviour in children is similar to normal behaviour in the way it develops — following the same psychological laws and principles. Unfortunately — and it is the case with all forms of learning — the very processes which help the child adjust to life can, under certain circumstances, contribute to maladjustment. An immature child who learns by imitating an adult will not necessarily understand when it is undesirable (antisocial) rather than appropriate (pro-social) behaviour that is being modelled. The youngster who learns usefully on the basis of what are called 'conditioning' processes to avoid dangerous situations, can also learn in the same way (maladaptively) to avoid school or social gatherings. A parent may unwittingly reward (reinforce) immature behaviour by attending to it. And many problem behaviours can be seen as a consequence of the child's *failure to learn* social skills or other successful ways of coping with the demands of his environment. An example here might be the rude and utterly selfish child who is 'stuck' at an earlier infantile, self-centred stage of development.

use of psychology

If problems, by and large, are the result of learning the wrong strategies for dealing with life, parents and professionals alike can draw on psychology — the science of mental life and behaviour — for basic principles such as learning and development, in trying to prevent or remedy a child's problems. This approach should appeal to parents and teachers, since they are very much involved, day-to-day, with children who are learning as they develop — not only good habits, useful skills and information, but bad habits, fears and escapist fantasies. It is reassuring to realize that what has been learned can be unlearned; and what has not been learned may be capable of being taught.

It would be helpful to parents and teachers, if we could list factors X, Y and Z (for example inconsistent discipline, maternal rejection or being an only child) as invariable causes of emotional complaints A, B and C (say, disobedience, juvenile delinquency or shyness). Unfortunately, life is not that simple. This kind of analysis is too vague and too general to allow us to put right the particular problem, or to prevent problems from developing in the first place. Human actions — whether simple or elaborate, normal or abnormal — are brought about by *many* influences rather than a single factor.

prevention is better than cure

When considering problem behaviours, we have to bear in mind the irksome fact that not only can a particular environmental background or type of child-rearing philosophy produce a certain kind of emotional problem in one child and another kind of emotional problem in another child, but that it may result in no exceptional behaviour at all in a third youngster. The arrival of a new baby in the home, for example, may be the occasion of a variety of emotional upsets in the 'dethroned' older child, ranging from babyish behaviour such as clinging, lisping, and a return to bed-wetting, or to aggressive displays such as temper tantrums. The advent of a new baby in another home may be the cause of a quite different pattern of behaviour, such as an increase in the older child's helping behaviour and sense of responsibility.

In searching for causes of problem behaviours, researchers and theorists have focused on the early influences in children's lives, particularly during the first five or so years when they find most of their emotional and social sustenance within the bosom of the family. The young are thought to be particularly impressionable at this stage of life, learning their first lessons and enjoying (or suffering) so many new experiences. The saying 'as the twig is bent, so inclines the bough', expresses the notion of predisposition. It is thought that early childhood experiences are not ephemeral but determine later behaviour and attitudes. Not surprisingly (if often unjustly), one is still likely to hear the phrase; 'There are no problem children only problem parents.' It reflects the fact that parents and the family are the most

the search for causes

important representatives of society that the child encounters during his formative years. The mother and father have the task of transforming — by example and training — a totally dependent, self-centred infant into a more or less self-supporting, sophisticated and responsible member of the community. This 'civilizing' process is called *socialization.*

temperament: difficult babies Not all infants are as co-operative as they might be in this process of socialization. Parents are sometimes taken by surprise by the 'difficult' temperament of their newborn baby, and by his resistance to changes of routine and even the simplest training requirements.

This is what one mother told me about her baby:

> From the first day that I saw my adopted son Paul I realized that he was more lively than his sister Janis and wouldn't be content to be in a room by himself. He would scream; and I went through endless months wondering if I was feeding him incorrectly, whether he had a pain or was unhappy. Meanwhile, other problems were emerging. He would never sleep during the day like other babies, and eventually wouldn't sleep at night either; and when I went to cuddle him he would scream, bite or kick and this showed itself particularly at bathtime and changing time.

Certain temperamental attributes can seriously worsen relations between parents and children; and it is possible to demonstrate different styles of temperament in babies soon after birth. Some children have inborn characteristics — irregularity in biological functions (feeding, sleeping, passing motions), unadaptability, hypersensitivity, a tendency to withdraw in the face of new situations, powerful and frequent bad moods — which make them particularly difficult to rear. They are more prone than easier babies to develop behaviour problems later on.

The characteristic way in which a child behaves can arouse a mixture of emotions — pride, resentment, guilt, or helplessness — in parents. In the case of an active child, an energetic, active woman may welcome him — to her there is nothing 'excessive' in his behaviour. However, a quiet, relatively passive mother might find the same child exhausting and indeed unlovable. In many ways a child's behaviour can have almost as much effect on his parents' actions as their behaviour has on his. Influence is not a one-way street. Indeed, some parents get overwhelmed. They may alter, willy-nilly, the style in which they intended to bring up their child. The impact of the child's noisy unwillingness to adapt to changes in routine may be greatest on parents who have personal problems of their own. This is because they ascribe the difficult behaviour to their own feared 'inadequacies' or possibly interpret it as a rejection of themselves by the child.

The temperamental make-up of another group of children is such that it usually makes early care remarkably easy. They are mainly positive in mood, very regular, low or mild in the intensity of their reactions, rapidly adaptable and unusually positive in their approach to new situations. These children frequently enhance their mothers' sense of well-being and of being 'good' and effective parents. Mothers tend to characterize such infants as 'easy' babies. Even these easy children, who generally thrive on the widest variety of life situations and demands, can, under special circumstances, find themselves vulnerable to adverse influences. When they adapt to inconsistent and unpredictable parental demands, their easy adaptability, usually a temperamental asset, can become a liability. **easy babies**

We saw earlier that the child's response to his environment is more than a simple or passive reaction to his environment; he is *actively* engaged in reaching out to shape and influence his small world. Erik Erikson wrote that a family brings up a baby by being brought up by him. **personality**

Some children, as they grow older, are very extrovert and outgoing; they may differ widely, by nature, from introverted and inward-looking children. Other youngsters are highly individualistic in temperament and rebel against some of the standards that are imposed upon them. And we must not forget that they sometimes do this with justification; not all our standards and demands are reasonable ones. We tend to say behaviour is normal when it conforms to the behaviour of others. All is well if the child learns to conform to what is generally done.

It is rare, quantitatively speaking, for small boys to play with dolls and tea-sets rather than cars and guns. We encourage and train children to stick to what is perceived by society to be 'appropriate' actions for their gender.

Described baldly like this, normality suggests a very grey world where a child must be more or less indistinguishable from his peers, where to strive to be adjusted is to strive to be average. On the one hand, society claims to generate individuality, but at another level it fears the manifestations of individualism.

learning to be a social being

The words learning and training keep recurring; indeed, learning *is* the key word or concept in this book. The vast majority of human responses are learned responses; man and woman (whatever else they may be) are creatures of habit. This is not surprising, considering that our brains and nervous systems are so much more complicated and subtle than those of the species where instinctual behaviours are found in the most complex and stereotyped forms. What is important from our point of view is that the brain and nervous system determine not only *what* we learn, but how quickly and how efficiently we learn the lessons of life. The family too is important, training the child's mind. It has the first and primary responsibility for the infant. And what it achieves, as we saw earlier, is nothing less than the transformation of a biological organism into a social creature: a truly 'human' being. Nothing could be more fundamental than this to social life.

A child is protected and taught by the family. This teaching includes not only physical skills — among them, walking and feeding — but cultural skills too, from good manners to handicrafts. The patterns of co-operation and conflict which a child learns through family relationships teach him how to relate to groups outside the family, initially neighbours and schoolfriends, but later to wider groups. One of the most important cultural skills a child learns is language, the tool which is central to all further learning processes. Language enables us to develop and transmit values, norms and moral judgements. From his earliest years in the family, a child is shown what is right, praiseworthy, acceptable, and what is wrong, ridiculed or punished.

If learning is as important as is claimed here, parents will naturally wish to know whether *early learning,* when the infant is malleable and inexperienced, is different in any way — even more significant — than learning that takes place at a later stage of childhood. They may well have heard or read that there are 'critical' or 'sensitive' periods in a child's life, when he shows a heightened susceptibility to the effects of his environment and is therefore vulnerable to adverse experiences and learning situations. The young have always been said to be more easily influenced than their elders. What is the evidence for this?

There is, in fact, little reason to suppose that infant learning is acquired more easily than later learning. Nor is there any indication that it is better retained or more resistant to forgetting. In fact, experiments suggest that infants and young children are strikingly *inferior* to adults in many dimensions of learning.

There is, basically, an optimistic message for parents, teachers and therapists: studies do suggest that early learning is of importance for its foundational nature, but there is good reason to be sceptical about the rigidity of the structuring of character which is thought to occur during infancy. The fixity of the child's psychological attributes at a very tender age seems to have been exaggerated. Early learning experiences do not appear to set the child on an inevitable 'tramline route' for his later development. Of course one can trace certain continuities from early childhood to adulthood. An orientation toward achievement (to take one example) can be identified fairly early on and it tends to remain a feature of the child's progress toward maturity. (Remember, these are generalizations; they do not apply to every individual case, nor is there anything inevitable about such findings.)

There are also discontinuities between childhood and maturity — attributes in maturity which could not have been predicted from a knowledge of the young child. For normal children, personal characteristics and, indeed, most areas of behaviour, do not begin to crystallize or stabilize until the early school years are reached. And even then, only moderate correlations (associations) with adult behaviours emerge. The view, commonly held by workers in the field of mental health, that early

the child is father of the man. . . . or is he?

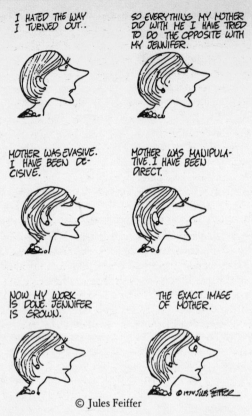

© Jules Feiffer

characteristics remain relatively unchanged seems to be true only of a specially vulnerable section of the population.

This must be reassuring to the mother who worries a great deal about 'mistakes' she has made in dealing with her child, or about severe emotional upsets the child has suffered. The important thing is to prevent these negative influences being repeated to a point at which their transitory ill-effects become chronic and ingrained.

I have mentioned already that there are great differences in the vulnerability of particular children to early adverse experiences, and in their resilience afterwards. These differences may be due to genetic factors, or to some kind of minimal brain injury. This brings us to the machinery of mind — that all-important control system, the brain.

This is the supreme instrument which gives men and women their flexibility and seemingly infinite capacity to learn. The basic elements of this system are thousands of millions of nerve cells (neurones) designed to sense, store and transmit information. The system attends selectively to what is crucial in the individual's ever-changing surroundings, regulating countless adjustments required in his interaction with the environment. It stores and integrates vast amounts of information, and exercises choice over how and when to react to particular situations.

the brain

Should there be any abnormalities, owing to hereditary influences or damage sustained before, at, or after birth, the individual would find himself in an extremely vulnerable position. Most of us, fortunately, can rely on a dependable service from our brains. But the effects of brain malfunctioning do not always show themselves in obviously handicapping problems like mental handicap, cerebral palsy, blindness or deafness. The original injury may be so slight that there are no neurological signs to make the disorder easily recognizable. Yet the insidious and cumulative effects of the malfunction, and the fact that it so often goes undetected in childhood, put a child suffering such a defect at a grave disadvantage. This is especially so when his ability to learn — the most crucial of his capacities — is adversely affected.

The brain is part of what is called the central nervous system. There is another bodily system — the autonomic nervous system — which plays a part in the child's emotional life. We will return to this later on. For the moment we need to look at the influence of socialization on the child's emotional well-being. Most theorists agree that an infant under the age of three months is incapable of 'true' emotion. This is because of the close links between social and emotional development. The sorts of emotion called delight, love, anger and jealousy, depend upon *social* awareness — a consciousness of self and of others. Social awareness is not present in the newborn child; it develops gradually out of the child's interactions with his family. Furthermore, it is a fragile plant — subject to distortions in its growth if certain psychological nutrients are absent or of the wrong type.

emotional development

Psychological problems are very much bound up with the child's social and emotional development. The child's favourable or unfavourable perception of himself — his self-image — and his perception of, and relationship with, other people, are important indications of the sort of adjustment he is making to life. So many of the difficulties with which a youngster has to cope are social ones — getting on with his brothers and sisters, or with other children of the same age, with teachers, and with his own parents, and, by no means least, getting on with himself. He needs to like himself, to rely on himself, and to know himself — understanding his own limitations and taking maximum advantage of his capabilities.

'there are no problem children . . .'

Parents and teachers play a large part in determining the child's self-image. Observe a child with a very poor opinion of himself and, more often than not, you will be able to find evidence of parents who resort to severe and continual criticism; and you will not see many instances of praise and encouragement. I referred earlier to the popular saying: 'there are no problem children, only problem parents.' This aphorism is far too simple and all-embracing in its claims, but nevertheless the insight it contains can be gleaned from some cases of people seen by my colleagues and myself (the names are imaginary).

Mrs Prince brought Leon to the clinic because of his timidity and 'clingingness'. The psychologist greeted Leon in the waiting room, offering him her hand and saying 'You come with me Leon, to the playroom. Your mum will wait here for you.' The boy came forward quite willingly. Next thing Mrs Prince jumped up and said in an agitated voice, 'Oh I don't think Leon will leave me, he gets so upset!' On hearing these words Leon burst into tears and clung on to his mother's hand.

Mrs Collins was convinced that speech therapy was making Annette worse. 'Whenever she comes out she goes berserk!' Observations of Annette at the speech therapy group showed her to be quite reasonably behaved. However, as soon as she saw her mother in the waiting room, she would misbehave. Mrs Collins responded to her grossly disruptive behaviour by making a fuss of her and sympathizing with her for 'all she'd been through'.

Mr and Mrs Webb were concerned that David was deceitful; they complained, too, of his shoplifting. The psychologist asked what it was he mainly took? 'Sweets and games' they answered. David made little attempt to conceal the stolen goods. When apprehended he would be scolded and told it was wrong to steal. Yet he continued, off and on, to repeat his misdemeanours. The psychologist asked David what happened to the sweets and games. He replied cheerfully: 'After tea me mum and dad and me sister sit down and play the games; and we eat the sweets.'

In all of these cases parents are unwittingly contributing to their child's difficulties. Let us ask the 'how' question: 'How does this come about?'

3

Learning to be a problem child

learning to
behave

How, precisely does a child come to acquire his
capabilities, and conversely, those actions which his
parents and teachers might call his 'incapabilities'. 'He's
incapable of listening to what I tell him!' 'Deborah is
incapable of telling the truth!' The vast majority of a
child's behaviours are learned and this includes the
problematic ones that adults find so reprehensible or
worrying. Children have to be taught how to behave
normally, that is, in a socially appropriate manner. To do
anything well demands good training; two persons are
involved: a learner and a teacher.

Parents, as teachers, are faced with an infant who has
to learn all about social life and who begins pretty well
from scratch. Generally speaking, they do not have the
'benefit' of a formal training in parenthood, although
they may have the enormous advantage of having had an
informal induction into parenthood by the experience
gained from watching and helping good parents of their
own. School teachers, of course, do receive a training —
hopefully a good one.

Fortunately we are not wholly dependent upon what
we are taught; being human, we have tremendous
capacity to use our intuition and commonsense and work
things out for ourselves. Without a training in child-
rearing, most parents bring up their offspring to be law-
abiding, social adults.

Robust and adaptable as children are, it is not necessary
for them to discover their way around their world entirely
by trial and error. We can save them a lot of time, and
circumvent some distressing mistakes, if we prove to be
— as parents — wise guides and mentors. To this end we
need first to know the basic principles of learning, as aids

to teaching children and bringing about change when necessary. It would also be useful to be familiar with some of the major principles and findings from the field of child development. This knowledge will indicate how (and when) to teach the child desirable behaviour and the means to help him 'unlearn' undesirable behaviour that he has picked up along the way. We also need to know how, once the desired behaviour shows itself in the child's repertoire, we can get him to maintain it. Good habits are so easily lost.

It must be emphasized that learning theory only tells us *how* to teach, not what to teach! Deciding what is desirable for your youngster is a question for your values as a citizen, individual and parent.

When experience leads to a relatively permanent modification of behaviour, attitude or knowledge, we say that learning has occurred. Memorizing a formula, recognizing a face, reading music and becoming fearful of doing maths or going to parties, are all examples of learning. We have to distinguish between *learning* an action or behaviour and actually *performing* it. Basically, as far as the child is concerned, there are three preliminary questions to be answered:

the nature of learning

1 Does he know *what* to do?
2 Does he know *how* to do it?
3 Does he know *when* to do it?

Now he may know the appropriate behaviour or skill and when to produce it, but still he does not perform it. So there are four more questions:

1 How can I get him to do what I want him to do?
2 Now that he does it, how can I encourage him to continue doing it?
3 How can I get him to stop doing what I don't want him to do?
4 Now that he has stopped doing it, how can I encourage him to desist from doing it?

What you have to remember is that behaviour can be strengthened and behaviour can be weakened. A behaviour will be strengthened (that is, it will be more likely to occur again) if it is followed by a reward. A

reward is anything that makes a child's actions worthwhile! A behaviour will be weakened (that is, it will be
less likely to occur again) if it is not followed by a reward.

**the ABC of
behaviour**

This is where the ABC of behaviour will prove useful.

A stands for *Antecedents* or what set the stage for (what led up
↓ to) the
B which stands for *Behaviour* (or what the child actually does);
↓ while
C refers to the *Consequences* (or what occurred immediately
after the behaviour).

What we have is a rough and ready rule of thumb:

Acceptable behaviour	+ reinforcement (reward)	= more acceptable behaviour
Acceptable behaviour	+ no reinforcement	= less acceptable behaviour
Unacceptable behaviour	+ reinforcement (a reward)	= more unacceptable behaviour
Unacceptable behaviour	+ no reinforcement	= less unacceptable behaviour

the C term

All these examples illustrate how B *depends* upon C;
consequences help to mould or shape behaviour. Parents
(and teachers) influence behaviour by manipulating the
consequences of behaviour. The technical term for this
learning principle is instrumental conditioning; the
person's action is instrumental in producing a favourable
outcome.

It seems paradoxical to begin with the C term of the
ABC equation, but, as you will see, instrumental
conditioning is crucial to learning; it is the form of
learning most essential to our understanding of the effects
of children's *own* behaviour on their learning and
subsequent actions.

It is nicely illustrated by an experiment which Dr
Yvonne Brackbill conducted on the smiling responses
(our B for Behaviour term) of eight three- and four-
month-old infants. She studied the babies for two or
three sessions a day over several days. After she had
measured how much smiling the babies normally
displayed, she carried out the conditioning sessions.

During these sessions she stood motionless and expressionless. As soon as the baby smiled, she smiled in return, began to speak softly and picked it up. (These rewarding actions were the positive 'reinforcement'.) The experimenter measured the frequency of smiling throughout. There was a steep increase in the frequency of smiles produced by the infants subjected to conditioning. By contrast, a baby who was put through the same sequence as the others (but without reinforcement) showed no increase in smiling. In other words C (attention) increased B (smiling). Even tiny infants can be conditioned or, in a sense, 'trained' to increase the frequency of their smiling.

By removing the rewards (that is, by no longer giving attention) their newly acquired behaviour (increased smiling) can also be reduced to their previous (pre-conditioning) level. This is called 'extinction', or 'extinguishing' behaviour. Don't be alarmed! They didn't stop smiling altogether; they simply returned to their former natural rate of smiling.

If the consequence of a behaviour is rewarding (that is, favourable) to a child, that behaviour is likely to increase in strength. For example, it may become more frequent! Put another way: If Pat does something, and as a result of his action something pleasant happens to him, then he is more likely to do the same thing in similar circumstances in the future. When psychologists refer to this pleasant outcome as the 'positive reinforcement' of behaviour, they have in mind several kinds of reinforcers: *tangible* rewards (e.g. sweets, treats, pocket money); *social* rewards (e.g. attention, a smile, a pat on the back, a word of encouragement); and *self-reinforcers* (e.g. the ones that come from within and which are non-tangible — self-praise, self-approval, a sense of pleasure). For instance, if you say 'Pat, that was nice of you to let Sally have a turn on your bike. I am very pleased with you', Pat is more likely to lend his bicycle again. (Note: we are dealing in probabilities not certainties.)

first principle: positive reinforcement

Here then, is a form of learning in which the frequency of a behaviour (which occurs quite spontaneously in the individual) is increased by following its appearance with a reward (that is, by reinforcing it). If it does not occur spontaneously, you will have to *prompt* it, and then reinforce it.

The whole issue of the nature and timing of reinforcement is complex. What we do know is that the time intervening between a response and its reinforcement is very important. The shorter the interval, the more the response is strengthened for future occasions. If the interval is too long, learning does not occur. It is of little use promising a young child a reward (for some good deed) which won't eventuate for a week; it is not likely to have much incentive or teaching value. Long deferred punishments, likewise, are ineffectual. Of course, older children are better able to understand delayed incentives. Symbolic rewards such as stars on a star chart, bridge the gap between action and a promised reward (say, a football match).

The reward should *follow* the desired action not precede it. This has been called Grandma's Rule: 'First you wash the dishes, then you play outside.' Not the other way around.

applications   Let us take an example of the unwitting reinforcement of disruptive behaviour in a four-year-old boy, James. He had been brought to a clinic because he was extremely difficult to manage. His mother told the staff that she was helpless in dealing with his frequent tantrums and disobedience. James often kicked objects or other people, removed or tore his clothing, called people rude names, annoyed his younger sister, made a variety of threats, hit himself and became very angry at the slightest frustration. He demanded attention almost constantly, and seldom co-operated with his mother. He was found, on examination, to be overactive and was thought to be possibly brain-damaged.

After observing the mother and child in the home, the psychologists noted that many of James's undesirable behaviours appeared to be maintained by attention from his mother. When the boy behaved objectionably, she would often try to explain why he should not act in such a way; or she would try to interest him in some new activity by offering toys or food. James was occasionally punished by having a misused toy or other object taken away but he was often able to persuade his mother to return the item almost immediately. He was also punished by being placed on a high chair and forced to remain there for short periods. However, such disciplinary measures were usually followed by tantrums which were quite effective in maintaining the mother's attention. What the clinicians are looking for in this type of problem is the relationship between the individual's own activity and the rewarding results it produces; those behaviours (in this case James's attention-seeking disruptive behaviour) that led to satisfying consequences tended to be repeated under similar circumstances.

I have often heard a mother say, as this one did: 'Carol must be allergic to me. The very moment she sees me she plays up, no matter how good she's been before with other people before I appeared on the scene.' Technically speaking, the mother's presence represents a discriminative stimulus for Carol's disruptive behaviour. A discriminative stimulus signals the availability of reinforcers — lots of lovely rewarding attention. But what happens when the consequences of actions are the opposite of satisfying? In other words, what are the practical applications of the principle of negative reinforcement? (I shall return to this issue later in the chapter.)

It has been found that there is a positive relationship between the number of times a child's actions are reinforced when learning a new repertoire, and the number of times he will perform that action during the 'extinction' phase (that is, when there is no more reinforcement (rewarding) of the actions. The greater the number of reinforcements that are given during the learning phase (in the Brackbill experiment, the amount of attention given), the greater is the number of responses made during the extinction phase (that is, the more unrewarded smiles there will be before the previous state of affairs — a normal rate of smiling — is restored). Here, then, is an important psychological principle: the strength of an association between a stimulus and a response is a function of the number of times that the association has been reinforced. Let us look at this in practical terms.

Suppose a child cries when he is made to go to bed, and his mother, who cannot bear to see his tears, gives in and lets him stay up late. After several similar scenes with the same outcome — mum giving in — she finally appreciates that she has been encouraging or reinforcing an undesirable habit. The situation now roughly parallels the end of the learning phase in our 'smiling baby' experiment; for the child has also discovered, of course, that crying is instrumental in obtaining his reward — staying up late. The mother decides to stand firm and prove herself impervious to his tears. She now makes the child go upstairs to bed no matter how long or heart-rendingly he cries. How long will it take to extinguish his crying habit? This will depend largely on how often the mother has previously let him have his own way. We can see from this example how 'bad habits' may be reinforced.

Of course, we can also reinforce 'good habits' when they are present, with social approval and encouragement. And by reinforcement training, we can instill those habits that are absent from the child's repertoire of behaviour.

© King Features

In day-to-day situations, it is on only the odd occasion that the mother says 'good boy' or smiles in approval when her child behaves appropriately or well. In fact, there is evidence that what is referred to as 'intermittent reinforcement' (the occasional reward) is a more potent method for *maintaining* the frequency of desirable behaviour than reinforcement presented for every 'correct' response made. The manufacturers of 'one-armed bandits' (fruit machines) have cleverly used this principle in the schedules of reinforcement programmed into the machines. You win just often enough to keep you at that machine.

We know that it can be very helpful to look at difficult behaviour by analysing very *precisely* the behaviour itself, what led up to it and what happened immediately before *and* after.

Some parents remember to reward (or in psychologist's jargon 'reinforce') desirable behaviour as below:

are you making her behaviour worthwhile?

Antecedents	Behaviour	Consequences
Marjorie was asked to put away her toys.	She did so.	Her mum gave her a big hug and said thank you.

Marjorie is likely to tidy up her toys when asked again.

Some parents persistently overlook or ignore their children's desirable actions:

Antecedents	Behaviour	Consequences
James asked Dennis, his brother, for a turn on his new bike.	Dennis got off and helped James on to the bike.	Nil! Mother made no comment. James rode off without a word of thanks.

It won't be surprising if Dennis doesn't share his things next time around.

Some parents unwittingly make undesirable behaviour worthwhile:

Antecedents	Behaviour	Consequences
David was told to leave the television off.	He kept putting it on.	It was eventually left on — to give people a bit of peace.
Anna was having breakfast.	She kept getting down from her place.	Mum followed her round with a bowl of cereal, feeding her with a spoonful whenever she could.

In both of these instances, the child's unacceptable actions were rewarded — by getting his or her own way. In other words, the child received positive reinforcement for behaving in an undesirable manner — which made it even more likely to occur again.

Some parents make undesirable behaviour unworthwhile:

Antecedents	Behaviour	Consequences
Johnnie wanted to go to the park; Dad said there wasn't time before tea.	Johnnie kicked and shouted, lay on the floor and screamed.	Dad ignored his tantrum; eventually Johnnie calmed down and began to play.

second
principle:
negative
reinforcement

Behaving in a manner that *avoids* an unpleasant outcome leads to the reinforcement of behaviour, thus making it more likely to recur in similar circumstances. If your child does something you do not like, such as losing her temper too easily, you may *increase* her ability to think first and hold her temper, by penalizing her consistently for failing to do so; in this way you are providing what is called 'negative reinforcement' for her efforts to 'keep her cool'. You may not have to apply the penalty if she believes your threat because of your record of keeping your word. For instance, if you say, 'Donna, if you do not think first, but lash out at your sister, I will not allow you to watch the television', then her resolve to think first and desist from hitting out will be strengthened.

Positive and negative reinforcement techniques give parents and teachers four training methods: reward training, privation training, escape training and avoidance training. In a sense you are saying the following:

Reward training:	'If you do the desirable thing, I will give you a reward.'
Privation training:	'If you don't do the desirable thing I will withdraw a reward.'
Escape training:	'If you do the desirable thing I will withdraw a penalty.'
Avoidance training:	'If you don't do the desirable thing I will present a penalty.'

applications

If a desired behaviour (and for that matter, an undesirable action) is not reinforced it is likely to reduce in frequency, and perhaps vanish altogether ('extinguish').

If your child does something you would like her to continue doing, for example, talking to you, asking questions, pointing things out to you, smiling and generally communicating with you, and you ignore her persistently, then this behaviour is likely to diminish and perhaps even disappear. She will be discouraged. (You will see how we make use of this principle for therapeutic purposes later on.)

If your child does something, and as a result of his action something unpleasant happens to him, he is less likely to do the same thing in the future (the undesired behaviour may be *decreased*). In practice, 'punishment', as we all know of this technique, is so complicated, that it needs a chapter to itself (chapter 17).

Many of the problems of childhood are not due to the child learning inappropriate responses, but are the consequence of the child's failure to learn the appropriate behaviour or skill. Here is an important difference in the nature of behaviour disturbances in children and adults. Many behaviour problems in children (especially in the early years) are associated with inadequate skills of behaviour control. These deficiencies are often connected with the activities of eating, sleeping, elimination, speaking and expressing aggression. In most instances the problem arises because the child has failed to develop an adequate way of responding — for example, in controlling anger (tantrums), in learning to control wetting (enuresis), and in learning to articulate speech smoothly (stammering). The over-aggressive child has failed to learn the socially desirable restraints over his hostile acts.

failure to learn

The reason why we look at A (Antecedents) after C, so to speak, is that it seems that the antecedents of a behaviour, its cues or triggers are of rather less central significance than its consequences. Nonetheless, these antecedents are very important, and if you think about and watch the settings of your child's behaviour, it may be that he or she behaves in a non-compliant way, or has a tantrum on some occasions but not others; that is, some situations seem to act as cues to him to behave in a particular way.

the 'A' term

People tend to tailor their behaviour to the particular places and the different persons, in, and with whom, they find themselves; and in the case of children, this chamelion capacity often leads to misunderstandings between home and school — each blaming the other, when (more often than not) they are difficult in the one setting but not the other. A child tends to look around him, consider the rules, the firmness of the adult, how other children behave, and what is expected of him. Then he adapts his behaviour accordingly. If your child displays awful behaviour with you, ask yourself: 'Is there anyone to whom she shows her better side?' If so, there may be something worth learning from him or her.

the
development
of stimulus
functions
Meaningful stimuli are vital because tney direct our behaviour. Or to put this another way, it is crucial for the individual's survival that he *learns* to respond appropriately to stimuli. For instance, we can rely on most car drivers to respond to the stimulus of a red traffic light by stopping. If we could not, chaos would ensue. We can depend on the vast majority of parents to respond to the stimulus of a crying child by caring for his needs; otherwise children would not survive.

Psychological laws often take the form of statements about the relationship between events called stimuli and responses. These are called stimulus-response (S-R) laws: 'Given stimulus Y one would expect response Z.' Or more economically: 'If Y then Z'. We can make use of these laws to make reasonable predictions about adult and child behaviour in given situations and conditions, and are thus in a position to suggest ways of changing behaviour that has gone wrong, as in the case of extreme fear. Many of the connections or associations between stimuli and responses are learned on the basis of conditioning processes. Children also learn — most particularly — by watching!

observational
learning
The child learns much of his social behaviour (and many other complex acts) by modelling himself on his observations of the significant people in his environment, imitating what they do and say. This form of learning, which is based on cognitive (intellectual) processes rather than training by means of external reinforcements, is called 'observational learning'. Very young children are restricted to instantaneous imitation, whereas delayed modelling of complex behaviour requires symbolic abilities that emerge in the second year of life.

do as I say,
not as I do!
The child's ability to imitate also has its negative aspects. It plays an important role in the acquisition of undesirable deviant behaviour. We often forget that children are just as influenced by their parents' behaviour as by what they actually say. The effects on children observing aggressive models have been demonstrated in a series of experiments. The 'aggressive models' (adults) exhibited unusual forms of physical and verbal hostility towards a large inflated plastic doll. In contrast, the 'non-aggressive models' sat very quietly, totally ignoring the doll and the

various instruments of aggression that had been placed in the room. The nursery-school children who had observed the aggressive models, displayed a great number of precisely imitated aggressive responses, which rarely occurred in the other ('control') group which observed non-aggressive models. In addition, the results indicated that models observed on film were as effective as real-life models in transmitting hostile patterns of behaviour.

The example given above is a very simple one, but even such apparently simple patterns of learning are difficult to analyse. Psychologists are not certain why some models have an almost irresistible influence over children while others are ignored. Deficiencies in imitation may be due to inadequate attention to the modelled activities (one thinks here of the hyperactive child); inadequate retention of the stimuli ('I keep forgetting, Dad'); motor inadequacies ('I'm all fingers and thumbs with the sewing needle, Mum'); or lack of motivation ('I don't see why I should!').

With this type of learning (and another which we will come to) we are less concerned with the *consequences* of behaviour, but more interested in the *antecedents* of behaviour, i.e. what goes before, or leads up to, the particular action. For example, a child might learn vicariously to fear a teacher because he has observed him treating another child harshly. All of this is not to deny the importance of the C term (consequences) in observational learning. A child's imitations — actual performance — of various socially-approved behaviours are given even greater impetus by praise and encouragement; in other words, they are reinforced by 'social' (or 'symbolic') rewards. He will also be more likely to imitate if he sees that the model's actions have rewarding or prestigious consequences. (Think of the many television characters, watched avidly by children, who achieve outcomes favourable to themselves by violent means!)

These symbolic rewards regulate behaviour. The child is likely to be willing to obey distasteful rules because he wishes to have his parents' approval or avoid their disapproval. Their words of approbation increase his self-esteem. And, in this way, he develops patterns of behaviour which conform to the social norm. Not all human behaviours require external reinforcements; children often learn to solve problems simply for the pleasure of solving them. Successful imitation may contain its own rewards. Many of our activities and strivings are in this sense, self-reinforcing.

applications

Modelling has been used successfully to teach masculine behaviours to a boy who was ceaselessly jeered at for his gender identity confusion — an effeminate style of walking, gesturing, sitting and so on. His misery evaporated as he acquired — by observational learning — more acceptable boyish mannerisms. Preschoolers have overcome their fear of dogs by watching a child pet, feed and play with a dog. Similar methods have helped children to master their terror of the dentist. Parents often model calm behaviour in the surgery, for the benefit of their offspring, even sitting in the dentist's chair to indicate its safety.

classical conditioning

There is another form of learning which occurs on the 'A' side of the ABC equation, in the main. Let us take a simple example. It would not be surprising if a dog responded to a slight pinprick applied to his leg by lifting and thus withdrawing his leg. The withdrawal of the leg is called a respondent — it is an example of an innate and involuntary behaviour (withdrawal) regularly elicited by a specific stimulus (pinprick). It would be surprising if he responded in the same way to the sound of a bell.

However, if an experimenter arranges that a dog regularly hears a bell, just prior to receiving a pinprick to his leg, the animal will (after several pairings of bell and pinprick) lift his leg to the bell alone! This is an example of classical conditioning. The conditioned response is formed when a stimulus (the bell), originally neutral with respect to a particular (and natural) response (lifting the leg), is paired a number of times with the stimulus eliciting that response (pinprick), so that the previously neutral stimulus itself (the bell) comes to elicit the response.

Now let us illustrate human conditioning with the example I mentioned earlier, of mothers who have the nerve-racking chore of taking a small child to the dentist. Over a number of such visits the child's behaviour and response to the situation may change very markedly. On the first visit the youngster (if he has not already been indoctrinated by an anxious mother or a worldly-wise brother) may sit quite calmly in the waiting-room and smile when introduced to the dentist. However, he cries when the first alarming drilling of his teeth takes place. On succeeding visits the child does not wait until the drill is presented before beginning to howl. On the second visit he may yell the moment he sees the dentist, and on successive occasions it may be enough just to see the building containing the consulting rooms for the tears and screams to begin.

At first, the sight of the dentist (visual stimulation) was more or less neutral in its effect on the child. The distressing (aversive) stimulus provided by the drill, on the other hand, elicited crying. After the sight of the dentist had been followed by the frightening drill stimulus one or more times, the formerly innocuous visual stimulus (the dentist) acquires the characteristics of the distressing stimulus, and the sight of him is enough to provoke tears.

Conditioning sometimes produces quite unexpected and unwelcome results. Some mothers use orange juice to help their offspring get rid of the taste of an unpleasant medicine. Not surprisingly the orange juice itself is liable to acquire (by association) the aversive properties of its 'fellow-traveller'. Adults are not immune to the influences of conditioning. The person who tends to munch sweets and biscuits while watching television is likely to find, after a few weeks, that he develops a craving for food within minutes of switching the set on, no matter how recent his last meal. In other words he has nurtured a minor compulsion, or, if you like, a thoroughly 'bad habit'.

Many of our attitudes, our tendencies to react positively or negatively to people, ideas, situations and objects, are acquired quite unconsciously on this basis. The mere thought of some event (like experiencing a dentist's drill) can produce an involuntary response (a shudder of horror). You may blush to think of some embarrassing incident which made you hot with shame long ago.

To help you gain confidence in dealing with difficulties which arise from faulty stimulus control, here is an example of the method used to stop a ten-year-old girl being untidy. The behaviour of the child was used to reinstate appropriate cues for her to attend to, so as to

some applications

learn tidy habits. Her mother complained to a psychologist that for two years her daughter had annoyed her by a habit of tossing her coat and hat on the floor as she entered the house. On what seemed like one hundred and one occasions the mother had insisted that the girl pick up the coat and hang it in its place. These irritating ways were changed only after the mother, on advice, began to insist not that the girl pick up the fallen garments from the floor, but that she put them on, return to the street, and re-enter the house, this time removing the coat and hanging it up properly. The principle at work then is that the child must be made to perform the required act while she is attending to the stimulus which is to control it. In the example, the mother had been getting the response out in the presence of the wrong stimuli. The stimuli which were meant to control the response were those present *immediately* after the child entered the house. What was going wrong was that the 'tidy' response was being repeatedly and merely evoked in the presence of a stimulus — essentially an inappropriate one — the mother saying 'Please pick up your coat.' There was a need for the cues to occur at a much earlier stage.

It is important to remember the role of the parent in faulty stimulus control. So often the problem results from a lack of proper communication between the adult and the child. It may be necessary for the parent to give more assertive, unambiguous verbal signals (e.g. commands). Some parents give their commands in the form of a weak question ('Darling, will you put your toys away for mummy?'), their eyes glazed with the expectation of the defeat that usually results. A parent (or teacher) may be ineffectual because he or she over-reacts to certain situations. A mother may feel depressed, hostile or anxious. Relaxation training could help her to remain calm and competent in these circumstances.

toilet training: bed-wetting The question of toilet training and the problem of enuresis (bed-wetting), mentioned earlier in the chapter, provide interesting examples of *conditioning* in the training and treatment of a potential childhood problem. At eighteen months of age most children are physically mature enough to hold their urine for between one and two hours without much leakage. Potty training might take only a few days if your child is ready. Remember there are large individual differences in this readiness! The association between voluntarily passing urine and sitting on the potty should be made relatively easily if you remember to pot your child regularly. In the first few weeks it is up to you to anticipate his need and suggest sitting on the potty. Keep the training 'low key' and praise success. Sixty per cent of children are dry by two and a half years.

A very high level of skill is needed before the bladder can be properly controlled during sleep. Some children find this a difficult skill to learn, just as some children find it difficult to learn to swim or to ride a bicycle. It is perhaps not surprising that some children do not learn bladder control as infants, or easily lose (especially when under stress) their ability to control the bladder at night. We should perhaps be surprised that so many do manage to learn such a complicated skill. It is likely that unpleasant experiences make the learning of bladder control more difficult.

The ability to stay dry at night usually occurs *after* learning to stay dry during the day. Nearly ninety per cent have that skill at three years of age. Some children do not begin to develop nighttime control until after their third birthday so there is no need to worry if your child is somewhat slow to achieve success. Whether a child has been wet all his life, or has more recently lost control over his bladder, he needs special help in the difficult task of learning bladder control. (This applies to children over the age of five — an age at which a majority might be expected to be continent at night.) The child will usually be examined first by a doctor in case there is a physical cause for his bed-wetting, although this is rare. When a child wets the bed, it seems that his brain is not properly aware of the amount of urine in his bladder, allowing it to empty automatically while he is asleep. The child cannot help this.

The device known as the 'enuresis alarm' (or bell-and-pad) has been developed to help children (with the supervision of a professional) to overcome the problem of bed-wetting. Basically, the alarm is made up of a pair of detector mats on the bed, connected to a buzzer next to the child's bed. As soon as the child begins to wet in his sleep, the buzzer sounds. The use of the alarm produces two actions — stopping the stream and waking — whenever the child's bladder begins to empty automatically during sleep.

Gradually the child's brain learns to connect these two actions with the feeling of a full bladder. After a time, the brain becomes more aware of the amount of urine in the child's bladder — and itself begins to take the two actions of contracting the muscles and waking the child when the bladder is full. Eventually, the child is able to sleep without wetting, waking up on his own if he needs to use the toilet at night.

Night (and day) wetting can sometimes be brought to an end by the use of a simple incentive programme — a star chart — for dry beds (or pants). When a negotiated number of stars is achieved the child receives a special treat or privilege, or exchanges them for small items such as crayons, plasticine and so on — at a fixed tariff.

In most instances it will not be necessary to make a special effort to train your child to control his bowels and to use the potty. He will automatically learn of its use by passing a motion while doing his wee. It is important not to engender fear, embarrassment or shame if it does become necessary to institute training. Calm, matter-of-fact association of potty and passing a motion (by regular potting) should do the trick. Perceptive parents can 'read' their child's need to go to the toilet. Frequent anticipation of your child's intentions will facilitate learning. Remember that it is rare for children not to achieve control. Some take longer than others, as is the case with all developmental skills. About ten per cent of children can be expected to be soiling still at three years of age. By four years this has fallen to only three per cent.

cognitive learning

We cannot leave the topic of learning without a brief mention of cognitive learning. The categories mentioned so far take little account of such crucial human attributes as insight, reasoning, explanation, logical argument and other ways in which we come to modify or correct our view of things. The assumption is that the psychologist simply can not 'talk' anyone out of being afraid or antisocial. Yet there is no doubt that cognitive learning does occur since people can be encouraged to behave differently as a result of being told that this or that is the case, or by receiving instructions to do something in a particular way.

Learning is not simply something that happens to the individual, as in instrumental conditioning, but something which he himself makes happen by the manner in which he handles incoming information and puts it to use. The main difference between this model of learning and the ones we looked at earlier is that they do not pay enough attention to the element that comes in between, namely the learner's own behaviour (B). This behaviour is not simply something brought forth by a stimulus and strengthened, or otherwise, by the nature of the reinforcement that follows. It is, in fact, a highly complex activity which involves three major processes: the acquisition of information; the thoughtful manipulation or transformation of this information into a form suitable for dealing with the task in hand; and the testing and checking of the adequacy of this transformation.

What people say to themselves influences their behaviour. Faulty thinking can bring about 'faulty' actions, and may be revealed in what children tell themselves ('self-talk'). So changing (by discussion and debate) their self-talk and (hopefully) their cognitions, you can benefit the way they act and feel.

Self-talk is a major preoccupation of all of us when we are beset with trials and tribulations. 'I can't cope any more . . . I'm in a terrible mess . . . There's no hope . . . O, what am I to do?' Self-talk is often accompanied by symptoms, such as listlessness, weepiness, sleeplessness and social withdrawal and fear. A feeling of control is of particular importance in coping with fear; children can be taught to make statements to themselves ('I feel brave', 'I *can* do it!') which help them, in turn, to manage their feelings. Distortions and illogicalities in thinking may lead to resentment and despair.

To help children (and indeed, parents, at times) we examine and dissect some of the faulty reasoning underlying the self-talk: the exaggerations ('No one loves me . . . there's no hope!'); the need to be all-competent, to show no weakness, to be acknowledged and loved *all* the time, to be for ever right. Counselling on such illogicalities, the prompting and practising of new self-talk ('I can manage. . . . I'm a good mum'; 'Think first, act afterwards . . . keep cool') may bring some relief; teaching problem-solving skills has longer-term benefits.

applications

PART II

Social training within the family

Socialization has, as one of its main objectives, the preparation of children for their future. Social development is a life process founded upon a paradox; we are both *social* and *individual* creatures. We associate with others in a multitude of ways, but ultimately we stand alone in the world. The basic biological impetus of all living beings to adapt, by modifying the self and modifying the environment, is so fundamental to childhood that we tend to overlook its manifestations. The business of adjusting to life and its various demands, is reflected in two interrelated processes called *assimilation* and *accommodation.* Assimilation involves a person's adjustment of the environment to himself, and represents the individual's use of his environment as he perceives it; accommodation is the converse of assimilation and involves the impact on the individual of the actual environment itself. To accommodate is to perceive and to incorporate the experience provided by the environment as it actually is.

One might say that 'mature' social development is the achievement of a balance between assimilation and accommodation, as between one's self-centred needs and the altruistic concern for others. This process begins during the first year of life — a year that is foundational but *not* irreversible for the child's development. What is so fascinating about this first year is that within the space of 365 days, such momentous events take place, that by her first birthday, the previously asocial newborn could be said to have well and truly 'joined' the human race.

Discipline becomes a very real issue in the child's

second year of life, although the foundations for good disciplinary practices should have been laid down much earlier. Notions of right and wrong, a code of behaviour, a set of attitudes and values, the ability to see the other person's point of view — all of these basic qualities which make an individual into a socialized personality — are nurtured in the first instance by parents.

'No son of mine is going to stand there and tell me he's scared of the woods'
Copr. © 1932, 1960 James Thurber. *The Seal in the Bedroom*, published by Harper & Row.

At the very foundation of normal development is the child's emotional tie to his parents and their bonding to him. Erik Erikson proposes that the essential task of infancy is the development of a basic trust in others. He believes that during the early months and years of life, a baby learns whether the world is a good and satisfying place to live in, or a source of pain, misery, frustration and uncertainty. Because the human infant is so totally dependent for so long, he needs to know that he can depend on the outside world.

If a major task is, indeed, the development of a sense of trust in the world (derived from parental affection and the prompt satisfaction of needs), mistrust and a sense of insecurity are the emotional problems which potentially have their origins in the neglect of the child's needs during this phase of life. If parents are rejecting and neglectful, he may see his world not as a manageable and benign place, but as threatening and insecure. Let us therefore look at that all-important bond of love.

4

The bonds of love

All infants need to become attached to a parent (or parent substitute) in order to survive. The child's growing bond of love and loyalty are a great source of joy to her mother and father; but such ties of affection also serve a utilitarian function. The respect and the good-will she feels (this applies to teachers as well) enhances all the adults' efforts to teach her. The fact that she is 'on their side', so to speak, makes the task of teaching — and learning — much easier.

There is the other side of bonding: the parents' commitment to their offspring. When all goes well — and it usually does — an attachment is cemented between a mother (say) and her baby, a relationship implying unconditional love, self-sacrifice and nurturant attitudes which, for the mother's part, are quite likely to last a lifetime. Obviously, a great deal is at stake in the success of attachment processes: child-to-parent and parent-to-child.

There is a fly in the ointment. It is a commonly held belief (which can be very worrying to parents) that infants who are deprived of *continuous* maternal care and love — undoubtedly evident in the history of some of the older children who are emotionally disturbed — are invariably affected adversely in their ability to form bonds of affection, and in other ways as well.

Behaviour which is characteristic of infantile attachment may readily be observed in its many forms in human children as well as in the young of birds and non-human mammals. Examples of chicks, ducklings, goslings following a person have been seen by many people in nature films. You may have seen a television film of an ethologist at work, with a straggling line of ducklings following him about as if he were their mother. These misguided infants have become 'adoptees' of a human

what is infantile attachment?

being through being exposed to him rather than their parent, shortly after hatching. Although normally attached to their natural mother, such infants can become attached with ease to a substitute parent or (in the laboratory) to a moving inanimate object.

This type of early learning is referred to as imprinting. The newborn of mammalian species capable of loco-motion soon after birth — as are most herbivores, such as cows, horses, or deer — also appear to form attachments by exposure to figures in their immediate environment, which usually, of course, happen to be their mothers. Other young mammals, including mon-keys and apes, show strong ties to their mothers and sometimes also to other individuals. It is by no means certain whether these attachments can be explained in terms of imprinting.

Much has been written on the subject of the ties of affection of human infants to their parents, particularly in the context of what was called misleadingly — because it represented an over-simplification — 'maternal deprivation'. The most influential writings have been those of John Bowlby. He argued that the child's strong attachment to its mother was necessary for normal, healthy development. At that time he thought that deprivation of maternal affection, or *protracted* maternal separation, was liable to result in maladjustment which could show itself in a variety of ways, including delinquency. Bowlby's later view, following an examina-tion of detailed research findings, was that the child's separation from its care-giver did not inevitably result in the maladjustment of the child. This is not to deny the vital importance of the presence of a *mother-figure* (a nurturant, stimulating parent) — especially before the age of about five years — in facilitating the child's healthy psychological development.

Needless to say, parents are concerned about the effects of an early separation brought about by a baby going into intensive care, or by the mother going out to work or to hospital, when her child is young. In order to consider these matters properly, let us begin at the very beginning.

becoming an individual   The beginning of the baby's 'separate' or independent existence takes place at birth, when he ceases to receive all his sustenance through the umbilical cord. But at this stage he is not psychologically separate from his mother. The infant does not conceive of himself as a person, and certainly not as an individual separate from other persons. He and his surroundings merge; he does not clearly distinguish 'things out there' from internal impressions or feelings. The crux of the matter is that the child has limited self-awareness, as we know it. The mother (generally) will shape most of the infant's early encounters with his world, and these encounters will give him social awareness. For this to happen the child must first become attached to his mother or some other care-giver. We can only speak of a child as a person when he becomes aware of himself as a separate individual — a social being. Later, to become a person in his own right, he must detach himself, at least in part, from his mother's protective cocoon, and develop a point of view of his own. Like a space-ship, which has to force itself out of the earth's gravitational pull in order to make its journey, a child must move out of safe orbit around his mother and strike out to find his own place in the world.

In the development of attachments, the first year of life is the crucial one. Within 12 months, almost all babies have developed strong ties with the mother, or a mother-figure. And a good thing too! Humans have a long period of helpless infancy; they could not survive without continuous protection. The newly born infant is dependent on the loving, stimulating presence of a parent, not only for physical survival, but also for psychological integrity. She develops a bond of love, binding herself to her parents and her mother and father to her. When and how does all this happen?

Psychologists observing this bonding process have found it useful to conceive of (say) the mother and child, while they are interacting with each other, as a single 'attachment system'. This attachment system is almost always at work, especially in the early days of a child's life. Mother and baby are seldom out of each other's minds; what happens to one has its 'ripple' effect on the other: matters that strongly affect a mother usually having some sort of repercussions on her baby. We cannot analyse a child's so-called 'dependency' problems, for example, without also describing the mother's behaviour towards her child (see chapter 5).

The baby particularly enjoys human company; he is

genetically 'programmed' to respond in certain ways to the world around him. That is, he is born with a particular type of physical and psychological equipment which makes him sensitive to certain kinds of stimulation in his surroundings. For example, the human face in movement 'triggers' a smile in young babies. As every mother knows, her baby's smile — more than anything else — binds her to him with a deep feeling of joy and love. A baby attracts and keeps his parents' attention by crying, smiling, babbling and laughing. And the more attention he gets, as we saw in chapter 3, the more he will babble and smile.

Even in the first days of life, a baby is soothed and quietened by social contact — being caressed, rocked, talked to, or just picked up. Within his first weeks he begins responding to people, even though he can not distinguish one from another. If anyone approaches, he changes his position, tracks the person with his eyes, grasps a finger, reaches out and stops crying when he catches sight of a face or hears a voice. All this encourages attachment.

By about four months, a baby generally behaves in much the same friendly way towards people as he did earlier, but he will react more markedly to his mother. He will smile and coo and follow her with his eyes more than he will other people. But although he may be able to recognize her, there is not yet a bond which makes him behave in such a way as to maintain close proximity to her in particular — the real meaning of attachment. Attachment behaviour is best seen when the mother leaves the room, and the baby cries or tries to follow her. It is also evident when not just anyone can placate the infant. At six months, about two-thirds of babies appear to have a close attachment to their mothers, indicated by separation protest of a fairly consistent sort. Three-quarters of babies are attached by nine months. This first attachment is usually directed at the mother; very occasionally towards some other familiar figure.

During the month after children first show evidence of an emotional bond, one-quarter of them show attachment to other members of the family, and by the time they are a year and a half, all but a few children are attached to at least one other person (usually the father) and often to several others (usually older children). The formation of additional attachments progresses so rapidly in some infants that multiple attachments occur at about the same time. By one year of age, a majority of children show no preference for either parent and only a few retain their mother-centredness.

Professor Rudolph Schaffer writes that the child, by his first birthday

. . . has learned to distinguish familiar people from strangers, he has developed a repertoire of signalling abilities which he can use discriminatively in relation to particular situations and individuals, and he is about to acquire such social skills as language and imitation. Above all, he has formed his first love relationship: a relationship which many believe to be the prototype of all subsequent ones, providing him with that basic security which is an essential ingredient of personality development.

This relationship is disrupted when the family is torn asunder, a tragedy we look at in chapter 19.

Obviously mothering is of vital importance to the baby, but is it critical *per se,* in the 'feminine' sense of the word? Would good care from male *or* female, mum *or* substitute, do just as well? We look at the issues of mothering and fathering in a later chapter. What concerns many mothers is their freedom of choice to go out to work because they want to, or have to, or for a mixture of motives. Need they succumb to the tyranny of guilt?

Sadly, there have been some doom-laden speculations and peculiar interpretations of the research literature, **should I go out to work?** which have caused needless worry to mothers about the day-to-day separation forced on them by the fact of working in a society that does not provide proper facilities for working mothers. As Michael Rutter says:

Bowlby's writings have often been misinterpreted and wrongly used to support the notion that only twenty-four hours' care day in and day out, by the same person, is good enough. Thus it has been claimed that proper mothering is only possible if the mother does not go to work and that the use of day nurseries and creches has a particularly serious and permanent deleterious effect.

Mothers often feel guilty at handing over their child to someone else for a large part of the day. They feel that, somehow, the daily separation may be doing him harm. It is reassuring, then, to know that there is no evidence that children whose mothers work suffer adverse effects. But there is a most important proviso: finding *good* substitute care for the child. And it is critical that a mother feels confident about her motives for working, and is not crippled by nagging doubts. Parents should be painstaking in their provision of substitute care. The evidence suggests that children of working mothers do not suffer, provided that stable relationships and good care are provided by the care-givers. However, for parents who retain serious doubts about the wisdom of working, it is probably best (where they have a choice) to err on the side of caution, at least while the child is very young.

Good day care need not interfere with normal mother—child bonding. The use of day nurseries does not appear to have any long-term adverse psychological or physical effects. Children of working parents are no more likely to develop emotional problems or turn into delinquents than children whose mothers stay at home. An investigation of working mothers showed that the only children to suffer were those who were sent from pillar to post in a succession of unsatisfactory and unstable child-minding arrangements. They tended to be attention-seeking and clinging.

On the whole, children who go (say) to a high quality nursery may stand to gain socially and intellectually by becoming more independent and by coming into contact with other children in day care. Mixing with other children broadens the range of a child's social behaviour. The more he has to adapt to a variety of other individuals, the more his repertoire of social skills will grow. He has the opportunity to learn how to give and take, solve conflicts and to co-operate.

The important thing to remember is that a good mother—child relationship does not depend on being together every minute, day in, day out. It depends on what happens between them when they *are* together and the quality of care given. A loving mother who can enjoy the company of her child after her day's work can have a less fraught relationship with him than a mother who is lonely and resentful about being 'trapped' at home all day or always anxious and unhappy because she cannot make ends meet.

There are other separation experiences — also at times involuntary — which bring in their wake, anxiety and heart-searching for mothers. This fear arises out of a widespread belief in the theory of maternal bonding. This is the view that mothers become bonded to their infants through close skin-to-skin contact during the 'critical' hours and days following birth. To bond or not to bond has become a matter of great concern. What will happen if the newborn infant is ill, or hospital arrangements are inflexible, so that the baby is separated from its mother during this critical period? Could a chance separation from her baby really put a blight on a mother's love? Could the baby's development be adversely affected? **to bond or not to bond**

Sadly, this belief about the ties of affection is also quite likely to engender apprehension and pessimism in would-be adoptive parents. The social work and paediatric literature is full of dire warnings about the consequences of failures or distortions of mother-to-child bonding. They have been blamed for a variety of problems including unsuccessful adoptions, children's failure to thrive, infantile autism, and, notably, child abuse. Thus, it is not only parents, but people in the medical and helping professions who are concerned about the implications of the bonding theory for the care of premature or disabled infants.

The eminently sensible and humane idea of allowing a mother and her new baby to get to know one another by early and frequent interaction, becomes oppressive when the permissive 'ought' is replaced by the dogmatic 'must'! It is well to remember that the bonding doctrine is only one of the most recent milestones in the long history of child care precepts and practices. Ideas and prescriptions for the early management of children are like fashions, or even fads; they wax and wane. So let us look for some hard evidence to help us make up our minds about these issues.

The notion that this special tie, the loving, caring attachment of mother to child, develops rapidly during a **maternal bonding** relatively short sensitive period, is similar to the phenomenon of imprinting mentioned earlier in this chapter; it too has its origins in ethology. Ethologists study animal behaviour in the natural environment. The idea that human mother love depends on an imprinting-like process derived from some early experiments with female sheep and goats. These animals appeared to learn the smell of their babies in a rapid manner immediately after birth (a phenomenon called 'olfactory imprinting') and thereafter would reject, by butting away any lamb or kid other than their own. Additional support seemed to come from comparisons of human mothers who had little or no direct contact with their newborn infants, with those who had extended contact. The early results suggested that the former were less attached to their babies.

Mother-to-infant attachment is typically shown by the mother behaving in certain ways towards her baby; gazing, fondling, vocalizing, smiling, touching, putting her face close up, and the like. But we have to be careful about these assumptions. Such forms of behaviour are more often observed among English-speaking mothers and are less evident (although not entirely absent) among Spanish-speaking mothers. In some cultures, girls get customarily much less attention than boys. In attempting to define precisely what bonding is, the mother might be thought of as 'attached' to her infant if she consistently, over an extended period of time, reports that she loves her child, feels responsible for him, and has a sense of their mutual belonging. This is all very well, but actions are more eloquent than words. By this token, a mother in bonded to her baby — demonstrates her love for him — if she looks after him well (being aware of his needs and responding to them), and gives him considerable and considerate attention.

the evidence   In the book *Maternal Bonding,* I (and my colleagues) review the arguments and evidence for the maternal bonding doctrine. Carefully controlled scientific work from the USA and Sweden on mother-to-infant attachment, which relies on mothers' words and actions, *does not* support the far-reaching claims for the bonding theory! Contrary to a variety of strongly held beliefs, there is no clear-cut evidence that events around and soon after the time of birth can seriously distort the development of the infant's personality, or interfere with the growth of maternal love and attachment.

If there are any initial differences in attachment behaviour between mothers who have extended contact with their babies and those who have little or no contact, they soon disappear with time. Even the animal studies (and it is always foolhardy to draw close parallels between animal and human behaviour) fail to support the theory of bonding. It would be interesting if the rapid kind of bonding which is said to occur in human mothers could be observed in our nearest mammalian relatives, apes and monkeys. No such thing, in fact, has been reported for any species of mammal. What about the sheep and goats so often quoted in the bonding literature? Recent studies in the USA have shown more clearly how the she-goat functions after birth. What happens is that female goats butt away any incorrectly 'labelled' young, that is all those that are contaminated with alien smells. Any young, on the other hand, that are free from the 'wrong' smells, or those that have been freed by some means from them, are accepted and allowed to nurse at any time. It cannot therefore be argued that in these particular animals, maternal attachment is brought about by contact occurring immediately after birth.

fostering and adoption

Foster mothering does sometimes succeed in animals; and the use of adoption and fostering for the substitute care of human children has been a spectacular success. Acceptance and adoption of the young do not necessarily occur immediately or even soon after birth! A foster or adoptive home is a child's substitute family. If the bonding view were correct, it would hardly be possible for foster or adoptive parents to form attachments to their charges. It may well be that it is possible to look after children satisfactorily without ever becoming attached to them. But as children may need both care *and* affection if they are to thrive, then it is clearly better for them to be looked after by persons who show affection and whose affection stems from attachment. Tragic 'tug-of-love' cases have occurred because foster parents *have* grown to love their charges.

**what about
fathers?**

The bonding doctrine would seem to imply that paternal love is of a different order and quality from maternal love. The fact that a female gives birth does not necessarily mean that she invariably cares for the baby. This is so even in some animal species; male marmosets, to take one example, carry the infant at all times except when the infant is feeding. There have been variations among human groups. Anthropologists tell us that children may not be the special responsibility of their parent at all in some societies; they may be reared by all the members of a group living together under one roof or in a small compact housing unit. Contemporary Western society is witnessing a massive increase in the number of single-parent families in some of which the father is the care-giver.

Fathers, of course, *do* become engrossed in their infants and develop powerful bonds of affection. Common sense, personal experience, and experimental evidence, tell us so, and it happens (in most cases) without the benefit of skin-to-skin contact shortly after birth.

**coping with
handicapped
children**

The question of bonding sometimes arises when mothers have to cope with special problems in caring for handicapped children. Skin-to-skin contact soon after birth is of no more relevance to the acceptance or otherwise of a physically or mentally handicapped baby than it is to a non-disabled infant. Helping the family to accept such a baby calls for tactful counselling over a long period, starting when the medical facts have become clearly established. After the initial shock, mothers tend to react in a variety of ways. Whether they initially reject the diagnosis, whether they initially reject the infant, whether they are initially excessively loving, they all tend to ask for more information. Thus, *informed* help is needed to enable the mother to cope and also to develop an attachment to her infant which is conducive to effective mothering. Fathers, too, need continuing help. With such help, and with time, both parents learn new skills, while their feelings and motives are gradually modified.

**allaying
parents' fears**

There is really no need for nurses or mothers to attach any special importance to skin contact. What is required is what seems sensible in the given circumstances. The aim is, of course, to be kind to the mother; but being kind will mean much contact in some cases and little contact in others. Everything should depend on what suits best all concerned; the mother, the infant, the father and the hospital staff. Not only do most (but certainly not all) mothers like contact, but it also facilitates lactation and breast feeding, and provides an opportunity for the mother and infant to get to know each other. However, if the mother is ill, or the baby premature, then no harm is done by keeping mother and baby apart until the time when they are both fit and well. No mother should feel deprived or guilty if early skin-to-skin contact has not occurred.

What the mother believes with regard to such matters as contact and separation, the sensitive period, and bonding in general, *is* important. Mothers acquainted with these ideas — and there are now many such — tend to be anxious lest they are not properly bonded to their children, and hence that their mothering is not as good as it should be. The proper message to the anxious mother is 'stop worrying'. It is bad enough that many mothers are made to doubt, needlessly, the true quality of their maternal feelings. It is unjust and unnecessary to blame the lack of maternal bonding for all sorts of ills.

It is not uncommon at professional case conferences to hear a tragic case of child abuse explained in terms of a failure, absence or distortion of bonding, and due, in turn to an early experience. There is simply no evidence at all that children are abused by their mothers because the latter have not been successfully bonded to the former. But there is plenty of evidence that child abuse and neglect occurs in certain types of deprived homes and social environments: amongst the better-off it is associated with psychiatric illness. If child abuse or failure-to-thrive is ascribed to lack of bonding, the prospects are made to look unjustifiably pessimistic. Once, however, the situation is assessed in much broader terms there is indeed much scope for remedial action.

It is true that *immediate* affection for the newborn is more likely to occur when the confinement is uncompli- cated. In view of this, it might be worthwhile to forewarn mothers in antenatal classes so that they do not need to worry if they feel initially detached from their babies, as this appears to be a fairly common occurrence. Some 40 per cent of mothers of first-borns have been found to express an initial indifference to their infants, a state of mind which soon evaporates as they get to know their offspring.

It is reassuring to realize that there are striking variations in the way that maternal feelings arise and grow. Mothers generally expect to have positive maternal feelings towards their infants at the time of birth. In fact, some mothers do report an instant love towards their newborn babies, even a bond for the foetus in their womb. When subjective and objective reports of the development of mother love are scrutinized, however, it becomes apparent that the growth of maternal attachment is usually a *gradual* process.

The practical advice to parents who have had an enforced separation — at whatever time — from their children is: 'Do not spend time worrying needlessly.' From the adult's point of view, your so-called 'bonding' need not be impaired, unless you talk yourself into a crisis. Those separations in the maternity hospital need have no ill-effects. From your child's perspective — where the separation occurs later in life — he may be upset for a short time, but he will soon recover if you appear your usual self and avoid fussing over him in nervous expectation of the worst. We know that the child's separation from its care-giver does not inevitably result in the maladjustment of the child. Brief separations are fairly common for all children and seem to have little adverse effect.

We appreciate, more clearly now, that the older child may be able to maintain an attachment in the parent's absence over quite long periods of time; that the stimulation necessary for development is dependent on the amount of adult—child interaction; that attachments are made early on to persons other than mother if they are responsive to the infant's needs and signals; that it is possible for good mothering to be given by more than one person, provided the care-givers remain constant and do not number more than about five; and that mothering need not be provided in the child's own home, but seems to be on the whole best provided there.

In no way has the discussion in this chapter meant to 'downgrade' the vital importance of the presence of a mother-figure in facilitating the child's healthy psychological development. The debate on the originally very pessimistic message about 'maternal deprivation', can now be informed by some useful critical reviews of the evidence. They reach the more optimistic conclusion that early experience is no more than a link in the chain of development, influencing and shaping behaviour less and less powerfully as age increases. What is probably crucial is that for some children, early learning and experience (of an adverse kind) is *continually* repeated and reinforced, and it is in this way that long-term effects appear. Later problems and deviance are very often the result of later experience, not only early learning experiences. So do not be discouraged by 'mistakes' or one-off 'bad' experiences. With sensitive and sensible handling, your child should get over the crisis and eventually shrug it off.

5

The spoiled child

Young mothers are subjected to many warnings about the dangers of spoiling their offspring, and thus encouraging bad habits and indiscipline. Here is a voice coming to us over the centuries:

> The children now love luxury. They have bad manners, contempt for authority, they show disrespect to their elders and love to chat in places of exercise. They no longer get up when their elders enter the room. They contradict parents, chatter before company, gobble up dainties at the table, cross their legs and are tyrants over their teachers.

The querulous voice belongs to Socrates. Apparently fourth-century teachers, like their twentieth-century counterparts, had to cope with disruptive pupils. Yet it is the allegedly contemporary phenomenon — a breakdown in discipline — which is blamed for many present-day problems: disruption of school life, drug and substance abuse, the drop out, rebelliousness towards authority, the rising numbers of delinquents and, to top it all, sexual promiscuity.

Obviously, the older generation has always looked askance at the lack of discipline, and obedience and respect among the young. The reasons are not hard to find. Obedience to rules — whether they are laid down by convention, codified in laws, or hidden in our consciences — is a prerequisite for social living. All parents and teachers are beset at one time or another by disobedient children. But there is disobedience and *disobedience*! Parents and teachers are more sensitive to the breaking of certain kinds of rules than others. Many of the 'conduct problems' (as they are called) involve what might be called moral rules, and it is when children break these rules that parents get most perturbed. Youngsters are forbidden to lie, steal, cheat and hurt others. A child who has been punished severely for committing these sins may be surprised when he overhears his mother telling a 'white' lie to avoid lending her neighbour the lawnmower, when she surreptitiously picks a cutting from a shrub in the park, when his father gets off the bus without paying, or when he gives him a painful hiding.

Despite all the inconsistencies of parents as moral teachers, children still have to learn, on the one hand, the conventional rules of good manners and of correct behaviour at school, and, on the other, the rules concerning sympathy and respect for others, keeping faith, honesty, and so on. The latter *are* moral issues. Parents and teachers sometimes treat the former as if they were too, but there are important distinctions; it is a pity to give the same weight to both.

Socrates' words have a particularly poignant resonance to them, in the light of contemporary parents' uncertainties about child rearing. Parents are pulled in two directions; if they are too permissive, the child will become (it is said) an overly dependent 'satellite' to his parents or a self-centred unpopular and wilful tyrant. But if they are too restrictive, authoritarian and punitive, their discipline will produce slavish conformity in a neurotic, submissive, even obsequious nonentity. What are the facts?

the dependent child

The term 'spoiling' is obviously a matter of interpretation. Can one, for example, really spoil a child by allowing her to display her dependency needs, for example, crying to be picked up. Among the things she needs in abundance, are human attention, stimulation and intimate company.

Now an overly dependent child is one who (inappropriately for her age) needlessly seeks help and approval from adults, and also makes excessive demands for physical proximity to, and contact with, her parents. The mother who has an accepting and tolerant attitude towards dependent behaviour, is also likely to be, in general, affectionately warm towards her child, gentle in toilet training, permissive about the sexual curiosity she shows, unlikely to use physical punishment for dependent behaviours, and tolerant when she is angry and aggressive towards her parents. Such a mother tends to be responsive to her baby's crying, usually (or in some cases, always) picking up the baby immediately. Such responsiveness is not associated with a later 'clinging' type of dependency in the children. Many of the mothers are often irritable, and punish their children when they hang on and cling on to them. Their irritable scolding while pulling themselves away from their clinging children increases the frequency of such dependency.

The trouble with dependency needs is that every child has savoured the delights of being cared for; even the most reluctant mother has to minister to certain of her child's wants. So the child knows what it is missing and craves for more — especially if she is not specifically discouraged by punishment. This is where dependency training differs from training in sexual matters. Children are almost never encouraged, that is to say rewarded, for displays of sexual behaviour; they are likely to be consistently punished or at the least, ignored. But with dependency, because of her sheer helplessness, the child will be rewarded occasionally with some signs of nurturance. If the parents withhold or are meagre with their attention and care, but do not actually punish dependent behaviour, they are likely to intensify the child's needs for attention and care. The more a child is 'pushed away' (figuratively speaking) the more she clings for dear life.

One would expect that more severe forms of rejection would lead children to suppress such behaviour. This is reflected in the finding that aggressive boys who have undergone a good deal of parental rejection show much less dependent behaviour than non-aggressive boys who have been accepted by their parents. There seems to be a balance in child-rearing, an avoidance of extremes, within which the child thrives. If rejection represents one extreme, so does excessive care, colloquially referred to as permissiveness and (even more perjoratively) as spoiling.

permissiveness Permissiveness has become an emotive word in our vocabulary. When adults wring their hands and bemoan the 'permissive society', they forget that they are passing judgement on themselves. They carried out the socialization of the youngsters they now deprecate.

The word 'permissiveness' has a technical meaning, and also a popular meaning. It is misleading to use the term without knowing what is going on within the family. Thus a child who is permitted to do pretty well what he likes against a background of 'couldn't-care-less' or hostile attitudes from parents, is very different from the child who is given this freedom against a background of parental support and love. The word 'permissiveness' is sometimes used as if it defined the extreme end of the freedom dimension — a licence for a child to do whatever he wishes. Yet there are all kinds and degrees of permitted freedoms. Interestingly, many parents who say they are against permissiveness in discipline, would probably accept (as democratic citizens) the philosophy of maximizing the things permitted to the individual, allowing him as much personal freedom as is possible without interfering with other people's rights and freedoms. Unfortunately, this notion of balance rarely seems to enter their consideration of permissiveness in discipline.

According to the psychologist Diana Baumrind, the technical meaning of calling someone a 'permissive parent' is that the parent attempts to behave in a non-punitive, accepting, and affirmative manner towards the child's impulses, desires, and actions; to consult with him about policy decisions and give explanations for family rules. Children of quick-responding mothers cry less with the passage of time than those left alone.

The evidence suggests that it is well-nigh impossible to 'spoil' a child during the *first* year of his life. However, it is possible to sow the seeds, in parents' attitudes, for 'spoiling' their offspring as he gets older; if they feel compelled to give in to his every whim — reasonable or unreasonable — this could become habit-forming! We then tend to hear the word 'spoiled' applied to the children of such indulgent parents.

If spoiling occurs, it may be the result of a parent's anxieties arising from over-protective attitudes, and may take the form of excessive father—child or mother—child contact. In such a case, the child may sleep in the same room as (say) his mother for years. She tends to fondle him excessively, watch over him constantly, and prevent him taking risks or acting in an independent manner. She fusses a lot about his health by over-medicating and over-dressing him. His mind is made up for him more

the 'brat' syndrome

often than not. In return for absolute obedience, she may
over-indulge his every whim, in an attempt to prolong
his childhood and keep him tied to her apron strings.
Over-protective mothers (and fathers) are this way for a
variety of reasons. The child may be particularly
'precious' because he is frail, or because he followed a
sad and long series of miscarriages. Parents frequently
alternate between dominating and submitting to the
child. Such 'smother love' is frequently cited among the
causes of emotional problems.

If the child is brought up in this way he is quite likely
to turn out to be a 'lovable little tyrant' in mum's and
dad's eyes; but a 'spoiled brat' in the view of others. The
others see an exploitive character using every device,
through charm, wheedling, coaxing, and bullying, in
order to get his own way. Unless this is stemmed by
reality experiences, the child could continue into adult
life to play the part of the beloved tyrant, encouraged by
ever-responding parents. The incessant babying might
leave the *enfant terrible* with a permanent illusion of
omnipotence.

It has been said that parents and teachers (not to
mention everyone else) tend to fall somewhere between
two extreme points of view in their views of the essential
nature of children. These attitudes — which do not
always function at a conscious level — affect the way
they tackle various child-rearing tasks, especially the
disciplining of children. At one extreme, there is a
pessimistic view which sees 'original sin' at work
everywhere, not least within the developing child. Inside
the child, so to speak, is a power-mad, scheming little
demon which must be suppressed at all costs. Surveillance and discipline are the watchwords of what might
be called the 'nip it in the bud' school of thought. Here is
a very pessimistic view of human nature! At the other
extreme is an idealized notion of the child as a sort of
'noble savage'; this view sees original virtue at work
within the developmental forces shaping the child. Any
interference with natural, instinctive or spontaneous
developmental processes is wrong. 'Nature knows best;
freedom is all', summarizes the essence of this romantic
but optimistic view of child development.

The above views are nicely illustrated in studies of parent—child relationships which have made it possible to reduce the rich variety of parental behaviour to two main underlying independent dimensions of parental attitudes: (1) attitudes which are 'warm' (or loving) at one extreme, and 'rejecting' (or hostile) at the other; (2) attitudes which are restrictive (controlling) at one extreme, and permissive (encouraging autonomy) at the other.

The combination of *loving and controlling* attitudes is indicated by behaviours which are restrictive, over-protective, possessive or over-indulgent in content; *loving and permissive* attitudes are shown by actions which are accepting, co-operative and democratic. The combination of *rejecting and controlling* attitudes is indexed by behaviours which are authoritarian, dictatorial, demanding or antagonistic; *rejecting and permissive* attitudes are indicated by actions which are detached, indifferent, neglectful or hostile. Children's reports of their parents' behaviour suggest an additional factor: a dimension of firm versus lax control. It is possible for children to perceive their parents as firm but allowing independence at one and the same time; or indeed, lax but still controlling.

The results of the various combinations of these parental trends are many. There is evidence to suggest that strict, autocratic (undemocratic) adult domination and restrictiveness will produce a conforming child, but will handicap him in initiative. Such a child may turn out to be rather passive, colourless, unimaginative and incurious — burdened, in addition, with shyness and a sense of inadequacy. The children of domineering parents usually lack self-reliance and ability to cope realistically with their problems, and later on fail (or are slow) to accept adult responsibilities. They are apt to be submissive and obedient and to withdraw from situations they find difficult.

According to Diana Baumrind the restrictive or authoritarian parent attempts to shape, control, and assess the behaviour and attitudes of the child according to a set standard of conduct, usually an absolute standard, motivated by theological considerations and formulated by a higher authority. She values obedience as a virtue, and favours punitive, forceful measures to curb self-will at those points where the child's actions or beliefs conflict with what she thinks is right conduct. Children should be indoctrinated with such values as respect for authority, respect for work, and respect for the preservation of traditional order. Such a mother does not encourage verbal give and take, believing that the child should accept her word for what is right.

the golden mean

Research into child-rearing techniques suggests a happy medium — a golden mean — which is not always easy to achieve in practice. The extremes of permissiveness and restrictiveness entail risks. The child with warm, permissive parents is brought up and trained mainly through love, good models to identify with and imitate, and giving of reasons, and the opportunity to learn for himself (by trial and error) how his actions affect others. A variety of studies tell us that well-adjusted children tend to have parents who are warm, nurturant, supportive and reasonably controlling; they also have high expectations. Diana Baumrind has produced evidence for the assertion that firm control is associated with independence in the child, provided that the control is not restrictive of his or her opportunities to experiment and be spontaneous.

Healthy personality development and satisfactory social relationships can be described in terms of a balance between the child's need to make demands on others, and his ability to recognize the demands which others make on him. A blend of permissiveness and a warm encouraging and accepting attitude on the part of the parents, fits the recommendations of child-rearing specialists who are concerned with fostering the sort of children who are socially responsible and outgoing, friendly, competent, creative and reasonably independent and self-assertive (admittedly Western values).

The balance is perhaps best illustrated in the philosophy of what is called the 'authoritative parent'. These parents attempt to direct their child's activities in a rational manner determined by the issues involved in particular disciplinary situations. They encourage verbal give-and-take, and share with the child the reasoning behind their policy. They value both the child's self-expression and his or her respect for authority, work and the like. The evidence, according to Diana Baumrind, points to a synthesis and balancing of strongly opposing forces of tradition and innovation, divergence and convergence, accommodation and assimilation, co-operation and independent expression, tolerance and principled intractability. All this means that in the case of the mother (for example) she appreciates *both* independent self-will and disciplined conformity. Therefore, she exerts firm control at those points where she and her child diverge in viewpoint. But she does not hem the child in with restrictions. She recognizes her own special rights as an adult, but also the child's individual interests and special ways. The 'authoritative parent' affirms the child's present qualities, but also sets standards for future conduct. She uses reason as well as power to achieve her objectives. Her decisions are not based solely on the consensus of the group or the individual child's desires, but she also does not regard herself as infallible or divinely inspired.

Authoritative parents facilitate the development of competence and self-reliance in young children by encouraging responsible, purposeful and independent behaviour. This may sound all very well in theory, but what about workaday practice? This authoritative parent sounds too good to be true — a paragon of textbook virtues. No mother or father could stick to this philosophy in practice with any consistency, even if they had the desire to do so. Nevertheless, it does represent an approach to child-rearing which many parents wish to emulate or approximate.

Most parents find it somewhat difficult to know when, how, and how much, to discipline — a matter we tackle in chapter 15. Mothers and fathers need to be firm and unbending at times, tough as well as lovingly tender and also flexible at crucial moments. They also need to know when to move from one modality to the other. Children can be exhausting and exasperating, and parents often feel they are not so much raising a lamb as training a tiger.

Three-year-old Clare was a small tigress when thwarted. We can witness a series of confused and confusing adult reactions to her defiance. The episode began when Clare sat on a delicate coffee table in an absent-minded way.

to obey or not to obey . . .

She was asked politely and gently by her mother (Mrs Brown) not to sit on the table. She ignored the request. She was then told — more loudly — by Mrs Brown to get off the table, but she continued to ignore her mother. Mrs Best (her gran) then lifted her off the table, laughing at her 'naughtiness'. She ran round the room and climbed back on the table. She was lifted off once more by her mother and lightly smacked. She screamed, stopped, ran round the room and climbed back on the table. She was lifted off once more, smacked harder, and told not to go there again: she yelled more loudly, stopped to look toward her mum and gran, then ran back to the table. All of this was accompanied by a commentary about her behaviour from the two women — angry on the part of mum, and amused on granny's side. The sequence was repeated several times until, with great ferocity, she hit her mother on the head with a doll. She was told by Mrs Best to 'love mummy better'. This she did with a hug and kiss and then immediately returned to sitting on the table. She was ignored and eventually came off the table in *her* own time.

Children like Clare demand support from their parents, but they also try to limit the restraints parents put upon their pleasures. They want it both ways. Although children often act in ways which seem unreasonable and troublesome to their elders, from their point of view, adult behaviour is often just as unreasonable and incomprehensible. A mother insists on her small child going to bed at a certain time, in spite of all her protests, because she knows she needs enough sleep to keep healthy and alert. In the child's eyes, her mother is insisting she gives up her intriguing play, isolating her from the rest of the family, for no good reason.

Growing up and learning the way she ought to feel and behave, what she ought to value, means that the child has to give up a lot of things she enjoys. She finds herself, in a sense, drawn one way or another between two 'magnetic poles': recognizing and adapting to the needs of others, on the one hand, and imposing self-centred demands on the social environment, on the other. An extreme lack of balance in reciprocity between self and others in either direction gives rise to unsatisfactory social relationships. Obviously the youngster will often clash with parents who are preparing her for life by striving for a happy medium.

Here again there is that balance, this time in the demands of the child and the demands of parents. The ideal balance is about a compromise between sometimes incompatible mutual demands, and about a style of life which maximizes the mutually rewarding possibilities of the parent— child relationship. This balance, if it is achieved, is established over a long period of time — during the process of socialization. It begins with obedience training.

The earliest signs of obedience begin to appear in the last quarter of the baby's first year of life. It consists in heeding and complying with the mother's simple commands and prohibitions such as 'Come here!' and 'No, don't do that!' Some infants may, on occasion, display an inner-directed obedience to commands given *previously* by the parent. Such a baby shows primitive self-control when he stops himself in the act of reaching out for the forbidden television control buttons, perhaps accompanying his act of self-denial with a shake of the head (imitating mum) or a vocal 'No! No!' It doesn't take long for problems of disobedience to appear. These are not simply the problems due to the absence of obedience. They are more likely to be wilful acts of rebellion; a deliberate countering of the mother's will. Negativism (as such behaviour is called) is an exaggerated form of resistance when the child becomes stubborn and contrary, often doing quite the opposite of what mother wishes. To put it graphically, the child goes through a stage of sheer 'bloody mindedness'. It begins at about 18 months and reaches a peak at around three years, after which it begins to decline. The 'terrible' twos and threes are notorious with parents for their noisy confrontations. They are clashing head-on with natural, but trying, egocentricity!

the beginnings of obedience

Most of the scrapes a child gets into as he begins to explore his immediate world, the house and garden, happen because he does not know enough to realize what will happen if he puts his hand in the nettle patch or treads on an upturned garden rake. But some of the hazards occur because of his egocentric tendency to think of himself as invulnerable. For instance, a child may become so fascinated by watching a car backing up

egocentricity

the drive that he fails to realize the danger of being in its
way.

Parents can observe the development of a less self-
centred view (de-centring, as it is sometimes called) in
their child's play. Like the use of language, playing with
others requires a child to be aware of them as persons
like himself with feelings and needs which he must
recognize and accommodate. The readiness to make the
necessary sacrifice of egocentricity at about three years
of age seems to depend on the formation of a rudimentary
but coherent conscience. You may hear the stirrings of
the inner voice of conscience at work in your child's
conversations: 'Oh all right, you haven't had a turn; you
have a go on the swing.' It is known that in order to play
mutually a child must be able to *enjoy* empathy with, and
concern for, others.

Adults can enhance this process by being around to
encourage sharing and helping actions and by insisting
on fair play. Children of three can be very aware of, and
sensitive to, the fairness of co-operating and sharing, but
they may not be so good at re-establishing these
conditions when they have been shattered by (say) a
quarrel. An alert parent can get them back 'on track' as
long as he or she does not become too intrusive. Mutual
play has an important contribution to make in the gradual
move away from egocentricity — something recognized
in the development of play groups and nursery schools.

The pursuit of altruism, unselfishness, co-operation,
sensitivity and helpfulness as attributes for your child
will be aided if you set an example and, in addition,
respond to their manifestation with words of praise and
encouragement. Repeated prompting will lead to them
becoming established habits. Eventually the child's
recognition of his own empathy becomes self-rewarding.
To this end you can play an important part by pointing
out the injustices, cruelties, selfishness and thoughtless-
ness which arise (unwittingly) from the child's limited
capacity to empathize. Explanations and reasons are
provided and the kind of propositions which begin with:
'How would *you* feel if . . . ?'

We are not judging the child when we say he is
egocentric in his early years, because as he grows up he
will begin to understand that others have a viewpoint
too. Sadly, not all children develop enough sensitivity to

other people's values and outlook. If you encourage your child towards a more unselfish view of the world by pointing out the other person's point of view, especilly your own, the attitude that his rights have to be balanced against the rights of others should be well rooted by the time he goes to school.

Parents who treat others, including their children with consideration, will need very little in the way of training sessions in manners. It is not unusual to hear people sneer at parents who place an emphasis on good manners. Such critics are commonly persons who pride themselves on their liberal and social consciences. While it is true that one can go overboard about manners and, especially, the formal and more banal aspects — good manners for appearance's sake — the underlying purpose of good manners would seem to be unexceptionable. Opening a door for a parcel-laden person; offering a seat to an elderly or disabled person; saying thank you for a kindness done, and please for a favour anticipated, all symbolize a concern for others and a sensitivity that reaches beyond oneself. These actions are the outward and visible sign that a child is beginning to sense that other people and their needs or rights matter.

good manners

Without a generally accepted code of manners, life would become rather brutish and nasty; parents have the task of passing them on to the next generation. We argued that manners and morality were different issues, but to the extent that good manners arise out of sympathy and caring attitudes, they shade into the area of moral concern. These abstract issues become real enough and worrying when your child brings home friends who seem rude and ill-mannered.

Every family has different values and rules of behaviour. Permissive parents may be quite happy to have their children playing boisterously with fragile and expensive ornaments if they feel like it, hurling abuse at them, or screaming with fury if they do not get what they want. What does your youngster make of it all, watching another visiting child flouting the rules and getting away with it? Difficult as it may be, it is probably best to inform the visiting child firmly that in your house you

rudeness in other children

expect your child (and him) to sit at the table to eat, and not walk around with his food in his hand.

It is more of a problem if a relative or friend who calls often brings along a spoiled child she is unable or unwilling to control. 'Please, darling, won't you be a good girl?' she admonishes ineffectually, adding 'You know Aunty doesn't like you playing her records.' And yet another record gets scratched by a manic stylus! Awkward though it is, you need to talk to her — sooner, rather than later — about the rules you have in your home for yourself and your children. Ask her for her help in solving an awkward problem. Explain that you have taught your children not to play the records without help. And it is now very hard to explain why they should respect other people's property as they see another child scratching the records — something for which they have been punished. Naturally they feel resentful when they see two standards operating side by side — one for them and a much more lenient one for the visitor.

All these things are, in a sense, a matter of tactics. It helps to apply tactical discipline, if the broad strategy of child care has been worked out. A set of coolly thought out guidelines allows one to deal with the unexpected 'crises' of day-to-day child management with a degree of confidence and objectivity. The philosophy that might underlie them is the subject of the following pages.

6

Knowing right from wrong

Children, in many aspects of behaviour — mannerisms, speech patterns, attitudes and the like — are small carbon copies of their parents; so many, indeed, that it seems we must be conformist by nature. Actually, as we saw earlier in this book, the transmission of attitudes and opinions and customs takes place through *teaching and learning* — the process of social training. Despite the general tendency of this process to produce uniformity of behaviour among the members of a society, failures and distortions of socialization sometimes occur. Such failures at times produce under-socialized or non-conforming individuals (children who are delinquent or psychopathic) and, on the other hand, over-socialized neurotic youngsters.

conformity

A child can be too obedient, too submissive to authority, be it the coercive influence of the individual or of the group. In deciding when conformity becomes excessive, it is necessary to ask to whom and how often the child submits, and in what contexts he is prepared to conform. Can he distinguish between the reasonable demands of those responsible for his care and training, such as parents and teachers, and the unreasonable coercions of, say, a delinquent gang? Does he stick up for his own rights or point of view, or slavishly give in to the wishes and attitudes of others? Hopefully the child will learn to discriminate between the desirability or undesirability of people, of particular demands and values. Here we are talking about moral values, in particular, and the development of character.

forming character

However uncongenial and difficult moral rules may be to keep, members of society cannot contract out. This is because — unlike the rules of other activities — moral rules are fundamental. They are concerned with the maintenance of trust, mutual help and justice in human relationships. This is what we mean when we talk about character. Unless this exists in some measure it becomes virtually impossible to continue any social activity. It is therefore not surprising that, though conventions and customs vary widely from one society to another, basic moral principles apparently do not.

These issues raise the whole question of self control. One of the great miracles (and headaches) for parents is the sequence of events whereby a child internalizes (takes into himself) the rules and controls that are necessary for social life. Immanuel Kant wrote that two things 'fill the mind with ever-increasing wonder and awe, the more often and the more intensely the mind of thought is drawn to them: the starry heavens above me and the moral law within me.'

the moral law within: the voice of conscience

Parents cannot always be on the spot to check the child. Eventually their voices and other voices (which enunciate social and moral values) are inside the psyche of the child so that what he now has the choice of heeding is his own voice of conscience. At such a stage he is generally able to restrain himself from doing wrong even when no one else will ever know about his misdemeanour. If he does give way to temptation he feels guilty afterwards. Not only can he be relied upon to keep the rules without constant supervision, but he will in turn, teach the rules to his offspring. At the same time he will endeavour to ensure that there are sanctions for people who break the rules.

It goes without saying that people's consciences are not equally strong. Going back to those first commands and prohibitions which are the foundation stones of conscience, it is apparent that some babies obey them more readily and consistently than others. And some parents convey them more effectively and constructively than others. Social learning theorists suggest that what a child acquires by learning and identification, is the parents' moral code and a willingness to act in accordance with the rules.

It could be said that the first and most important step in the socialization of the child occurs when he develops a *willingness* to do as he is told. What he learns will depend on the nature of the parents' demands, but it will be the development of an initial disposition towards compliance which may be critical for the effectiveness of all further attempts at training the child. If the child lacks this tendency he will remain in many ways unidentified with his society, regarding its rules and values from an uninvolved point of view. Parents need to encourage the child's natural bias towards fitting in with, and pleasing others, on the one hand, and, on the other, taking a firm line whenever he decides to be thoroughly antisocial.

Conscience is no simple or single entity. Some youngsters are highly moral in most if not all respects; others are scarcely, if at all, moral in any of them. Many children seem to concentrate or, if you like, specialize, in one or other of these components. Some young people (and, indeed, adults) are relaxed and easy going about their personal moral life, while generous in giving of themselves and their possessions in the service of others. Others spend their lives in a struggle to avoid committing misdemeanours or sins. Yet others lack sympathy and generosity; their personal conduct may not be all that scrupulous, but this does not deter them from moralizing and condemning the transgressions of others.

We do know that love alone is not enough in moral training! Precise teaching has to be provided in seemingly endless moral learning situations — with much attention paid to the detailed consequences of transgressions on the part of the child. Moral and social awareness and behaviour are influenced by:

moral training

1 Strong ties of affection between parents and children.
2 Firm moral demands made by parents on their offspring.
3 The consistent use of sanctions.
4 Techniques of punishment that are psychological rather than physical (i.e. methods that signify or threaten withdrawal of approval) thus provoking anxiety or guilt rather than anger.
5 An intensive use of reasoning and explanations (these are called inductive methods).

Resistance to temptation, and guilt on succumbing, contrary to what one might expect, do not necessarily go

timing is important

hand in hand. Those who are good at resisting temptation are not always the ones who experience the most intense guilt when they err. Whether or not parents bring out one or other of these facets in their children, depends on two things: the timing of the sanctions they administer for misconduct, and the nature of the explanation they provide when they do so. There is evidence to suggest that sanctions which are applied *before* a forbidden act (mind you, it is rarely possible for a busy mother to reprimand the child when he forms an intention to transgress) help to develop resistance to temptation.

To illustrate this question of the timing of punishment, puppies were trained not to eat a highly attractive food by being punished with a tap on the nose every time they went to eat it. However, some puppies were punished just before they touched the food, and others shortly after they had eaten some of it. When both groups of puppies had been given the same length of time in training, they were all tested by being made hungry and then being left alone with the forbidden food. The experimenter observed them through a one-way glass and was able to measure how long it took for them to 'transgress'. Those puppies who were punished just before eating the food 'resisted temptation' much longer than the others. The puppies which had been punished after they had eaten a bit of the food not only failed to 'resist temptation' well, but as soon as they did eat the forbidden food all showed the usual signs of doggy guilt. Their tails went down between their legs, and when the experimenter came back into the room, they slunk off into the corner looking distinctly guilty. There is evidence that the same principles work for children.

knowing right from wrong

There are many fine distinctions and subtle relationships that the child has to comprehend about matters such as truth, honesty and property. Parents would be acutely embarrassed (and often are) should their child tell the literal truth. Imagine the consequences if a neighbour asks whether the child likes her new dress, and she replies, 'No, you're too fat for it', or if she answers Aunty Mary's question ('Would you like to kiss me?') with an emphatic 'No!' Parents would fear that such honesty showed a lack of sensitivity and common sense.

Parents worry when they find their children lying,

stealing or cheating. They want to know whether such incidents are the early signs of some *character* defect or even the first steps on the slippery slope to delinquency? It is reassuring to know that such occurrences have all been observed as part of the behaviour repertoire of a majority of children — regardless of class, intelligence or even moral upbringing. As always, it is a matter of degree.

Many opportunities to lie, cheat and take things belonging to others occur naturally — in fact, quite innocently — in the course of childhood. Take, for example, a small girl who is addressed as follows: 'You *did* enjoy the party didn't you?' What can she say but 'Yes' even though she hated the party. She may be lying, but it is a 'white lie', and adults would approve of her tact. We all try to avoid hurting people's feelings by saying nice things when perhaps we do not mean them. Yet this is a mild form of hypocrisy — a socially acceptable brand of lying.

Learning to tell the truth, like the acquisition of other values, develops as a result of social training. To a young child, wrong is what parents forbid; right is what they allow. In time, he comes to realize that his parents disapprove of lying, cheating and other forms of behaviour, and may punish him if he does them. So (at least to a certain extent) he gives up such behaviours, in order to please his parents. Such social learning, like other learning, is part of the total process of cognitive (intellectual) growth. It comes from the child's increasing ability to make fine distinctions and see more and more subtle relationships. It is not surprising that unsophisticated youngsters by taking things literally, make mistakes with some of our more difficult and ambiguous moral issues.

Children have to learn the system of loyalties and values which allow people to stretch the truth in order to save face for the family. They will have to learn the hypocrisies and contradictions of society and, like so many idealistic adolescents, have to come to terms with many awful paradoxes. For example, he may be expected to lie and cheat for his firm (something called smart business practice). In many instances, children enter a Humpty Dumpty world in which words mean what adults choose them to mean.

I have listed some of the important influences on the child's moral development. The danger, as ever, lies in extremes. These conditions taken too far can lead to a neurotically guilt-ridden child. His conscience is fixed and rigid, his moral responses have a compulsive quality and are largely inaccessible to reasoning. His parents set an example by being very controlled and conscientious. For the child, *all* offences become personalized, because they become offences against parents. The parents make powerful use of sanctions that provoke anxiety in the child when he sees that they are disappointed and hurt by his transgressions.

The *authoritarian* youth's morality is influenced by his friends and other contemporary social relationships rather than his own reasoning and decision-making. His is an imperfectly internalized morality; his behaviour is controlled by the expectations of others. He finds democratic relationships difficult. His morality is a matter of obeying rules that are sanctioned by authority and tradition. Because his self-esteem is founded upon social status, his authoritarian character is strongly motivated to conform. He tends to come from a home in which a rather stern and distant father dominates a submissive and long-suffering but morally restrictive mother. Discipline consists of the harsh application of conventional rules. Relationships are conceived in terms of power rather than love. (Remember, these are research generalizations.)

The morality of the altruistic, autonomous youngster is internalized, and is based more upon the desire to live up to positive values than the fear of breaking rules. He is usually successful in resisting temptation, but when he does transgress his code, he deals with his short-comings in a constructive manner; his moral reasoning is based upon general principles which are rational and applied flexibly and with originality. His moral ideology is constantly developing. His upbringing is one in which democratic interactions with adults are frequent, where attachments to adults and to peers balance each other so that he is stimulated to grow between them, neither wholly identified with the one nor with the other. What he learns is that moral issues are of the greatest importance, that they are controversial, and that there is no way of settling moral disputes except through reasoning and the appeal to common values. He also learns that although he has no alternative but to live by his own standards, they are not absolute, universal or beyond revision.

It should be remembered that moral reasoning depends upon age and intellectual maturity and is not simply a fixed character trait. Young children show a simple and somewhat primitive view of moral issues. You would have no difficulty persuading them of the justice of the 'eye for an eye' (talion) principle.

Every parent has to deal with untruthfulness and it is often upsetting and perplexing. The most common reasons for childish lies are:

lying

1 The child is not yet certain of the dividing line between fact and fiction.
2 He is covering up his guilt or deficiencies.
3 He wants to avoid punishment.
4 He hopes for praise and affection.

In trying to judge whether your child is lying or not, take into account the way he sees the world. Childhood is a period of vivid imagination, fantasy and make-believe. For a small child with an active imagination, the borderline between fact and fantasy is not clearly defined. What he has wished and dreamed may sometimes be more real to him than mere fact. So if he comes and tells you he has been talking to a little goblin in the garden — 'he *was* there, truly, I'm not making it up!' — why not join in the spirit of the occasion, while at the same time indicating that you know it is all 'pretend'.

Many children have imaginary playmates for a while, usually around the ages of four and five. It may be a little boy who has to have his own chair at the table. These invisible friends need not concern you; they nearly always 'vanish' by the time the child reaches the age of ten. Young children use fantasy as a way of exploring relationships and situations (like going to school or hospital) and it would be a pity to spoil their fun or learning, because of an insistence on the most literal truth at all times.

Children lie, just as adults do, to escape the consequences of their misdeeds. Your small son has broken your favourite vase while fighting with his brother. He tells you that the cat jumped up on the table and knocked it over. Sometimes adults pressurize children into lying by over-emphasizing the need to do well in class. A girl who feels she is struggling to keep up with her classmates makes up stories about the high marks she earns or the praise the teacher gives her. She knows that if she tells the truth, her mother will be resentful and, perhaps, scathing.

Children often try to boost their prestige in a world where they feel small and insignificant by telling their friends tall stories about (say) the family's new sports car, which is really a battered second-hand purchase. They do this because they have learned from the adults around them that these things are the source of admiration and esteem. But sometimes children who 'lie' simply do not perceive the circumstances in the way you do and feel thoroughly misjudged if you call them untruthful. When two brothers fight, it is *always* the other one who started it. When two sisters cut and 'style' their hair, it was always the other one's idea.

As a child gets older and gains more confidence he normally finds he no longer needs all the little lies which bolstered his self-esteem. Of course some individuals go on lying into adulthood and may, in the end, have trouble distinguishing truth from falsehood.

Persistent lying is a danger signal. Make sure you are not aggravating the problem by being too harsh. If the punishment for breaking the rules is too severe, your child may be forced to go to great lengths to deny he has broken them. If a toddler accidentally breaks a treasured ornament and owns up, only to find you lose your temper, he is far more likely to blame it on the cat next time. The main step in teaching a child not to lie is to reassure him sufficiently, so that he does not have to resort to lies.

Finally, try to set him a good example. You may tell him what you call 'white lies' or 'fibs', from the best possible motives, saying that his budgie has 'gone away for a visit', instead of explaining that it has died. Not surprisingly, he will have trouble seeing why his lies are not acceptable while yours are.

taking things   Children grow up admiring the thief and outlaw Robin Hood, and a similar ambiguity of attitude is shown toward the act of taking someone else's property at different ages. Early on, for example, the child will quite happily take another child's toy because his concepts of property and 'stealing' are still vague. He is always being told to *share* things, and that is exactly what he is doing. Nevertheless it will not be long before he knows that it is wrong to take or use the possessions of others without their knowledge and consent.

Those acts of 'theft' which seem to become less serious in the view of the older child, involve hoodwinking persons in authority, keeping found property, and using the belongings of brothers and sisters. Fear of punishment is at the basis of young boys' moral judgements more frequently than it is with older boys. They, by contrast, give the unwillingness to injure others as the most frequent reason for their judgements.

If the child is to desist from stealing as an easy way of getting what he wants, parents should label such acts as wrong, and apply penalties if he continues with them. The youngster can be stopped more effectively from doing something (say, stealing) in the future, if he is checked or reprimanded sharply just before or at the time of taking someone's possession. If punishment follows some time after the pleasure of the forbidden deed rather than preceding it, it is guilt which is maximized and resistance to temptation which is minimized.

Apart from the crucial matter of timing, it is necessary to be aware of *what is said* by the parents when they admonish a child for misconduct; the explanation given is of vital importance. Wrong acts often do not differ from permissible ones in the physical sense, but only in terms of their meaning and content. The act of taking a child's toy and putting it in one's pocket may be either stealing or borrowing, and even sharing. Morally reprehensible acts have to be labelled as such!

Even after the child has learned that it is wrong to take someone else's property, the seriousness of his act of 'stealing' should be interpreted with caution. When a child has taken something, parents would be overreacting if they immediately invoke the disapproval of God or the threat of a policeman's punishment.

Explain the situation simply and unemotionally. Sermons and melodramatics are unproductive. You might try to look on your child's taking things — when young — as an act of immature irresponsibility or faulty learning rather than a 'juvenile mini-crime'. In the light of what was said about resistance to temptation, it is not surprising that it is the general consensus of psychological opinion that childish stealing is *not* effectively treated after the event by severe punishment. It is best not to push the child into further deception, telling lies, for instance, in order to escape censure. Where money is involved try to ensure that he has a reasonable amount of pocket money. Buy him a notebook and encourage him to 'budget' and record his spending. You could arrange for a bonus if he keeps to his estimates and refrains from taking sums of money.

stealing

There are two distinct cycles in juvenile law-breaking. The first involves theft, mainly petty in kind. It starts at about the age of nine or ten and persists to fourteen or fifteen. The second stage in juvenile law-breaking begins at about fifteen or sixteen and persists until about eighteen or nineteen. This stage involves rowdyism, some violence, taking away and driving cars, and so on. A child's stealing can only be described as delinquent if it becomes a *habitual* activity, and often it will be a gang pastime.

cheating

There is no awful general character defect which turns your child into 'a cheat'. If this was the case, then the child who cheats in class would be the same child who cheats at games and vice versa, and indeed, everywhere else. But this is not what normally happens.

It is not possible to divide the world into honest youngsters who never cheat and dishonest ones who do so all the time. Most of us cheat occasionally, whether it is the person who passes off a frozen cake as home baking; or the individual who claims expenses for a first-class rail journey when she travelled second-class. Yet, when eleven-year-old Sandy was caught cheating in a test at school, his mother was horrified. Her next mistake was to use a noun to describe his behaviour: 'He's a cheat!' Had she not brought him up to think that honesty was of paramount importance? Now he had been reported for cheating. His parents reacted as if Sandy had demonstrated extreme moral turpitude. They would have done better to say to themselves: 'He's been cheating in maths. Why does he need to do that? He is not very good at it, and we have been piling up the pressure on him to get better results, or else. . . .'

The first thing to do in this kind of situation is to put the cheating into perspective. Does your child regularly cheat? If not, and this is just a rare episode, then there is nothing to agonize about. Of course, that does not mean that you should simply shrug it off; he needs to know this is not the way you expect him to behave. But you will probably find that other children in the school have been found cheating. It is very catching; in some school classes cheating becomes the norm for a while, in others it hardly ever occurs. Critics of our competitive educational system question the wisdom of testing children; they would claim that the less able or less competitive youngsters are pressured into cheating.

Only about six per cent of schoolchildren *never* cheat. A child will cheat if he reckons the stakes are high enough, or the risk of getting caught is low enough. It has little to do with moral values at that age. If you ask children how they feel about cheating, those who cheat are just as likely to disapprove as those who do not.

A normal child cheats when he wants to cover up a real or imagined weakness. If he is self-confident and secure, he will not be tempted to cheat very often. If you find your child is persistently cheating, ask yourself why he feels he cannot rely on his own ability. Often the trouble comes from putting a child in unremitting, competitive situations, and only praising those who come out on top. Perhaps your child feels he cannot keep up with the rest of the class, in which case you could talk things over with him and his teacher.

The internalization of moral controls (the voice of conscience) takes place primarily through the child's acceptance of her parents. She and her parents strike an unconscious bargain; in return for the child's conformity to social requirements (e.g. rules), the parents give her love and approval. If the child fails to conform, disapproval follows. This is sometimes equated with a loss of love by children, and indeed, threatened as such by many adults. In time, she looks ahead to the consequences of her acts. If she is about to misbehave, a rising apprehension warns her that her parents might

to sum up

stop approving or even loving her. Thus, the inner
anxiety eventually results in the internalization of the
parents' morality. In learning terms this means the child
is self-reinforcing; approving her own 'good' actions and
punishing (by self-criticism and guilt) her 'bad' behaviours.
Reminders are less essential. The child has developed a
rudimentary conscience.

There is a more positive aspect; not only does the child
fear withdrawal of love, she also identifies with her
parents. She loves them, and she wishes to emulate
them. Children who fear the loss of love develop the
concept of 'must' but the 'ought' of behaviour comes
only through identification with parents and other moral
symbols.

A variety of family conditions undermine the operation
of these influences in the lives of some children.
Typically, children with persistent conduct (antisocial)
disorders come from families where there is discord and
quarrelling, where affection is lacking, discipline is
inconsistent, ineffective, and either extremely severe or
lax, supervision is inadequate. Often the family has
broken up acrimoniously through divorce or separation.
In addition, the children may have had periods of being
placed 'in care' at times of family crisis. The findings
described in this chapter — based upon many studies of
child development — present us with some practical
guidelines: these appear in chapter 15, in which we
discuss the issue of discipline.

7

Aggression and bad temper

Anger is a recurrent fact of life, for parents as well as their offspring. We have seen that children have to learn — sometimes rather painfully — the lessons of self-control. A young child has a repertoire of some 14 *coercive* behaviours, including temper tantrums, crying, whining, yelling and commanding, which they use (wittingly or unwittingly) to influence, often quite legitimately, their parents. At times influence develops into outright manipulation and confrontation.

This term is applied to the kind of training of children by parents, and, not least, *parents by children,* which is largely unplanned. Most children do not intend to reinforce their parents for nagging and scolding; most parents do not mean to 'reward' their offspring for displaying temper or for whining. But then people are not always conscious of the 'lessons' they are conveying to each other.

'accidental' training

One of the ironies you will find, if you try to analyse the ABC sequences of some of your confrontations with your child, is that you may be strengthening behaviours that you do not like and weakening (extinguishing) actions that you would really wish to encourage.

Here is an example: Pauline is arguing with her older brother; she wants the paintbox John is using. She whines and demands the paints. John refuses, so Pauline puts a few more decibels into a louder, higher-pitched whine. Irritated beyond words, mother orders John to hand over the paints to his 'poor little sister'. She has reinforced Pauline for whining and made the future use of such coercive behaviour more likely. The paint box is the reinforcer.

But that is not all, unfortunately. Mother was also reinforced by 'turning off' that distressing whiny noise. The relief (a reward) has made more likely her response of 'giving in' to whining. Doubtless, she would be quite indignant if we told her she was 'training' her child to be whiny, and that Pauline was 'training' *her* to take the unjust line of least resistance.

negative reinforcement In chapter 3 we referred to positive reinforcement. However, you would be well advised to look out for the accidental strengthening of undesirable behaviours by *negatively reinforcing* them. This is what we mean: anything that will 'turn off' a painful event (e.g. a child's whining) is strengthened. Most of us learn to *avoid* or get away from painful events. Here is a fairly typical sequence:

1 Tom annoys Chris by grabbing his toy.
2 Chris reacts by hitting Tom.
3 Tom then stops annoying Chris, thus negatively reinforcing Chris's hitting response.

Chris has coerced Tom into terminating his annoying behaviour. A vicious circle is quite likely to be set in motion, an escalation of attack and counter-attack. To continue the sequence:

4 Tom may, of course, react to Chris's hitting not by desisting from his grabbing at Chris's toy, but by hitting back in an attempt to terminate Chris's aggression.
5 Chris now responds to Tom's aggression with more intense counter-aggression.

This exchange would continue until it is interrupted by an irritated parent or until one of the antagonists is negatively reinforced by the cessation of warfare on the part of the other child. We can see how it carries within it the seeds for a perpetuation of aggressive behaviour in the child's repertoire.

Coercive behaviours decline steadily in frequency from a high point around two (the 'terrible twos') down to more moderate levels at the age of school entrance. The older 'aggressive' boy displays coercive behaviours at a level commensurate with a two- or three-year-old child and, in this sense, is an exemplar of arrested socialization. Because what usually happens is that with increasing age, certain coercive behaviours (e.g. whining, crying, tantrums) are no longer acceptable to parents; these behaviours then become the target for careful monitoring and sanctions, which in turn are accompanied by reductions in their frequency.

By the age of four, there are substantial improvements in children's ability to hold in check their negative commands, destructiveness and attempts to humiliate. By five, most children use less negativism, non-compliance, and negative physical actions than younger siblings. Such an increase in self-control in the maturing child is most welcome to parents. But let us look at some of the problems they may encounter along the way. Breath-holding is a fairly common example of infant behaviour which often betokens uncontrolled frustration or temper, but sometimes panic.

These 'bouts' occur when the infant or child holds his breath for so long (during the act of crying) that he turns blue and sometimes becomes unconscious. What usually happens is that the episode is triggered when the child is frustrated or suffers a sudden hurt. He cries for a few moments and then, after breathing out, holds his breath. He turns blue because he is not breathing in. Sometimes, after turning blue, he holds his breath for another 10 or 15 seconds and becomes limp — frightening the life out of his parents! Most children, at this stage, take a breath, and soon recover their normal colour. Although breath-holding is so alarming it is basically harmless. Nevertheless — and this applies to all emotional problems which have physical repercussions — it is *essential* to consult your doctor to make sure there are no underlying physical complications which require attention. Once your mind is relieved on this, it is wise to make as little fuss as possible about the breath-holding attacks.

breath-holding

Breath-holding bouts are fairly common in children from 12 months (or a little younger) to three or four years. Where breath-holding may have undesirable side-effects, is in the situation where your consternation about the attacks blackmails you into giving in to the child when you know in your heart of hearts that you should not do so.

All of this does not mean that you should let the bouts go unchecked. No medicines will prevent breath-holding, but you may be able to stop a particular sequence in its tracks by getting your infant to take a breath. A splash of

cold water, a firm pinch, or up-ending the child may do
the trick.

**my child is
aggressive!**

Aggressive outbursts (like headcolds) are a perennial
feature of childhood, nothing to get too excited about.
But some children, like ten-year-old Mark, are problems
because of the persistence of their aggressiveness, the
intensity of the malevolence they feel, and their inability
to control their tempers. Take a day in his life. (We
asked his mother and teacher to record a 'typical' day.)
He bickered with his brother at the breakfast table until
his mother slapped his face. His sister left for school
crying after he had hit her. At school, his teacher had to
reprimand him several times for tripping up and spitting
at the smaller boys in the playground. Back at home
again, he managed to upset a mother new to the
neighbourhood: making her son hysterical by squashing
a wriggly worm on his face. When complaints were
made, he embarrassed his mother by cheekily 'talking
back' to her, in front of the neighbour. The day ended
with Mark, miserable and lonely, excluded from a house
where all the children had gone to play.

Aggressive children make their parents suffer! They
make their teachers suffer! And other children —
particularly the less robust ones — also suffer at their
hands . . . not to mention their feet and the rough edges
of their tongues. In turn, parents of the 'victims' have to
cope with *their* offspring's tears and anxieties about
going to school, out to play, or to places where they will
meet with bullying or abuse.

Aggressive children — in many cases, frustrated
children — eventually hurt themselves; the unhappiness
which makes them aggressive is compounded when they
are shunned by other youngsters.

**what is
aggression?**

The trouble with portmanteau terms like 'aggression' is
that they contain so many meanings and cover so many
different activities. This is not the place to quibble over
academic definitions of aggression. What is really
important to remember is the fact that, as we progress up
the evolutionary scale, living creatures depend less and
less on reflex or instinctual patterns of behaviour and
more and more on experience and learning. Hence the
fascinating variety of possibilities in human behaviours.

15

How should I discipline my child?

For many people discipline is uncomfortably equated with the words 'punishment' and 'repression'. The result is that parents sometimes become tentative and inconsistent in disciplining their children for fear of seeming Victorian or overly intrusive. In fact, discipline is really about a process of training and guidance which helps children come to terms with the world inside and outside the family. The word does not pre-empt the methods, which can be mainly *positive*. Much of the time parents can, and should, rely on natural, spontaneous reactions to their children's behaviour. But intuition is not always enough in matters of discipline. If you can work out some broad strategy on discipline you can anticipate events rather than always be trailing helplessly after them.

the long view: a strategic approach

Think through your philosophy and attitude toward discipline and discuss them with your partner. It is undesirable that one parent has to act the 'heavy' while the other is always the 'nice guy'. If they cannot agree on matters of discipline, their child will soon 'divide and rule'. If father is trying to instil good table manners while mother is arguing 'what does it matter so long as he eats?'; or mother is trying to set up a sensible bedtime routine, while father says 'another half hour won't hurt', mealtimes and bedtimes will go on being a source of friction.

If you can follow a few tried and tested guidelines, based on research into the rearing and development of children, you may find your job less irksome. They will also serve as a reminder of some of the points made in earlier chapters.

**be clear
about your
priorities**

You should try to have a reasonably coherent idea of your aims and objectives in training your children. Discipline is a means to an end, not an end in itself. Parents have the right to have *their* needs considered as well as those of the child; parent—child relationships need to be balanced. To this end, Haim Ginott suggests that parents think of the child's behaviour as falling into three colour codes: green, amber and red.

> *Green* is the 'go ahead' code for the type of behaviour they want from her, the actions which they facilitate by praise and encouragement, for example, sharing her toys with another child or eating her meal without a fuss. They should include those individual attributes of the child — aspects of her personality which make her unique.

> *Amber* is for 'caution' behaviour, which is not encouraged but is tolerated because the child is still learning and making mistakes; for example 'decorating' her room's walls with finger paints or hurling her toys across the room in a moment of fury. Any sort of stress like moving house, illness or some upset in the family, may mean a temporary step backwards in her behaviour. Be understanding if she suddenly starts wetting the bed or crying after a nightmare during the night.

> *Red* is definite *stop* (No! No!) behaviour which needs to be curbed as soon as possible. Obviously anything which could be dangerous for her or for others has a red code: running into the road, touching the hot iron, biting the baby.

**foster bonds
of respect
and affection**

A bond of respect and affection is essential in parenting, and will also make the teacher's task much easier. The more respect and affection there is as a backdrop to disciplinary tactics in the home (and at school), the more notice the child will take of what she is told. It is helpful to make it clear that however cross or disappointed one is over something she has done, it is only *that* particular piece of behaviour the parent dislikes. It may seem obvious to the parent that she does not love the child any less, but it is not obvious to the toddler. Never say 'You've been naughty; mummy doesn't love you any more.' That is to imply that you disapprove of the child as a whole. Rather disapprove of the specific misdemeanour. 'Mummy doesn't like it when you pinch your baby brother. It's wrong to do that!'

Parents cannot always be on the spot to enforce rules, so the rules must become so ingrained — so much

There is no denying that inbuilt physical factors, such as hormones and brain mechanisms, are important in the aggressive behaviour of animals and humans. There are the internal bodily changes which occur during the so-called 'emergency emotions' — rage, fear, excitement and pain. During a crisis, the hormonal changes mobilize the energies of an individual in preparation for a vigorous fight or a flight for life. It has been possible (in animal experiments) to locate centres in the brain which are involved in the production of rage and aggressive behaviour. Previously placid humans, after disease or injury to certain areas of the brain, have become irascible and sometimes violent. In humans, the appearance of rage and anger is regulated by the highly developed cerebral cortex, which can either inhibit or give release to expressions of hostility.

aggression as a learned habit

This cortical control has led many distinguished scientists to be optimistic about human nature. They conclude that the important lesson to be derived from studies of aggression in individuals and societies is that there is no instinctive impulse to violence in human beings. The *feeling* of anger may well be aroused by involuntary processes, but humans are not stereotyped in their behavioural responses to the emotional state. Aggressiveness is a *learned* habit or appetite. The belief here is that social rather than biological characteristics determine the hostile acts and belligerence of individuals. This notion has infused the debates about the malignant effects of penny dreadfuls, comics, the movies and television on successive generations, with much solemnity.

watching television

There is insufficient space here to detail the complicated and inconclusive debates about the influence of television on children. There is some evidence that violent television programmes can lead to aggressive acts by children, and that such programmes influence the development of aggression, particularly in boys, and more generally in already vulnerable antisocial children. Why take a chance? It is better not to allow the television to become an electronic nanny or an irreplaceable friend to your child. Parents are discriminating about choosing a child minder, or about monitoring their child's playmates; they should be equally selective about his viewing.

**the develop-
ment of
aggressive
behaviour**

The child's aggressiveness arises as a natural, if tiresome side-effect of becoming socialized. From birth onwards, there are individual differences in assertiveness and passivity. These tend to persist in many children as they grow older. Rage appears in very young infants. The infant is intolerant of the thwarting of his desires and he tends to hit out when frustrated. Typical displays of undirected anger in young children include: jumping up and down, breath-holding, screaming, and so on. The younger the child, the stronger are its demands for the immediate gratification of all its wants. As the child gets older, random, undirected or unfocused displays of emotional excitement become more rare, and aggression that is retaliatory more frequent. It may consist of throwing objects, grabbing, pinching, biting, striking, calling names, arguing and insisting. A small child will perhaps bite when frustrated, an older child may hit or throw something at the frustrating person. It is not easy for young children to learn to 'wait patiently', to 'ask nicely', and to be generous, considerate and self-sacrificing. They try to get their way by fighting for it. The psychological restraints of naggings, frequent 'nos', and punishment, provoke resentment and possibly aggression. The child may 'get his own back' by indirect tactics; he 'gets on his mother's nerves' or irritates her by his refusal to eat or go to bed, or he inconveniently forgets to go to the toilet — wetting or soiling his pants.

'Are You the Young Man That Bit My Daughter?'
Copr. © 1932, 1960 James Thurber. *The Seal in the Bedroom*, published by Harper & Row.

Interference with the satisfaction of needs is only one of the many sources of frustration leading to aggression. Another common source is in the conflict of motives. Observations of children demonstrate that one of the most common causes of fighting is dispute over the possession of desired objects. Self-control also enters the picture. In older children, hostility is frequently inhibited from open expression; after three years of age, the more aggressive components of behaviour — like other coercive activities — begin to be less frequent, in both boys and girls. There is a reduction in temper tantrums. At nine, more than 50 per cent of boys, but only 30 per cent of girls, are having quite frequent explosions of temper.

Some of the differences in aggressiveness between boys and girls may be due to the fact that parents tend to disapprove more of aggression in girls; in our culture females are supposed to fulfil the role of submissive, gentle and nurturant creatures. Boys are expected to be assertive go-getters, so parents tend to approve aggression in their male offspring as 'manly'. Much of the time parents are quite unconscious of their 'reinforcing' behaviour. What we have then is aggression depending on the habits acquired during upbringing, on temperamental qualities moulded during the formative years, on exposure to aggressive models (such as aggressive parents), and on the indulgence or punishment meted out when anger has been shown.

There are several tactics for dealing with anger and 'blame' in frustrating situations, but three basic patterns have been observed: the 'anger out' reaction, in which the tendency is to blame others aggressively for misfortunes; the 'anger in' response, in which the tendency is to look within oneself for the responsibility for frustrations and to accept the blame; and, lastly, the defensive impunitive reaction, in which the frustrating situation is glossed over, its existence denied, and no blame attributed.

These explosions of temper are among the most intense and formidable outbursts of rage seen in children; the child works himself up to a pitch of frenzied excitement, during which he stamps his feet, hammers with his fists, thrashes his arms about, bangs his head, rolls about on

temper tantrums

the floor, and curses or screams. We have seen that it is quite normal for the two- or three-year-old to have such rages; these episodes often occur when mother has frustrated the child. At the moment of his rage he may really appear to 'hate' his mother; yet, more often than not, he seems to deflect his aggression by hurting himself rather than her.

Feelings of hate may reside alongside deep feelings of love, and this love—hate relationship indicates the complexity of human emotions. Many stricken mothers have heard their children say, 'I hate you' or, 'I hate my home', but they usually try to understand that frustrations evoke this protest, and appreciate that it is merely a ripple on the deeper waters of real affection. Paradoxically, if a child can say this he must feel safe, loved enough to let rip. In relationships between people, love and hate are opposite sides of the same coin. The rejected child or abandoned lover may respond with hate to loss and deprivation.

Detailed tips on the management of temper tantrums are provided in chapter 16. The way in which parents handle their child's aggressive behaviour can have an important bearing, in the long run, (as we shall see) on whether he is too submissive or too hostile. While no compassionate person would wish to heap frustrations on any child's head, if you try to protect him from all thwarting of his wishes, you may produce a person with a very low threshold for tolerating frustration. Some children are on a 'short fuse', quick to anger; every small provocation is welcomed as an opportunity to release a flood of hostile acts or abuse. Others are slow to react, and find it easy to 'sit out' frustrating events.

the coercive child

We examined, earlier on, the coercive process; the way a child learns to command all and sundry. Danny was such a child — a six-year-old boy who was brought to a clinic because of his frequent attempts to force his parents to comply with his wishes. He virtually determined his own bedtime, the foods he would eat, when his parents had to play with him, and various other household activities. The psychologists who described this case felt that it illustrated how successful mothers can be as 'therapists' for their own children (see Appendix II). A record was kept and a graph plotted of Danny's problematic ('commanding') behaviour, and was defined as any verbal or non-verbal instruction to his mother (e.g. pushing her into a chair, or making commands: 'Now we'll play this'; 'You go over there and I'll stay here'; 'No, that's wrong. Do it this way!'). Also recorded were actions labelled as 'co-operative behaviour' — Danny's non-demanding statements or actions. There was a marked predominance in frequency of the problematic over the co-operative behaviours during the assessment (baseline) sessions. The mother's reactions usually consisted of following Danny's instructions with such comments as 'OK, if that's what you think; am I doing it right, now?' We shall return to Danny's problem, but for the moment let us see how his mother let herself in for this predicament.

Many children with coercive problems seem to be arrested at a demanding (egocentric) stage of development — whatever their age. The period between approximately one and three years of age is a 'sensitive period' with regard to the development (and therefore prevention) of such conduct. These problems take root because of the inability of parents (for a variety of good and not-so-good reasons) to confront their child's early and 'natural' coercive behaviour in a manner that will launch him into the vital later stages of moral development and those processes of socialization which have to do with empathy and impulse control.

causes of coercive problems

The psychologist Gerald Patterson suggests the following reasons for the child's failure to substitute more mature behaviours for his primitive coercive repertoire:

1   the parents may neglect to teach prosocial skills (for example, they seldom reinforce the child's use of language or other self-help skills);
2   they may, however, reinforce the child's display of coercive behaviours;
3   they may allow brothers and sisters to tease or bully the child in such a manner that the only way he can terminate them is by answering like with like, namely, coercive behaviours;
4   they may use punishment inconsistently for coercive behaviours;

5   when they *do* punish, they are likely to do so in a feeble manner that lacks credibility.

first aid   Quiet thought about your 'management' (or disciplinary) strategies is essential, when you are considering the longer term, and how to prevent the extremes of aggressive-coercive behaviours. But what about 'coping' tactics for dealing with the day-to-day emergencies and irritations, as when Joan pinches Sally and Kevin kicks the next-door cat; when Dick ruins his party by terrorizing the other children. Something must be done — and done quickly. The problem about coping with situations is that there is no 'recipe' book with clearcut advice for you to consult. What suits one child won't necessarily suit another. So it is really a good idea to work out personal guidelines (preferably broad and flexible), for dealing with blow-ups. Anger begets anger, and Haim Ginott advises parents to acknowledge the fact that children will make them angry; that they are entitled to their anger without guilt or shame; that with one safeguard they are entitled to express what they feel.

That safeguard is that you do not attack the child's personality or character. The saying 'sticks and stones may break my bones but words will never hurt me' is not always true. It is possible to break a child's spirit with incessant criticism and harsh words. But what about physical punishment?

Ask yourself: if I hit my child for his aggressiveness, do I make him more angry, or fearful? How does he interpret my counter-aggression? Won't he come to the conclusion that 'might is right'; that physical punishment is a legitimate means of getting one's way, of controlling others, because *I* do it?

dealing with aggression

give him a chance to cool down

From what we know from research into the problem of aggressiveness, it seems that scoldings and chastisement, administered in the heat of anger, are likely to perpetuate the spiral of frustration—resentment—anger—aggression—counter-aggression. It is no use trying to reason with a child when he is in the middle of a tantrum. Turn away from the persistent tantrum or walk out on it. When he is calm again he should be told *why* his behaviour is unacceptable.

You can not always afford to ignore a child's aggression. Put your arms around him firmly so that he can not lash out. This is called 'passive inhibition'.

restrain him firmly and as gently as possible

The absence of mum at the party or teacher in the nursery-school playground may be a cue for some children that threatening or hitting other children is likely to gain them certain pay-offs (i.e. advantages such as the best playthings). In other words, certain 'stimulus conditions' provide signals to children that aggressive behaviour is likely to have rewarding consequences for them. You need to be aware of situations that an aggressive child might exploit — and act accordingly. One way, here, would be to provide adult supervision of play until it is no longer necessary.

reducing cues (signals) for aggressive behaviour

A penalty, or 'response-cost' programme (see Appendix I), provides conditions which signal to the child that his aggressive behaviour is *not* going to produce a pay-off. Indeed, it is likely to lead to negative outcomes (penalties). The provision of such discriminative stimuli as part of your tactics may bring aggression under control while you encourage more acceptable *alternative* behaviour.

providing cues for non-aggressive behaviour

Exposure to other people behaving aggressively may facilitate the imitation of such behaviour by the observer. An attempt to reduce the exposure of a child to such aggressive models (does he have aggressive playmates?) is likely to decrease the likelihood of imitative behaviour.

reducing the exposure to aggressive models

You could encourage acceptable alternatives to aggression by exposing your youngster to children who manifest such peaceable actions — especially when he sees that they serve to obtain rewards for these models.

providing models of non-aggressive behaviour

Aggressive behaviour may be instigated by a large variety of unpleasant (aversive) stimuli; by physical and verbal assaults of a painful, threatening or humiliating nature, and by deprivation of proper nurturance, rights and opportunities. Reduction of such aversive stimuli may be accompanied by a reduction in aggression. Another technique involves defusing provocative events by diminishing their power to arouse anger in the child. This is achieved by teaching the child to remain calm in

reducing provocative stimuli

the face of provocation (see Appendix I), and to use humour (and other methods) to take the edge off awkward confrontations.

skills training   Many children lack some of the critical skills required to function in a satisfactory manner. Consequently, they may behave aggressively in response to a variety of frustrations and humiliations. If such children can be helped to become more competent, then they may have less recourse to aggression. For example, you might teach your child the skill of being more assertive, that is, to protect her own rights in a capable and confident manner, without denying the rights of others by being aggressive or neglectful towards them.

time out   Children sometimes need time to bring self-control into play. A period in which to reflect on their aggressive behaviour and *how* self-defeating it is, may do the trick. Explain how it leads to further unhappiness for herself, not to mention others. It may be necessary to remove the child from a group (by letting her watch a game but not participate) if she persists in disrupting the fun. Other methods can be devised to make bad-tempered behaviour costly. Nothing defeats a 'scene' as effectively as removing her from her audience. This age-old and very effective method of taking the intransigent child away from the pleasures of social company has been blessed with a technical term 'time out from positive reinforcement' (see Appendix I).

A parent can be helped by psychologists to deal with a particularly awkward situation by her own efforts. In the case of Danny's mother — following the assessment sessions — she was instructed to be responsive to the child's co-operative behaviour but to *ignore* his commanding behaviour completely. She was successful in following these instructions. During the first two sessions, her frequency of responding to Danny's commanding behaviour dropped to zero, while her response to his co-operative behaviour increased steadily. Danny's behaviour during the sessions soon showed a change. The frequency of his commanding behaviour dropped considerably, in comparison to its rate during the baseline sessions, while his co-operative behaviour increased sharply. Interestingly enough, Danny's mother reported that she was much more comfortable with him during the concluding sessions.

Verbal abuse is a form of aggression but bad language may have more innocent connotations. If children learned speech as easily as they learn to swear, life would be simple for parents. They are fascinated by words they think are 'naughty' — words like bloody, fart or bum. Obscenities have a kind of fascination for youngsters and they can be certain of raising shrieks of laughter from their friends, just by saying them aloud. Parents sometimes get alarmed about this; needlessly, it should be said. Children pick up bad language not only outside the home but sometimes from those censorious parents as well. Children do not have the same need as adults to use bad language as a means of relieving their feelings; they have other ways of letting off steam. But they do enjoy provoking a fuss and palaver from adults. Over-reacting with shock and dismay when the child first comes out with a four-letter word is the best way to ensure he uses it again and again.

verbal abuse and bad language

To begin with, *ignore* any swear words or obscenities he uses. (You may remember that 'extinction' is the name for this method.) This may be enough to make him lose interest; if he does persist, discourage him briefly and matter-of-factly, explaining that such words offend some people, who will like him less if he insists on using them. Do not tell him that adults are allowed to swear but children are not. One of the attractions of swearing is that it seems a grown-up thing to do, like smoking, and this will only make it all the more tempting. When bad language becomes abusive, that is the time to adopt a very firm line. Time-out and response-cost may help, and these methods are described fully in Appendix I.

taking action

8

Social skills and relationships

Apart from the obvious skills such as learning to read and write, crossing the road safely, counting the correct change, and developing good judgement, there are certain skills which, because they are not obvious or readily taught, come hard to some youngsters. These are the social graces which many of us take for granted, simply because they are to a large extent unconscious. It is these skills that we use when we meet strangers, make small talk, encourage acquaintanceship, attract friends, fit in with groups of people, and negotiate countless other social interactions.

forming impressions of people In any encounter with a strange person — at a party, at school, or wherever it may be — the youth forms a basic impression of the other person — (say) a boy. She observes his actions, takes note of his voice and accent, follows what he says and how he says it, notices his mannerisms, and *particularly* pays heed to the way he reacts to what *she* does and says. He, in his turn, responds to her actions, correcting his approach if he sees signs of boredom, resentment or embarrassment, and so social interaction is created — a cycle of action and reaction. In this way the boy attempts to assess her attitudes and feelings towards him; he decides whether or not she likes him. She, in turn, tries to evaluate his sincerity and motives. Their conclusions help to shape their intentions and responses toward each other.

From early childhood we have to learn how to react to, and cope with, a multitude of people and situations. Many conventions shape our behaviour towards particular persons in particular circumstances — there are some things that can be said and others that cannot. A

familiarity of manner and address which is permissible
with one individual is frequently taboo with another;
there are sensitivities, about both topics and language,
which must be respected if offence is not to be given in
certain settings. We have to learn to predict and interpret
the behaviour of others.

In certain ways, at that first meeting, the youngster's
role is that of a detective — looking for clues, piecing
together fragmentary pieces of information — in order
to obtain a picture of the girl's personality and attitude
towards him. Unlike the detective, the boy accomplishes
much of his impression-forming at a more or less
unconscious level.

Youngsters who cannot get on with other children,
who are lacking in social skills, who are clumsy or shy,
often lead miserable and lonely lives. They may lack the
vital skills of social sensitivity and of forming accurate
impressions of other people — the foundations upon
which personal liking, leading to the attraction of
acquaintances, and thereby to friendship, is built. Those
children who are the most popular or influential members
of groups, and the most effective leaders, tend to have
these attributes in abundance. Of course there are
children who possess the requisite social skills, but have
little opportunity to practise them and thus gain
confidence. It is hardly surprising — in the light of what
has been said — that those who have problems with their
peer group early in life, tend to have severe difficulties in
adolescence and adulthood; they have been found to be
more likely to drop out of school, be identified as juvenile
delinquents later on, or have mental health problems in
later life. (Remember, this is a statistical generalization,
not a prediction in every case of poor relationships!)
Ratings of children's popularity (at the age of about nine)
by their peers are better predictors of later psychological
problems than school records, intellectual achievements,
teacher judgements, or any other type of measure.

Certain values — affection, loyalty, altruism, dependa-
bility — have always been associated with a good, mature
relationship. A friendly relationship is one which requires
a degree of self-awareness and social sensitivity. Obviously
a baby is not born with either of these qualities; he

**forming
friendly
relationships**

develops them gradually through his dealings with other people — parents, brothers and sisters, friends and teachers. His image of himself plays a part in all of this. It is shaped by the way he believes they see him, and the way he wants them to see him. If his immediate circle of family and friends is a happy, relaxed and outgoing one, providing love and appreciation — balm to his ego — he will have a good image of himself, and get along well with others. If, however, they always undermine his self-confidence with criticism or rejection, so that he feels unworthy and inferior, he will tend to have a poor self-image, be over-anxious and defensive. It will be an uphill task to form relationships with others. Nor can he get on (in a sense) with himself.

what are social skills?

Generally speaking, social skills do not simply apply to what a child does, for example, how 'good', 'compliant' or even 'friendly' he or she is — but to what they are able to do. The clearest analogy is with problem-solving, how we work out solutions to difficulties in a particular person-to-person setting. You would be asking: does my child have alternative courses of action ('solutions') which he can take, plus some means of choosing between them? Or is he tied to narrow, rigid and perhaps self-destructive modes of action? Aggression would be a classic example of this.

learning social skills

Without confidence in his social skills a child feels inadequate; he expects to fail and the more he anticipates disaster the more likely he is to fail. The most important foundations for learning social skills are the relationships which children form with adults and children and which teach him how to locate himself in a social world, form emotional bonds, and understand the social events with which he may be faced. In our culture a large number of these skills are acquired from learning experiences in the family. Mixing with children of his own age is necessary for learning about aggression, the development of sociability, moral values and sexual roles — a somewhat different range of experiences to those provided within the bosom of the family.

The aim of a psychologist is to increase an unskilled child's repertoire of possible actions within a social setting, making his relationships with other children both more constructive and more creative.

Here are some specific research findings about what makes a child socially successful or unsuccessful:

1 Children who are acceptable to their peers tend also to demonstrate sensitivity, responsiveness and generosity in their relationships with other children. They help others often; they frequently give attention, approval and affection to others; they give and receive friendly overtures and respond positively to the dependent behaviour of their peers; and they are sensitive to the social overtures of others.

2 Children who are not much liked by others, but are not particularly disliked, tend to be withdrawn, passive, fearful of social contact.

3 Children who are actively disliked by others tend to be aggressive. They seem to be locked in a vicious cycle whereby they learn that to get what they want they should be aggressive; this often succeeds in the short term (e.g. they gain a toy by using threats) but fails in the long term. Other children avoid and reject them. In this way, aggressive youngsters never learn alternatives to such actions, and become more and more reliant on their fists as their only social 'skill'.

4 Children who are well liked are better at seeing things from the point of view of another child; disliked children tend to be poor at this.

5 They have at their command more potential techniques for solving difficult (*and* everyday) situations involving person-to-person relationships. The processes underlying such skills are sensitivity to *when* problems occur, ability to work out alternative courses of action, and sensitivity to the consequences of their chosen action.

Immature, self-centred children are not always able to manage the give-and-take of friendship. What is called 'exchange theory' gives us pointers to why this should be so; it provides one method of evaluating friendships. Social interactions and relationships are compared to economic bargains or the exchange of gifts; they are seen as a ratio of rewards and costs. All activities carried out by one individual, to the benefit of another, are termed 'rewards', while detrimental activities — hostility, anxiety, embarrassment — are counted as 'costs'. If a child forgoes a reward (e.g. loses the approval of his family) because he engages in some form of social interaction (e.g. associating with a delinquent), this, too, is termed a cost. The ratio of rewards to costs is called the 'outcome'; if the outcome is positive, it may be said to yield a 'profit', if negative, it is termed a 'loss'. So, before we can be said to be attracted to a potential friend, the 'reward—cost outcome' must be above the 'comparison level', a standard against which satisfaction is judged. Selfish or aggressive people, by their actions, tilt the balance towards the loss or debit side.

Although this theory makes it seem as if all friendships are exploitive — and of course some are — it must be repeated that the emphasis is on mutual satisfaction of needs. There must always be some give-and-take; friendships which are too one-sided, selfish or exploitive, are not likely to last. To continue with the economic analogy, when costs soar and the balance-sheet is in fundamental imbalance, showing persistent losses, the friendship is likely to be in danger.

If you are worried about your child's inability to make or keep friends, carry out a small exercise in 'accountancy', based on discreet observations of your youngster's behaviour with other children; the trick is to look at things from the *other* child's point of view. Is your child being insensitive, too demanding, or disloyal? Is his company rewarding enough?

practical hints   *Teach him.* Teach your child to see the other's point of view (not necessarily at the expense of his own). Role-taking — the mental placing of oneself in the other person's position — is central to all forms of human communication. There is evidence that children engage in rudimentary forms of role-taking very early in life. Nevertheless, when children are confronted with perspectives that are different from their own, they often *assume* similarity where there is none. This leads to misunderstanding — mutual and at times painful.

Praise him. Praise your child for initiating social behaviour.

Model for him. Model *social* behaviour to a child; physically demonstrate the various ways of interacting socially with others. Demonstrate how he might make positive comments about another child; also show him how to play constructively.

Prompt him. Ask him to demonstrate something to another (e.g. how to work the fizzy machine); direct him to help, or seek help, of another.

Coach him. Coach your child in social behaviour — encourage him in social activity and describe or explain ways of interacting socially (e.g. when he is with children you have invited home). Here are some suggestions:

1 Encourage the child to adopt a sociable perspective (e.g. 'Let's talk about some ways to have fun with other kids when you play games'; 'One way to make a game fun for everyone is to take turns . . . when you take turns in a game other kids will have fun too and will want to play with you again').
2 Clarify what 'taking turns' means (e.g. 'During a game, taking turns means giving everyone a chance to play').
3 Encourage your child to identify some good and bad examples (e.g. 'Yes, waiting until others have finished before you begin would be taking turns'; 'Always trying to have first go or stopping others from having a try would not be taking turns').
4 Get your child to rehearse verbally some examples of sociable actions and then to recall them.
5 Give your child 'feedback' about the way he has learned (and later — hopefuly — performs) the social skill.

In this way you teach him to translate social concepts into social actions.

We go, now, beyond ordinary social relationships, beyond   **friendship**
friendly acquaintances and getting on with people, and look at children's friendships. There are rather special benefits in friendship. Reciprocated liking, the sharing of interests and life-experiences, a relaxed, uncritical and

undemanding association, produce a sense of warmth and well-being in what it only too often a rather cold and inhospitable world.

becoming
friends

How and when do children make friends? There is relatively little interaction with peers during the first year of life. Social responsiveness, at this stage, is mainly to adults and older brothers and sisters; but even at this tender age there are interesting differences in the nature of babies' responses. Some are 'cuddly', and enjoy being held and fussed over; others do not take to cuddling. Parents who enjoy a good cuddle may (mistakenly) interpret this aloofness — even resistance — to restraining physical contact as rejection, and feel quite hurt.

Children from six to eight months of age generally relate to their play surroundings rather than to play objects and playmates. Other children are usually ignored. When contact is made, and when it is friendly, it comprises little more than observing, smiling, or perhaps grabbing at the playmate. There may be angry conflict when the infant wants a toy which is in the possession of the other child. This anger tends to be relatively unfocused.

From nine to thirteen months, children respond more to play objects than to playmates. Fights over possession of desirable toys tend to be frequent and rather more personal; nevertheless the objects, not the playmates, are still the main focus, so true hostility has yet to appear. Babies begin to shift their attitudes towards playmates somewhere between 14 and 18 months. There is a decline in the element of conflict with others. For the 19- to 25-month-old children, play objects and playmates are more successfully integrated, and social interaction begins to predominate. Youngsters will modify their behaviour in order to adjust to their playmates' activities.

friendship
patterns

Children's interactions with peers are transformed soon after infancy by three changes in their psychological capacities: their increasing awareness of the symbolic significance of everyday events; their gradually emerging consciousness of moral obligation; and their growing ability to view social interactions as part of a system of continuing stable social relationships. Friendly contacts between children increase between the ages of two and five. During these years, children form their first friendships, generally, but not exclusively, with members of their own sex. Popular children can be distinguished as early as the nursery school phase. They are frequently sought out as playmates, while others are frequently ignored, and some are consistently shunned by their peers. However, in general, the interaction of pre-school or nursery-school children is characteristically more friendly and co-operative than hostile and competitive and, indeed, even the most aggressive youngsters at this stage make more friendly than aggressive overtures to other children. Friendships at this age are casual, transient and unstable, and they probably have few important or enduring effects on a child's personality.

Friendship patterns change with age. After five, the development is towards closer attachment to a few special children though, at this stage, peers in general also become very important. Previously, parents and family have been the main agents of the child's socialization. Now it is teachers, parents, peers *and* close friends who are the important social influences in the child's life. In many ways, children of this age turn their backs on adults and become immersed in the community of children. Even at this early stage, children tend to choose friends who have the same status as themselves, who live in the same neighbourhood or are in the same class at school, and who are about the same age. Most boys between the ages of six and eight ignore gender in their play — choosing girls on their sides in games as often as they select boys — but, at about eight, associations with members of the opposite sex decrease sharply until, at eleven or twelve, the segregation in play groups and at social gatherings is almost complete. When asked to name their best friends, youngsters often choose children with highly-esteemed personality traits. The older ones in this age range emphasize friendliness, cheerfulness, tidiness and cleanliness. The younger ones tend to stress externals such as a nice home, pleasant looks, and having money to spend.

The process by which people are initially attracted to each other and finally become friends, can be represented symbolically by a 'funnel' with a series of filters in it.

choosing friends

Each person has such a figurative 'funnel', with filters designed to fit his particular criteria for a friend. At the opening of the funnel is the first criterion, *proximity*, which determines the eligibles. Before any kind of attraction can be established, there must be opportunity for the children to come into contact. Ordinarily, friendships evolve out of some direct face-to-face contact. Children who live close to one another are more likely to become friends than those who live some distance apart, and children who interact frequently are more likely to become friends than those who interact rarely. Youngsters who live in isolated areas, or whose parents artificially isolate them from other children, may have difficulty in making friends. The pool of eligibles is too small.

After the constraints of the proximity factor, further filters will work to narrow the field gradually. In general, the filters select 'similar individual characteristics', 'common interests or values', and 'similar personality'. Someone who successfully passes through these filters becomes a friend. The second filter works on the basis that *like attracts like*. There is little or no evidence that opposites attract in children's friendships. Pairs of friends, in fact, tend to resemble each other in several respects: social maturity, age, weight, height and general intelligence. Friendly, energetic, capable, responsive and daring youngsters are attracted to each other, possibly because they understand one another and can fulfil their mutual needs. Thus, the second 'filter' suggests that birds of a feather do flock togehter.

Friendship choices are influenced to a significant extent by similarities in social background, religious affiliations and ethnic-group membership. The most significant influence on the formation of friendships is the *belief* that another is similar to oneself; this is more important than whether or not he is *actually* similar. Children also tend to choose as friends those with characteristics considered desirable in terms of the values of their group. Some children are attracted to others whose needs complement their own, although this is rare. For example, a dominant child may become friendly with someone who is predominantly submissive, but the principle that 'opposites attract' is the exception, not the rule. People usually choose others whom they perceive as choosing *them*. In other words, a person likes others whom he believes view him in a favourable light.

In middle childhood, friendships are fairly unstable; interests change easily at this period, and 'old' friends may be unable to satisfy new needs. The capacity for building lasting friendships gradually increases during childhood and adolescence. As the child grows older, interests become focused, and friendships are thus more likely to be enduring. Before the age of eleven or twelve, girls are more socially active than boys, and tend to establish more intimate and confidential relationships with each other. The capacity of the older child to form friendships, and to maintain them on the basis of meeting others' needs as well as his own, is thought to be a strong indication of developing social maturity.

It must be said that the lack of a friend during the school years is not uncommon. In a typical classroom, about one child in five turns out to be an isolate. None of their classmates chooses them. Not all children go out of their way to make friends; some actively shun other children. A few may have personality problems, as a cause or as a consequence of rejection. At the other extreme, most groups have a few popular members, chosen by many of their classmates. Popular children may have many admirers but few friends. Being singled out for admiration by many, may even tend to isolate a person from close personal relationships, especially if the qualities or accomplishments which earn popularity are envied by others who lack such gifts.

lack of friends

Children's temperaments vary, and so do their social needs. You may have one child who sticks to the same close friend for years and takes little interest in other children — another who has such a wide and changing circle of friends you can hardly remember their names. So long as they are both content with the way things are, there is no reason for you to interfere.

Most children naturally gravitate towards their own age group and there are good reasons for encouraging this whenever possible. A child who only has older playmates — the toddler in a big family, for instance — can get so used to being the one who has to fetch and carry, the one who follows meekly after the others, that

variations in friendship patterns

she has no chance to develop qualities of leadership and independence. Sometimes age differences can be useful. A bright child can benefit from being with older children where he has to make a little more effort to stretch himself and where he is not always the leader.

unsuitable friends   You can not choose your child's friends for her. The pleasant girl down the road may look the ideal friend for your daughter, but there is no way you can force them to like each other. If you disapprove (mildly) of a particular friend your child brings home, wait patiently for the relationship to fade out, rather than act the heavy-handed parent and try to force them apart. However, parents have become desperate because 'Johnny, down the road, has such a powerful and bad effect on Fred.' Parents have been known to sell their homes to get away from what they feel are the sinister influences of delinquent children. This is extreme, and parents can usually halt an association which is obviously having adverse consequences. Middle-class parents have more say than working-class parents about whom their offspring associate with. Suburban homes and gardens offer more 'protected' playgrounds than inner-city slum streets or the collective playgrounds of high-rise flats and council estates.

   Children belong to two societies: the society of adults and that of their peers. This is particularly the case as they approach their teens. Parents rightly concern themselves more, at this stage, about the 'good' and 'bad' influences in their children's lives. They worry about the company they keep, as they grow out of, and away from the family. One type of group — for example, a delinquent gang — can foster hostile, disobedient, uncreative individuals; another can develop confused, purposeless, drifters; and still another produces co-operative, flexible, purposeful, altruistic children. In turn, the atmosphere of the group is determined by the qualities of its leaders and those of the other group members. Research into juvenile misbehaviour demonstrates clearly the importance of supervision, of keeping a discreet track of what children are doing.

The short answer is yes; but the style of doing it is important. Try to keep a low profile. The type of child she mixes with can be important. And the degree of influence the friends have over her can be critical. The balance should not be allowed to tilt too far away from the family, and too far towards the peer group, if you are interested in having a say in your child's social development! This does not mean that you should keep your child under unremitting surveillance, but if youngsters are left completely unsupervised, they are quite likely to think of ways of getting up to mischief, and beyond that something downright illegal. Many of the parents of delinquent children just do not care what their children are up to, as long as they themselves are not bothered. It is surely worth the effort to get to know your children's friends and to be aware of the sort of groups or gangs they are associating with.

should I monitor my child's friendships?

Adrian, aged nine, the only child of rather elderly parents, refused to go to school, and would speak to no one but his parents. These problems (together with bouts of bed-wetting) had become worse of late. Always a solitary and timid boy at school, Adrian became noticeably more shy and preoccupied. At home, where he had previously been a precocious, domineering child — 'a lovable little tyrant', in his mother's words — he was pale and weepy. His mother was at her wits' end and couldn't cope with his fears of children and of social gatherings — which seemed to get worse day by day. We return to Adrian in chapter 10.

shyness and insecurity

Here we see shyness — social anxiety — in a rather extreme form. One of the strategies for coping in life might be called strategic withdrawal — or flight. This may not necessarily be physical withdrawal; it can take the form of a psychological 'retreat' such as avoidance behaviour, escape tactics and submission. Emotional forces (such as fear, anxiety or guilt) reinforce withdrawal or avoidance patterns of behaviour.

Submission is a tactic many of us have seen in animals. When animals of the same species fight each other, it often happens that when one is beaten it takes up an attitude of submission. It may emphasize its vulnerability by freezing into a defenceless position, by offering its throat to its opponent, or by cowering away, often with its tail between its legs. This acknowledgement of defeat may save the weaker animal from being overwhelmed. A child may characteristically adopt a submissive stance towards other children which says in effect: 'I am no threat. I am too weak to be worth attacking.' Such a strategy may work, more often it is self-defeating. If a child makes extensive use of the tactic of denigrating and humbling himself, he is likely to discover to his regret that bullies are only temporarily placated by such self-abasement. It may even be counterproductive, and encourage victimization because it reinforces the bully's sadistic needs.

There is a group of problems — the emotional problems — in which the emotional nucleus is a feeling of insecurity. An insecure child lacks confidence, feels uncertain, unsafe and anxious. His insecurity may show itself in the form of shyness and timidity; it may manifest itself in apprehensions about going to school, or hesitations in the hurly burly of the playground; it may show itself as a form of dependency, clinging to mother; or it may be revealed in a fear of teachers and other authority figures.

In meeting the many new and sometimes exacting and frightening challenges of life — at school, at play and on social occasions — the inexperienced, immature child is bound to feel some insecurity. A certain amount of insecurity in that sense is normal. However, most healthy children soon adapt to situations and get over their stage-fright. But in some children — vulnerable for a variety of reasons involving their upbringing and biological make-up — persisting uncertainty, apprehension, fear and a lack of confidence are so great that particularly sensitive handling (and perhaps professional guidance) are required.

a sense of security
Erik Erikson believes that if the child's essential needs are met, he will develop a 'basic trust' in the world, and thus evolve a nucleus of security and self-trust which is indispensable to his later development. How is this trust manifested in observable terms at this early stage of life? Perhaps it shows itself in the ease with which the baby feeds, in the depth of his sleep, and in the relaxation of his bowel movements. Later on it is demonstrated when

the infant will let his mother out of his sight without undue anxiety or rage. The baby who smiles easily is also thought to demonstrate security. The contrasting attitudes of trust and mistrust are very like the adult attitudes of optimism and pessimism; they can colour his outlook on life and, indeed, his personality. Of course that is not the entire story; other circumstances, occurring later in the child's life may engender a sense of uncertainty.

A child's shyness may reflect an insecurity when in the presence of adults or other children he does not know. We are not surprised when the young child goes through a 'shy stage', becoming bashful, timid, anxious and silly in the company of strangers. (At most ages, girls are more likely than boys to show signs of shyness.) Babies, at about the age of seven or eight months, usually become shy of strangers. This shyness is gradually overcome as the baby grows to feel less dependent on his mother, father, and others of immediate significance to him, but a majority of young children go on being a little diffident and apprehensive in *strange* situations. Children often experience conflict when confronted by strangers. They show by their overt behaviour that they are attracted to strangers — they try to make eye contact, to approach them, and to engage in further social inter-actions of various kinds. At the same time, their avoidance tendencies — a sign of apprehension — involve keeping distance or moving away, avoiding prolonged eye contact, various degrees of turning away the head, and of closing the eyes. Most children come through this phase of shyness sooner or later.

Although adults are generally eager to help those who are vulnerable, children tend to be more insensitive, and the shy or fearful youngster is quite likely to become the victim of taunting and ridicule.

The best way to deal with shyness of the day-to-day *remedies* variety is, first of all, to resist the temptation to express disapproval and anger. A sympathetic attitude is called for. A careful analysis should be made of the types of social situation which upset the child. There may be particular precipitating events (see chapter 3) which magnify the youngster's anxiety. Parental attitudes (such as over-solicitous concern about the child's well-being away from home) may have fostered the initial timidity. Lack of confidence may be caused by an exposure to older and more boisterous children. Reassurance is necessary — but may not be sufficient — in such cases. It may also prove counterproductive if not applied *selectively*.

Unfortunately, there is evidence that adults can unwittingly use reassurance to encourage the very behaviour they want to stop. This was well brought out in a nursery school class. One very shy child found himself almost completely isolated from the rest of the class and over a period of several days it was observed that he spent no more than ten per cent of his time close to and working with other children. The teacher was aware of this, and did her best to reassure and help the boy by talking to him and generally making a fuss of him. However, what she had not noticed was that she consistently gave the child her attention when he was alone, and never when he was with the other children. So a simple experiment was done. She reversed her practice. She now ignored the child when he was alone and paid a great deal of attention to him when he was working with others. After a fortnight of this, the boy was spending 60 per cent of his time in social activity, and was beginning to find this sufficiently interesting, in itself, for the teacher to begin giving him less personal attention.

Try not to worry if, at times, your child seems to have no companions at all. Young children can be very fickle in their allegiances and many children go through lonely patches. Some children are by nature somewhat introvert, and like to spend a certain amount of time on their own, and will not thank you for constantly trying to push them into the middle of an extraverted group. But if the isolation persists and your child complains of loneliness, she may need a little assistance from you. You may not be able to make her into the most popular child in the school but you can help her to form attachments to one or two youngsters, and that will be enough to give her the feeling of belonging she needs. Encourage her to develop hobbies she can share with others, to bring school-friends home. Take her to the park, the sports centre, and other places where she can meet other children. Make sure that when youngsters visit, your home is a good place to be. Nothing succeeds like success in social situations, so it is useful to introduce your child to really friendly children who will help to coax her out of her shell. The child's morale can best be built up by gradually introducing new children to play with her on her own familiar home ground, and then slowly intro-ducing her to outside groups, preferably small groups in the early stages. Praise and encouragement for her social endeavours will also help to build up her confidence.

for teachers

Some pupils show an extreme withdrawal from social participation. They reject group activity to an extent which is worrying. Excessive withdrawal may indicate the existence of a more general and complex psycholo-gical problem in the child. A withdrawn child may be overlooked in the classroom situation. The aggressive, destructive child is soon noticed because he disrupts the lessons and the equanimity of his schoolmates. But the withdrawn child is quiet, and therefore 'submerges' unnoticed (except in the case of the perceptive teacher) into the anonymous ranks of the 'good' and 'well-behaved' children.

Some children are withdrawn because they find it easier to 'retreat' into a world of fantasy, than to face reality when it is unpleasant. Withdrawal, in this sense, is a defensive strategy; the self defends itself against the unacceptable and frustrating facts of life (say, persistent failure at shcool or a conflict-ridden home life) by creating imaginary substitute worlds which are pleasant to 'dwell' in.

how to help

Practise your observational skills by making a mental note of what your pupil does. Even the most shy or withdrawn child actually makes many efforts to approach other people. However, when she does try to interest people in herself she is tentative and clumsy so they are likely to ignore her. Help her to gain confidence at school (or home) by *listening* and responding when she talks; make her feel she has something worthwhile to say. This will also contribute to the feeling that *she* is worthwhile. Try to find circumstances whereby she will also be reinforced by other people. 'Prime' mature children to befriend her.

Work out a 'balance sheet' of the child's 'credits' and

'debits' with regard to social acceptability. Next, divide the debits into those things that are irreversible (say, a physical disability) which the child can learn to live with philosophically, and those that are handicapping, but reversible (say, fatness).

the obese child   Children who are overweight frequently have a poor self-image. It is not difficult to see why, when one thinks of the teasing and bullying that afflict such boys and girls. Obesity has a high incidence among juveniles in Western society, and as the childhood variety is a predictor of obesity in adulthood with all its attendant adverse side-effects, there is a good case for doing something about it early on.

what to do   Prevention is better than cure. Bad habits may begin if babies are overfed or if goodies are popped into their mouths every time they express distress (no wonder we tend to eat when we are depressed). Parents may pass on their own casual attitudes to overeating to their offspring. Parents should be vigilant from the beginning. Where it is too late, behavioural management can help the child to reduce weight. You need to combine measures that increase your child's exercise, control his diet, and simultaneously *reinforce* these difficult tasks. You might draw up an agreement (contract) with him so that there are specific rewards (and penalties) for achieving (or failing to fulfil) particular targets of exercising and eating, and for reaching tangible, measured goals of weight loss. *Do* get medical advice about reasonable goal-setting for this weight reduction, and about healthy dietary and exercise targets. Food consumption *must* be restricted to specific times and places (no eating between meals or in the easy chair in front of the television). This is vital — a method called 'stimulus control'. Play your part by having no tempting foods (cakes, chocolates, crisps, peanuts, etc.) in full view, or, indeed, accessible. Model appropriate eating habits by setting a good example, and encourage him by praising his effort and successes. Teach him to say to himself 'I *can* lose weight!'; 'I will *not* weaken my determination'; 'I will *not* give up!', whenever he finds the exercise and the diet irksome. Your efforts should bear fruit. Remember that producing change is one thing; *maintaining* it is the really hard part! After reaching your agreed goal you must help your child to remain vigilant. Never allow him to become complacent!

Unfortunately, food (sweets, biscuits, ice-lollies) are powerful incentives for children, and parents, not unnaturally, make use of them in order to show affection, as a comfort, as a reward, or simply to keep them quiet. I have suggested, paradoxically, using an ice-lolly as a reward elsewhere in the book. Of course, too many sweet things will be bad for the teeth or engender bad habits. As in all things it is a case of moderation, keeping things in proportion. If an ice-lolly is a powerful incentive for overcoming a difficult problem, use it for a short time and then phase it out in favour of social rewards alone, namely praise and approval.

PART III

School and its problems

Perhaps William Shakespeare, remembering, wrote these words from the heart:

> . . . And then the whining schoolboy,
>   with his satchel,
> And shining morning face, creeping
>   like a snail
> Unwillingly to school.
>   *(As You Like It)*

We take for granted the early-morning routine of seeing the children off to school. So when a child refuses to go any more, it is a shock to realize just how dependent we are on the voluntary co-operation of youngsters for the smooth running of the daily household round. As with real 'rebellions', school refusal tends to catch those in authority by surprise. There is the age-old problem of what to do about the rebel once we have exhausted all the usual methods of persuasion, and the school refuser remains implacable in the face of threats, entreaties and bribes. A case in point is Mrs Thompson's predicament.

The breakfast scene in her home is a harrowing one. Everyone is upset. Jane is pleading not to be made to go to school. She says she has a tummyache and is feeling sick. Her mother is at her wits' end. On one pretext or another, Jane has already missed two weeks' schooling. Sometimes the excuse is that she fears physical education, at other times she says she feels unwell. She also hints at being bullied. Mrs Thomson alternates between anger at Jane's rebelliousness and anxiety over her obvious misery. She becomes panic-stricken if she threatens to take her by force in the car. Mr Thompson is short-tempered; the daily scenes, the fuss and tension are getting on his nerves. He has been telling his wife for years to be firm with the children, and now (as he told her they would) her chickens have come home to roost! He declares that he has washed his hands of the whole crazy business. Even placid Bill, the youngest, is weepy these days. (I should say that it is a minority of children who place their parents in quite this predicament!)

beginning school

Most parents have had to cope — and have done this successfully, by and large — with the occasional *reluctance* of their children to go to school, especially early on. For many children, going to school is the first experience of prolonged separation from home. For long periods each weekday, the child is removed from the familiar, comfortable routine of his home, from a playful existence with a nurturant mother near at hand, and is plunged into the more exacting disciplines and the hurly-burly of school life. During these hours there is no appeal to mother's protection and comfort; the mantle of authority has been handed over to strangers.

The child has been transferred from what one might call a relatively 'closed' system, where the rules and requirements are understood and predictable, to an 'open-ended' system where, for at least a few weeks, life is full

Experts recommend getting them into a
playgroup as soon as possible
© Norman Thelwell *Brat Race*, 1977, published by
Methuen, London.

of the unexpected, the unpredictable, and sometimes the unpleasant. The demands and stresses of the new situation, real or imaginary, are many; a child requires a good deal of flexibility and self-control to cope with them. Classroom life makes demands — notably on his concentration and his ability to keep still — of an order never experienced before. And there are those apparently trivial, but, to the sensitive child, extremely intimate functions, such as washing, eating, and going to the toilet, which have to be carried out with less privacy than he is used to. (The act of putting up his hand 'to be excused' may cause a child agonies of embarrassment.) He has to learn to get along with other children who have a point of view of their own; one which does not always take his feelings into account. As most parents could testify, it is around such apparently minor issues that many of the dramas, the smaller crises, of school life are enacted.

What matters, as much as the objective or real stresses inherent in school life, is the way the child subjectively perceives a situation. What, for one child, is a routine matter is something that may hold terrors for another. The introduction to school is like that. Some fortunate children take to school without hesitation. The outgoing, mature child may find school a welcome and happy diversion — particularly if he is bored or lonely at home. When children's mothers were asked at various stages from the ages of six to eleven whether, during the past year, their children had told them about any problems or difficulties connected with school, or shown any reluctance to go, they provided some interesting information. The children themselves were asked (at twelve) what they had liked and disliked about their present and past schools. A reluctance to go to school affected, at one time or another, a majority of the six-year-olds. This unwillingness decreased at seven, rose to a secondary peak at eight (when there was a transfer from infant to junior school) and then dwindled steadily until the children's eleventh year. Even then, one boy in three was still showing some reluctance. In all, a vast majority of the children studied were found to experience difficulties in the infant school. Nearly one half suffered problems of moderate or marked severity. At every age level, boys showed more negative attitudes than girls. Boys who were 'only' children tended to have most problems in adjusting to school.

The specific problems of which children complained most were those connected with teachers and school-work, though difficulties over school dinners and objections to the school toilets were also relatively frequent. Worries connected with other children and with problems in physical education were also expressed, but these were less often of importance.

settling down at school

Parents often feel uncertain about how to deal with their under-fives who are being difficult about settling at nursery school or playgroup. Much depends on the mother's attitude in sending the child. If she feels he is too solitary, meeting no other children of his age, or if she has to return to work, she will be confident of her motives for sending her child to a nursery school. In other circumstances, a mother may feel guilty about her actions, and the child's tears on being left at the nursery school seem like a reproach to her. The child is quite likely to sense his mother's conflict. Many difficulties can be overcome by a gradual, phased introduction into a play group or nursery-school life.

By three years of age, many children are ready to be separated from their familiar environments for reasonably short periods, but only if they have confidence in the adults they are left with, and if you have carefully introduced them to their care-givers or teachers. Your child may express reluctance for a few days or even weeks. Much of this display is for your benefit, however, and tears dry up the moment you have gone. Only the individual mother who knows her own pre-school child can decide whether to persist if she continues to protest for a long period; it may well be that she is not ready to be separated from you and needs more time to mature.

reluctance to speak

The business of starting your child at school, and keeping him here — in a reasonably happy and receptive frame of mind — may be the first emotional problem which you and his teachers have to face. Each child's reaction to school will depend on his maturity, his previous group experience, and how he has been prepared emotionally for this new phase of his life. Some children express their emotional reaction in a reluctance or, indeed, refusal to speak ('elective mutism') at school. This is often part of a refusal to talk in almost all social situations, despite having the mental and physical ability to speak and to comprehend spoken language. The problem may be related to tension and anxiety (due notably to pressure from high parental expectations) and/or the reinforcement of attention from parents and teachers. Fortunately it is responsive to broadly based behavioural treatment.

We have mentioned the term 'maturity', linking it with independence. It is more complicated than that. Maturity is a value judgement and therefore impossible to define in absolute terms. However, the mature person in Western culture is thought to be capable (relative to her age) of:

mature behaviour

1 Being flexible in the face of new situations; able to change when it is necessary.
2 Developing a point of view; her own outlook on things; being herself and capable of independent action and thought.
3 Showing a sense of humour.
4 Accepting reality.
5 Accepting herself, showing respect and liking (not narcissistic love) for herself, plus self-awareness.
6 Enjoying human relationships (i.e. able and willing to form affectionate, lasting and altruistic emotional attachments to other people).
7 Showing some concern for social problems (accepting the obligations and duties of living in a social community).
8 Being able to tolerate a certain amount of solitude.
9 Respecting other people's views and rights.
10 Working out for herself many of her own values; not passively accepting conventional wisdom at all times.

Mature, healthy children are curious and active, open to the world in a way that adults have often forgotten. They are quite the opposite of 'lazy' — a term that is often applied to children who are not doing well at school. Habits of diligence and capacity for work are justifiably encouraged in the youngster. Parents wish to prepare children for the realities of adult society. However, the point here is that if children are taught imaginatively, they do not regard 'lessons' as work. Watch children learning from a gifted teacher and you soon see their joy in discovery — even where difficult subjects are concerned.

There can be many reasons for falling behind at school. Children who have troubled minds because of *intellectual difficulties* or *emotional problems* (resulting from tensions at home) are very vulnerable to failure of concentration. *Physical problems* such as exhaustion or lethargy are quite common in children beginning school. Here, the concentration demanded of the youngster is something beyond his previous experience. With older children, the exhaustion may be due to late bed-times or unsatisfactory sleep patterns caused by bad health. *Interest* (the school curriculum is vital here!) and *motivation* are very important if the child is going to make efforts to work well. Perhaps the moral about 'laziness' is that parents or teachers who so easily use this dismissive word, are themselves being 'lazy' in not searching out the causes, at home or at school.

9

She could do better!

From very early in a child's life, effort, application and ambition are stressed and rewarded as positive values, and idleness is punished as a negative quality. The confusing thing about achievement, for a perceptive child — and they have a disconcerting way of seeing things very clearly before being encrusted with society's prejudices — is the lack of an obvious distinction between ends and means. Indoctrination with the virtues of success, work and 'busy-ness' makes it seem sometimes that the mere activity of 'working' is an end in itself — whatever the nature of the work.

Erik Erikson sees the major developmental task of the five to eleven age span as a sense of duty and accomplishment — laying aside fantasy and play and undertaking real tasks, developing academic and social competencies. The child is probably as amenable at this stage as he is ever likely to be, to learning and direction and *inspiration* by others.

Some children have the right raw material to attain reasonable standards in our achievement-geared society, but for a variety of reasons do not do so. They are called 'under-achievers'. The under-achieving child's academic performance is significantly below that predicted on the basis of a measure of intelligence or scholastic aptitude. There is a highly significant association (correlation) between maladjustment and under-achievement. Chronic under-achievement in boys of above average aptitude may begin in the primary-school classes. It is not so likely to show itself in girls until they reach secondary school.

Most under-achievers fail to find academic work rewarding, and, when they do work, they exert little effort. They tend to be easily distracted, they seldom complete their work, and they set themselves low

under-achievers

standards. Under-achievers generally find school unsatis-
fying, and develop negative attitudes towards teachers.
There may be faults in the school and the school system,
but we must not use them as scapegoats; that would be
too facile. The home environment is a most potent
factor in determining the child's attainment at school.

A parent's early encouragement of independence
promotes concern for intellectual competence in the
child. The educational aspirations of the parents for
their child, the literacy of the home, the interest of the
parents in the child's work, the physical amenities of the
home, the father's occupation, and the parents' own
education level — all have a bearing on the level of the
child's achievement. If the parents are not encouraging,
if they nag and are always negative and destructive in
their criticism, the child will be demoralized and will
give up. Why should he work hard when all his efforts,
good and bad, are condemned? His confidence will be
destroyed.

**'switched on'
to
achievement**

If a child is going to be successful at school he must
desire *and* strive to do what is required of him by his
parents and teachers, and also to do it well. Eventually he
has to develop his own standards of excellence. When
this incentive to do well comes into play — the child is
not born with it — it is called achievement motivation.
By the time children are at primary school, they show (as
teachers are well aware) marked differences in their
drive to achieve, and in the areas of endeavour in which
they show it.

What seems to facilitate achievement is an emphasis
on the child meeting certain achievement standards
between the ages of six and eight, and also receiving a
training in independence and mastery. She is likely to be
highly motivated if, in addition, she is held in warm
regard by both parents, who are ambitious for her but
not too dominating, and who have a strong, positive
attitude towards education.

*a note of
warning*

If unrealistic standards are set at home or school, it is not
long before the child becomes self-conscious about the
discrepancy between her performance and the expectations of adults. After all, they are supposed to know best.
A sense of failure very often manifests itself in a 'don't

care', obstinate facade behind which the child hides. A corrosive self-fulfilling prophecy comes into play. Tell a child often enough that she is stupid; criticize her whatever she does, even if it is commendable within her own lights, and in the end, she will *really* act and thus 'become' stupid!

For many children who have been condemned at school, the great release comes when they go out into the workaday world and have to earn a living and perhaps support a family. They find new incentives and rewards for their efforts, and they surprise themselves with their capacity for hard work and application.

They can no longer be labelled backward — they cope with life's demands. This is also the case for those many worthy children who are a little short on the much prized (and somewhat over-rated) quality 'brightness'.

she's not so bright!

There is no doubt (but much misunderstanding) about the contribution of 'intelligence' — that elusive attribute — to the child's attempt to adapt to his environment. Nowhere is this more marked than in the school situation. Of all the qualities of human beings, mind is thought of by many as the most important. To be found wanting in general intellectual competence is, according to that view, the most devastating of handicaps. Consequently, for many less grossly impaired (and therefore more aware and sensitive) youngsters, any label implying mental impairment or educational subnormality (no matter what euphemism used) can be the most shattering of stigma.

Nothing gives a greater shock to parents than the news that their child is mentally handicapped. It usually comes to them after a long period of uneasiness, a vague apprehension that something is not quite right. It is difficult to lay down guidelines on how best to aid and encourage a mentally handicapped child at home. This is not the place to describe in full what is available to such parents. However, the bibliography contains references to helpful books. Parents need to strike a balance — giving the child every opportunity to make the fullest use of her abilities, while making allowance for her disabilities. Targets set to help her learn better speech, manual dexterity or social skills, must be realistic ones. The goal should be beyond the child's present attainment, so as to provide a challenge, but not so far ahead as to reinforce her sense of failure. Clear instructions and patience are required in any learning situation. Coercion should be avoided.

Elizabeth Newson and Tony Hipgrave (see references) point out how handicapped children are likely to encourage their parents to be too protective, both because they *are* more helpless and because they often like routine and letting things be done for them. If parents do too much for their child the message they are giving her is that she is incapable of doing things for herself. They are teaching her to be helpless. She needs to adopt a 'can' attitude to herself, not a 'can't' or 'won't' one.

Although the problem of handicap has always been with us, a number of developments in our society have re-emphasized its importance. One is the increasing complexity of society and the demands it makes on its members, and another is the emphasis on compulsory education. Both of these have served to alter the definition of intellectual handicap and to bring within the category persons who would not previously have been considered handicapped. Recently, the growing realization by educators that more than 50 per cent of the jobs in our society do not require schooling beyond primary level has meant a growing emphasis on the integration of the less grossly-handicapped youngsters into the community, to which they rightly belong.

the measurement of intelligence

It is possible to arrange problems in order of their difficulty for children of various ages, and to divide them into sets appropriate for children of four, five, six, and so on. When a child is tested, the examiner puts increasingly difficult tests to her until she cannot answer any of the questions for a given age-level; from these results the examiner works out the child's mental age and Intelligence Quotient (IQ). In this way, a child's performance can be assessed in comparison to that of a 'normal child' of a particular age. The child could then be said to have a mental age (or the intelligence) of a five-year-old or a six-year-old, or whatever it may be.

sex differences in intellectual activity

There are some interesting differences in the nature of intellectual functioning in boys and girls, although it is difficult — not to mention unrewarding and foolhardy

— to distinguish between heredity and environment as causes of these differences.

Intellectually, girls get off to a good start — being slightly ahead of boys during the first four years of life. On average, they literally have the first word — and, one might note, in view of the longevity of females, the last one too! They are more articulate. They learn to read more easily (girls are also on a quicker physical developmental timetable than boys). The intellectual differential soon vanishes at school, although girls still excel on verbal fluency tests — using more words, telling longer stories and, in fact, giving support to the stereotype that females talk more than males. In secondary school, boys draw ahead of girls on mathematical skills. Boys (in their teens) do better than girls of the same age on tests of spatial ability and, to some extent, on tests of abstract, analytical types of reasoning. The reasons for these differences are matters of debate, but undoubtedly, girls are severely disadvantaged by a process of brainwashing which suggests that certain careers (e.g. scientific and engineering ones) are more appropriate for males than females. These findings are all based upon scores obtained from intelligence tests and this is where the trouble begins. IQ tests do have their limitations and should be interpreted, and acted upon, by experts who fully understand their ramifications.

We know that children develop at different rates in a variety of spheres of life. It is no use comparing all the time; there is a wide range of differences which is quite normal. However, the really slow developer — be it physically, intellectually or emotionally — may face special difficulties in adjusting to school life. And these difficulties of adjustment are not necessarily confined to the opening phases of school life. The school environment is one which, all the time, is evolving towards greater complexity. It therefore continually increases its demands upon the child; demands for greater and wider mastery of intellectual, social and physical skills.

Change is a significant factor in the schooling process; long periods of slow, almost imperceptible movement are punctuated by phases of rapid, dramatic change when — as in the transfer from junior to senior school — there may be separation from old friends and familiar teachers,

the slow developer

and new subjects have to be assimilated. There are so many facets to school life — any one of them capable of providing a crucial challenge — that awkward and sometimes distressing adaptations may be required of the child at any stage in his school career.

Playgroups and nursery schools, on the other hand, are usually sufficiently small and informal to permit a flexible scheme for introducing the child to school — perhaps allowing the mother to remain near at hand for part of the morning. There is evidence that children who experience the more gradual transition, via nursery school, to the demands of formal education, are less liable to suffer from emotional problems like school refusal, than others who go straight to infant school. There is a lot of play, and a gentle guiding of the child into group situations, new routines and co-operative activities. 'Learning' is very broadly conceived, and the attainments that are emphasized are those that bridge the gap between skills that have been acquired at home and skills that will be required at 'proper' school.

the classroom For a large part of each weekday, the child lives in her classroom. Her relationships with her teacher and with her classmates are major aspects in her adjustment to school. She will spend some 15,000 hours in secondary school alone! Each classroom has its own social and emotional structure; this structure is implicit in the sort of questions a child is asking herself when she finds herself in a new class. These questions are: 'What is expected of me?'; 'What can I do and what can't I do?'; 'What will happen if . . . ?'; 'Who do I like?'; 'Who don't I like?'; 'Who likes me?'; 'Who doesn't like me?'; 'Who does the teacher like?'; 'Who's the most popular one?'. After the relationships within the classroom have settled down, the answers to these questions give the child her position in the structure of the class, and have a bearing on her psychological well-being.

Who does well in the classroom? First there is the youngster who, when she first enters the classroom, possesses a generous helping of the following attributes: she is a child with vigorous health, intelligence, and well-developed social skills. She is likely to have a good opinion of herself, and the ability to gauge accurately her effect on others, to perceive correctly the quality of their approaches and responses to her. Nothing succeeds like success! And nothing fails like failure. The child who is short on some of these qualities is quite likely to be labelled 'lazy'.

This phrase rolls easily off the tongue when adults are exasperated by a child's failure to achieve some goal dear to their hearts. The term 'lazy' is a Pandora's box containing a multitude of society's dislikes; in our 'go-getting', hustling and bustling, achievement-orientated society, a casual attitude towards competition and winning is a cardinal sin.

she's just lazy!

If what is really meant by 'laziness' is passivity, lethargy or inactivity, then it is understandable that it is regarded as undesirable. The apathy of an unwell youngster is often mistaken for laziness. If a child is to be successful at school, good health is vital; it provides the basis for the stamina demanded by long hours of concentration in the classroom. Regular attendance at school depends upon it, and effective learning, in turn, depends upon reasonably consistent presence at lessons. Some subjects are hierarchical in structure; that is, one step is logically preceded by, and dependent upon, another. So the child who misses a series of lessons (particularly the child who has chronic, recurrent illnesses) may experience great difficulty in catching up. Subjects like mathematics, which tend anyway to attract negative emotional attitudes, may (in the absence of an understanding teacher) become the focus of intense anxiety for the vulnerable child. Even the regular attender may not be able to learn efficiently if she is tired or apathetic.

Physical problems are not only responsible for undermining scholastic endeavours; they may themselves be the consequence of emotional disturbance. If a child shows physical lethargy and a lack of interest, she may be depressed. In its milder forms, depression may show itself as a lack of physical energy and well-being. In its more severe manifestations, the child tends to be irritable and bad-tempered, and, when it is at its worst, she sleeps poorly, lacks an appetite, and is always dejected, apathetic and lifeless. The child who is (for whatever reason) depressed refuses to meet the challenges of life, feels helpless, sad and useless, she ceases to strive and to use

depression

her full effectiveness in whatever sphere of activity she finds herself. An essentially emotional problem like this is often mistaken for a physical one. Depression is fairly rare during childhood, but more of a feature of adolescence. Whatever the age, a referral to a Child and Family Guidance Clinic (see Appendix II) is the wisest move.

physical damage to the brain

Although it would be foolish to try (as the ancients did) to locate 'mind', like some geographical feature, in the body, all that is really known of mental functions links them with the process of thinking; and it is impossible to conceive of thinking occurring in the absence of the brain or central nervous system. The brain, like a machine, can go wrong; but, unlike most machines, its standards of reliability are remarkably high and it goes wrong only rarely. This is amazing when you think that during each and every second of waking life, more than 100 million electrical impulses flow into the brain. Even when we are asleep, more than 50 million neuronal 'messages' are being relayed, every second, to and from the brain and different parts of the body. It can have its functions adversely affected by injuries (such as a blow, a fall or some penetrating wound), oxygen deprivation (for example, asphyxia at birth), infections, tumours, degenerative diseases, and mechanical trauma (brought about by difficulties during birth).

Brain injuries can have an influence on the emotional stability of the child, on motor and sensory abilities. They may also impair the processes she relies on to interpret the messages from her environment and those which co-ordinate her reactions to such information. Apart from the adverse consequences for the child's emotional intensity and control which can follow directly from injuries to the brain, the physical difficulties (e.g. clumsiness and over-activity) so often associated with brain damage may provide another (if indirect) route to emotional maladjustment.

Parents and teachers are often told that a particular child's difficulties at home and at school are 'a result of brain damage', suffered perhaps as early as at birth. This is no more helpful than for a GP to tell a mother her child is 'physically ill' when she takes her along for a diagnosis of her aches and pains. Certainly no programme of rehabilitation — remedial teaching or behaviour modification — could be planned on the basis of such a vague diagnosis as 'brain damage'. The cluster of symptoms which includes overactivity, motor inco-ordination, distractibility, impulsiveness and perceptual disturbance, applies to only a very small proportion of the cases of brain damage in the general child population. What we get is a variety of brain-injured children, with quite different problems, whose conditions call for careful individual analysis.

So many children with school learning problems fail to show any positive evidence of neurological damage or dysfunction, that a term *learning disability* tends to be used. It reflects educational rather than medical criteria. The child with a learning disability exhibits a difficulty in one or more of the basic psychological processes involved in understanding or using spoken or written language: listening, thinking, talking, reading, writing, spelling, arithmetic. He or she is also quite likely to be clumsy.

the clumsy child

The problem of severe clumsiness or poor motor co-ordination involves a discrepancy between the mind's intention and the body's execution. This difficulty illustrates how a problem, initially physical in its origins, can have emotional repercussions. It occurs in some one to two per cent of children in the population, being more common, by far, in boys. Such a problem will be evident in a child's awkwardness of movement, her clumsiness at gym and sports, and her difficulties with the fine muscular control demanded by writing. She may suffer a great deal as a result of rebukes from parents and teachers for her 'ham-fisted' and ungainly behaviour, and as a consequence of teasing and mocking from her playmates. Or her maladroitness may be accepted fatalistically by parents and teachers as being 'just one of those things'.

Because there are no obvious or dramatic neurological signs and symptoms of brain malfunction, the underlying condition often goes undetected. As a result, the clumsy child tends to receive less sympathy and understanding than other handicapped children. Not surprisingly, she becomes more diffident about attempting manual skills and, consequently, is often accused of laziness or misbehaviour, and even suspected of being mentally dull.

Punishment and scorn are frequently her lot at school, making her life there thoroughly miserable.

Clumsy children are often of average or above average intelligence, but sometimes their intelligence is focused into very narrow and specific activities; they often develop rigid and stereotyped ways of getting things done. They generally improve considerably in late childhood and adolescence, but a majority still remain somewhat awkward. Some boys with this handicap are inclined to girlish games because they find gymnastics and sport an ordeal. Exclusion from such 'manly' pursuits may also bring problems in its wake. Because they seem 'odd', clumsy children tend to become 'outsiders' — left out of social group activities. It is not difficult to imagine the frustrations suffered by a clumsy child in a bustling, overcrowded classroom. Her difficulties are, in fact, very real. They affect fine finger movements, so that she has difficulty in doing up buttons, in writing neatly, or in drawing. She also experiences problems in gross bodily movements, which means she cannot hop, throw or run in a co-ordinated manner. As a result of this difficulty in perceiving shapes and in copying designs, she may be very slow in learning to read.

difficulties in learning to read

The ability to read is the key to all kinds of learning as well as a source of information and great pleasure. When a child has a *reading age* of somewhere around nine (this should not be taken too literally!) she can do just that: use reading to obtain information and satisfaction. Whatever method is used to teach reading (and schools vary) different children progress at different speeds; several experience difficulties.

Parents are often worried about reading, and there are many causes of difficulties. The following points should be noted:

1 We assume that all children are mature enough to begin to learn to read at the age of six. Some children are late developers and are not ready.
2 Children who are well below average in intelligence may make very slow progress at reading.
3 Poor teaching or poor teaching conditions may be causes of reading problems. Teachers may be uncertain about the best way to teach reading.

4 Some children have missed a lot of school because of illness.
5 If a child is not reading, she may not have had a reasonable opportunity to learn.
6 Reading difficulties may be a result of emotional problems. Many children find learning to read impossible because of tensions produced by preoccupations, worries and depressions which may have nothing to do with school. Often children who are intellectually bright have reading difficulties; their reading age fails to match their mental age (IQ). The causes could be emotional or some quite specific difficulty.
7 Poor reading skills are sometimes manifested if the child comes from a home where learning is discouraged. Parental attitudes are important. The parents of severely backward readers tend not to have read to them. Some may be illiterate.
8 Hearing or visual disabilities can make reading difficult for a child. If a child has something wrong with her eyes or ears she must obviously be taken to a doctor. But — contrary to popular opinion — poor eyesight is unlikely to be found to be a major factor in reading problems.

Reading is not simply the ability to 'bark at print', that is, the ability to translate symbols from a printed page into recognizable speech sounds. A child is truly reading only when she understands what she is reading. Some children seem to be able to see all the letters in a word but cannot make sense of them, just as a diagram of an electrical circuit is a meaningless jumble to a layman but makes perfect sense to a qualified electrician. They may have difficulty with sounds as well — and with the task of fitting the spoken word to the written word.

dyslexia

The term 'developmental dyslexia' — not every specialist agrees that there is such an entity — is often used to describe such an awful dilemma, especially when all the causal possibilities given above are eliminated during the psychologist's assessment. An abnormality is left which some scientists think may be inherited. It is argued that some children are poor at reading and spelling because they are 'born that way', rather like the notion that some

have no ear for music. A significant proportion of
dyslectics are left-handed.) Certainly there seems to be a
history of poor reading in the families of children labelled
as dyslexic. Because the essential work of reading takes
place in the brain, not the eyes — even blind people can
read raised type of braille — doctors assume that any
physical cause of dyslexia must involve some abnormality
in the development of the brain. Some scientists point to
the child's first environment — the womb — when the
brain is most susceptible to its environment. The foetal
brain may be influenced by hormonal and other factors.

The first thing that makes a psychologist suspect that
a child is dyslexic is her very bizarre spelling — so
strange that it looks like a foreign language. For example,
she might write the sentence: 'The boy had a dog' as
'The dop uib a bod.'

Often dyslexic children confuse letters of similar shape,
and write 'b' when they mean 'd' or 'w' for 'm'. This
reversing of letters is a common fault in young children
and is, in itself, nothing to worry about in a child up to
the age of seven or so, but if it persists it may, in rare
cases, be a sign of a serious problem.

Whatever the cause of reading problems, schools
normally organize some form of remedial teaching,
perhaps with a specialist part-time teacher. It is wise for
parents to get professional advice from an educational
psychologist if a child is having prolonged difficulty with
reading. This would follow consultation with the teachers
and headteacher. You can be sure that your offspring is
by no means the only one with a reading problem; about
10 per cent of all eleven-year-olds are to some extent
backward in the development of reading, though not all
of that 10 per cent are in any sense dyslexic. (There is
something of a temptation to label poor readers with this
fashionable 'diagnostic term'. If used in a facile manner
it could lead to pessimistic thoughts: 'Nothing can be
done about it . . . It's a fault in his brain.' The experts
can help!) You can be of great assistance to your child
with her reading difficulties, but *do* get advice from the
school on how best to do it. You do not wish inadvertently
to compound her confusion. It is reassuring to know that
countless dyslectics have overcome their handicap and
achieved success in many fields of endeavour.

teachers and pupils

Let us turn our attention from the 'consumer' of training to the teacher herself. When a child starts school, teachers become a significant part of her world. A teacher's behaviour has an enormously influence — affecting the emotional and social climate of the classroom, and even the quality of the relationships among the pupils. It also affects the individual child's behaviours, moral attitudes and intellectual performance. The primary-school teacher influences not only the child on whom she is focusing her attention, but the onlookers as well. If she delegates some of her authority and power, and if her acceptance of the pupils in the classroom is widespread and not confined to a few 'pets', she is able to increase the social and intellectual interactions between her pupils. In this way she is able to reduce conflict and anxiety in the children. Such democratic behaviour can stimulate independent working habits, independent thought, and a sense of moral responsibility.

It is no exaggeration to say that the teacher holds the key to children's happiness at school, and therefore to the effectiveness with which they learn. Twelve-year-olds who were questioned about the schools they had attended, saw them prmarily in terms of how the teachers had treated them. The qualities they appreciated in a teacher were helpfulness, clear explanations, firmness in keeping order, fairness, humour, kindliness and good manners towards the class. They resented anything they saw as unfair: shouting, ranting and grumbling in the class, confusing instructions, boring teaching, physical punishment and, most of all, humiliation of individual children. In any school, teachers are bound to vary, and different teachers suit different children. Inevitably, there is an element of chance in all this. In general, from about the age of seven on, it is probably good for a child to have to adapt to teachers of varying personalities.

consulting his teacher

Occasionally situations arise where child and teacher seem really incompatible. If your child persistently complains of unfair treatment, this should not be ignored, though what she sees as unfair may take on a different colour when you know all the facts. School work can cause a great deal of anxiety to parents, teachers and children — and anxiety often leads to irrational behaviour. If this point is reached, a talk with the teacher may clear up misunderstandings and enable her to alter her approach to the child. It is important for you to show the teacher that you realize that her job is not an easy one, that there are many children besides your own whose needs she has to consider. Her view of the situation as well as that of your child, is being sought.

school morale and atmosphere

Michael Rutter and his co-researchers demonstrate very convincingly that children do better at school — in all sorts of ways — when the curriculum and approaches to discipline are agreed to, and supported by, the staff acting together. Attendance at school is better and delinquency less frequent in schools where there is such accord and where courses are planned jointly. Group planning provides opportunities for teachers to support and encourage one another; continuity of teaching is also enhanced. Much the same is found with regard to standards of discipline. Exam successes are more frequent and delinquency less common in schools where discipline is based on *general* expectations set by the school (or house, or department) rather than left to individual teachers to work out for themselves. School values and norms appear to be more effective if it is clear to all that they have widespread support. Discipline is easier to maintain if the pupils appreciate that it relates to generally accepted approaches and does not simply represent the whim of an individual teacher.

teacher rules, OK!

The particular rules which are set and the specific disciplinary techniques which are used, are probably much less important than the establishment of some principles and guidelines which are both clearly recognizable and accepted by the school as a whole. For all that, rules — or better, *thoughtful rules* — are crucial. The pupil needs to attend to the consequences of his academic and social performance in order to make progress. One of the most important of these consequences is the *feedback* he receives from the teacher as to whether the academic answer he gives is correct or incorrect, and in the case of behaviour, appropriate or inappropriate. The feedback may be direct and immediate (praise or reprimand in the classroom); it may be less direct and more delayed (annual prizes for work or sport); or it may be quite indirect (like putting up children's work on the walls).

The most immediate and direct feedback in the form of praise or approval has the strongest association with pupils' behaviour, according to the researches of Michael Rutter and his colleagues. Prizes for sport are associated with good attendance only, but prizes for work are quite unrelated to any of the outcomes the research team measured. The amount of punishment used, shows only a weak, and generally insignificant, influence on such things as conduct, school attendance, and so on. The greater the punishment the worse — generally speaking — the outcome.

Cues (rules) inform the pupils about what is required of them. Here are a few guidelines for teachers:

1 Negotiate rules. Discuss the rules and the reasons for them, with children who are old enough to participate in such a process. Rules are more likely to be obeyed if they are perceived as fair and seem to have a purpose. It is surely not demeaning (where possible) to engage pupils in the formulation of *their* classroom rules.
2 Negotiate a set of classroom objectives and clarify the part played by rules in facilitating these objectives.
3 To be effective rules should elicit responses which the pupils are capable of making.
4 Emphasize rules that offer beneficial outcomes for appropriate actions.
5 Select a few essential rules only — ones that can be enforced, and reinforced.
6 Praise pupils who follow the rules, identifying the precise grounds for the praise.
7 Rules *alone* are unlikely to be effective. Group and/or individual reinforcers (privileges) might be built into the curriculum.

Some teachers arrange a competitive points system, one half of the class (say) competing with another for points and an eventual prize or bonus. Such 'team' endeavours can be highly successful but they carry the danger of group coercion against the individual.

10

Absent without leave

Why is it that children like Adrian and Jane (we met them in earlier chapters) develop school attendance problems when faced with difficulties? Why, for example, did Adrian refuse to go to school following an incident of bullying (the event which he blamed for his fears), while Colin, another victim of the same persecutor, resolutely soldiered on? If Adrian's problem was reluctance only and not outright refusal, it would be normal enough. It is reassuring for parents to know that their offspring are not unique in making excuses to get out of school; as many as 80 per cent of 'run-of-the-mill' children experience difficulties, at one time or another in going to school, and express varying degrees of reluctance to attend. Some 'try it on'. Parents usually know by the 'look' of their child whether he is feigning illness. If this seems likely, a carefully, diplomatic enquiry into the child's school life may indicate a sensitivity which may be overcome by parental support or perhaps by a word to the teacher.

There is a group of children whose determination goes beyond mere reluctance to set off for school. They dig their heels in, and not even weighty authority, in the person of the school head teacher or the Education Welfare Officer will budge the adamant refusers. We saw how Jane's parents had been trying unsuccessfully, and for some time, to get her to go to school. In addition — and here is another symptom of the serious attendance problem — Jane is suffering from anxiety in connection with a number of other topics which most children cope with fairly well. Like quicksilver, her anxiety is apt to move about, changing shape — now attached to one object (her mother's health), now jumping to another (a sarcastic teacher), and then another (the playground bully). Her apprehensions are not soothed by reassurances. She has recurrent physical symptoms, which tend to clear up at weekends, or even (and this is particularly maddening) shortly after parents have reluctantly agreed to keep her at home. Is she, then, a malingerer or a rebel? This tremulous child is neither, experiencing as she does all the mental and physical suffering of an anxiety attack. She does not choose to stay away from school; the fact of the matter is that she *cannot* go, because of some overwhelming dread of the school-going process.

Research shows that it is certainly not mere dislike of the place that causes school refusal. There is no difference between the attendance records of children who like school and those who dislike it; the cause must be something much more serious and fundamental. There is greater appreciation nowadays that persistent school refusal is a very real emotional disturbance, not simply a moral or disciplinary problem concerned with malingering. Some refusers may even *want* to go to school, but find that they simply cannot go through all the necessary motions.

There are several possibilities inherent in the circumstances of school life and any of these is capable of making a child fearful for quite *reasonable*, objective reasons: the size and routine of the school; examination stresses; experiences of classroom failure; disturbed relationships with teachers and school-mates (sometimes involving extreme fear); parental pressures and expectations; and intellectual disability. School children, aged eleven, tend to worry about failing a test; being late for school; being poor spellers; being asked to answer questions; being poor in reading; getting a poor report card; being reprimanded; not doing as well as other pupils; being poor at maths and drawing.

Most children manage to cope with the difficulties listed above without refusing to go to school. In this sense the 'phobic reaction' seems disproportionate to the observer. Nevertheless the phobic child's terror is real enough to him. It may not even be the school. The phobic child, in many instances, has a fear of leaving mother rather than of something at school. This is why the term 'school phobia' can be something of a misnomer; 'school refusal' is preferable. At least the school refuser's parents know he is absent; he is, after all, safe at home.

There is another group of children whose parents

condone their absence from school. They may be helping at home, working somewhere, or simply being elsewhere — anywhere but school. For various reasons (economic, or hostility to school) the parents collude with the child. There are other non-attenders whose parents do not know where they are, let alone about their absence. Truants — who go off and amuse themselves — are much more like rebels. Their activities are frequently delinquent. And there are differences in their personality, social and family background, and school performance.

In Adrian's case, a careful assessment revealed a chain of events possibly explaining his problem. Given his introverted type of personality and an over-reactive (volatile) autonomic nervous system, he was particularly prone to learn 'maladaptive' (self-defeating) patterns of behaviour. Take the situation, in which he was set upon by a bully during the lunch-break. The chance association of the playground, the time of day, etc. with the terrifying attack, caused Adrian to feel particularly anxious at lunchtime, in the playground, and so on. He made the effort to approach the playground, but immediately began to feel panicky. Avoidance of the area led to relief from anxiety, and it is in this way, perhaps, that the habit of avoidance became reinforced (negative reinforcement). His intense initial fear reaction spread to more and more aspects of the school situation ('stimulus generalization'). It developed to a point in which only avoidance of the entire school situation brought him relief from intolerable anxiety. The anxiety, conditioned as it was to various stimuli but not under conscious control, came into action despite Adrian's best efforts. There are several ways of dealing with such problems: a change of class could be arranged, and individual therapy can be applied. 'Desensitization techniques' offer a promising compromise between the difficulties of enforcing an immediate reintroduction of the child into school and the dangers of further delays.

An example of this approach is provided by the treatment of Jane's phobia. She and the psychologist would go to the school early in the morning when no one else was present. Jane was asked to report any feelings of apprehension. As soon as she did so, the therapist immediately took Jane back to the car and praised her for what she had achieved so far. The therapist and the child approached the school together in a series of steps graded from the least anxiety-provoking situation (sitting in a car in front of the school) to the most anxiety-provoking condition (being in the classroom with the teacher and other pupils present). She spent a few days working in the school library, and then moved back into a normal routine one subject at a time. At the end of a thirty day period of desensitization treatment, Jane had returned to school completely. The presence of the psychologist (with whom she had a good relationship) was considered as a strong positive stimulus evoking a positive emotional repsonse. The graduated re-entry into school-life ('exposure') was so designed that Jane's confidence in the therapist would counteract any fears aroused by each new step forward in the treatment programme. There were other problems to tackle as well, involving discussions with Jane. Nevertheless, the behavioural programme was central in the attempt to get her (and the other child we heard about — Adrian) back to school.

As with other emotional problems of childhood, the long-term prognosis (outlook) for school refusers is generally good. But some school refusers who have been untreated, or inadequately treated, have become work refusers in adolescence or adulthood. In very young children the problem is generally short-lived; in older children the problem may be more worrying and disabling, but again the prognosis is usually quite a good one. The earlier the treatment is initiated, the better the outcome, and the quicker the disappearance of the symptoms. Quick intervention, the seeking of help from experts, is always wise (see Appendix II).

the truant

The truant is a child who absents himself from school without a legitimate cause and without the permission of his parents or the school authorities. He is not really like that famous light-hearted, and rather roguish absconder, Tom Sawyer. Truants are characteristically beset by problems such as enuresis (bed-wetting), lying, wandering from home, stealing and aggression. Many delinquencies (such as shoplifting, stealing from cars, and so on) are committed by boys when they are roaming the streets during school hours.

Behind the truant's dislike for school lies a history of failure, often both academic and social. The child who is poor at schoolwork and who is constantly criticized by his teacher and called stupid, finds school a demoralizing experience. If he is kept down a year, he finds it boring, lonely and embarrassing to be with younger children and to be doing repetitive and familiar work. Because over-age children generally fail to get social acceptance in the class, the repeater makes few friends, and this increases his distaste for school. On average, truants are below the majority of their schoolmates in mental ability and in attainment at reading, arithmetic and other school subjects; this is not always the case, and a few truants may be of exceptional intelligence. Truancy is as powerful a deterrent to high school success as a low IQ. In general, a child's attendance record at school is a very good predictor of his adult adjustment.

those at risk Often, family conditions are intolerable for the truant. Homes tend to be overcrowded and dirty, often concentrated in uncongenial slum settings. Parents may have little interest in their children's welfare. Their offspring may even lack adequate clothing; they are often kept out of school for no good reason. Most of them lack affection or a close tie with a parent who will demonstrate good standards or a positive attitude to education. Many have slept out at night or run away from home. Children who truant are apt to feel lonely and miserable, becoming unsociable and unable to perservere at anything.

The truant has learned, over a period, that the best escape from tensions at home — so often the place of harsh punishment and the scene of rows and rejection — *is* to escape; in other words, the best way to cope with frustrations is to avoid their source. So he wanders away from school (where he feels he is disliked by teachers and children alike) in the same way he wanders from home (where he also often feels unwanted). He may amuse himself as a solitary; or he may look for congenial companions who also crave excitement and a distraction from their feelings of depression and discouragement. It has to be said that truancy may represent a *rational response* to an unimaginative and irrelevant school system, in far too many cases.

Children without notable 'hangups' may also truant on rare occasions — for a dare, to escape an exam or a threatened punishment. Firm parental pressure, reassurance about children's fears, and understanding of their transient difficulties at school, are sufficient to keep all but a small minority of rather seriously disturbed children regularly at school.

Children who truant, may come with their parents for professional help, as did a sixteen-year-old American girl named Claire. In an attempt to correct this, her mother had stopped Claire's pocket money, use of the telephone and going out on dates, but had not made it clear how these privileges could be regained. When treatment started, the school attendance officer was involved. If Claire was present at all her classes during a day, he would give her a note. This note was exchangeable, with the mother, for certain specified privileges. It was stressed also that when Claire brought a note home her mother should praise her. Over a period of seven weeks the improvement in behaviour was so marked that notes were gradually reduced and then stopped entirely. Before treatment, she had been absent on 30 out of 46 days, whereas, for three months after it commenced, she truanted on only two occasions, and not at all over several months following its termination. Some improvement in her performance, attitude and interest in school was also reported. *coping with truancy*

Special educational units — small in scale and informal in style, have been set up in some cities to deal with more intractable cases. Education Welfare Officers have (among other duties) the responsibility to investigate persistent non-attendance at schools. The schools themselves have evolved different ways of coping with these (and other) problems. Some have instituted special pastoral care units. Whatever the methods devised, teachers with pastoral care responsibilities might well ask a series of questions about the child who misses school a great deal.

These questions (see table 1) are what we call 'push/pull' questions. In making an assessment of a complex problem like school refusal it is helpful to have a guide to the factors that require investigation. The first conceptual aid is to assess the push—pull factors in school attendance. Many children feel reluctant at times to go to school. Their parents 'push' them into going, sometimes simply by their being there, i.e. they do not have to exert undue pressure. But there are 'pull' factors: *vital questions*

Table 1 To get a child to school and keep him there ('push' and 'pull')

Has to wake up on time	Get bathed, dressed, breakfasted	Leave the house on time	Make a journey	Enter the school gates	Go to assembly	Stay in the school	Go home at appropriate time

Does he wake on time? If not, why not? Does he get enough sleep? If not, why not (going to bed late; lying in bed unable to sleep because of morbid preoccupations, tense, depressed)?

Anyone to structure his day at home, e.g. supervise getting him ready ('push')? Is he sick/anxious/panicky?

Any reason he needs to be at home (care for a sick member of the family; parents keep him at home to look after siblings, etc.)? Is he afraid to leave home because concerned about his mother's health, afraid of an accident befalling her (preoccupation with illness and death)? Does he suffer from separation anxiety? Is he depressed, overwhelmed by apathy, helplessness, inertia?

Is he teased/bullied on the way to, or at school? Is a bus journey difficult because of claustrophobia? Is his clothing adequate for school? Is there anything to keep him at school (interests, friends)? Deviant models (peer group) for truanting, ie, children who lead him astray? Other 'pull' factors absent? (Is he under-achieving grossly at school, bored; lacking in any self-esteem?) Does anyone really know him or take an interest in him at school?

the authority of the school, the presence of friends at school, the interest provided by a good school (and conversely the boredom of being at home or elsewhere on one's own). In any assessment of persistent non-attendance at school the presence or absence, strength or weakness of these push-pull factors need to be evaluated. As a background to this analysis, it is helpful to list the potential crisis points in getting a child to school and keeping him there. It is useful to view this chrono-logically.

In the case of Barry, an only child aged fifteen, I had to intervene over a wide spectrum, as many of the push—pull factors in his life were absent or minimal. This meant, among other things, enlisting the help of a kindly neighbour to wake him up. When his mother was alive, she often had to 'drag' him out of a deep slumber. The father was on early shifts with a bus company and could not supervise the early morning routine. A series of school visits was also required to mobilize the personal interest of a teacher and educational psychologist in the fate of this lonely boy. The school was an extremely large and impersonal place. The treatment programme also involved discussions with the boy about his future plans, his social life (he was introduced to a youth club) and his grief over the loss of his mother. Joint meetings were arranged between Barry, his father, and me, to iron out misunderstandings, to work out a rota for household chores, and to arrange a 'contract' involving a loan for a moped if Barry returned to school and gave proof of his intention to attend regularly.

practical help: an example

Contract

Between Barry K and Mr. K.

Son agrees to:
1 Get up and make ready for school when aroused by the next door neighbour (every weekday).
2 Catch the 8 a.m. village bus to school.
3 Stay at school during school hours.

Father agrees to:
Lend Barry £20 towards the purchase of a moped.

Both parties agree to the following conditions:
1   The loan will be paid after Barry has been back at school for one month.
2   The penalty for missing school after that date will be the loss of the use of the bike for each day missed (unless there is a legitimate reason for absence from school).
3   The money will be returned at the rate of £1.50 per month out of Barry's paper-round money.

Signed:_____
                                    Father

Signed: _____
                                    Son

Witnessed by:_____
                                    Psychologist

11

'Hyperactive' children

'He never stops'; 'He's forever into things'; 'He's *so* fidgety!'; 'He flits from one thing to the other'; 'He never listens to me!' These are some of the anguished complaints we hear from despairing, exhausted parents with a highly active child. It is no joke coping with any child who is a bundle of energy, especially indoors on a cold winter's day. But there is another turn of the screw for some parents — yet a higher notch of activity which clearly (in intensity, persistence and inappropriateness) goes beyond anything which can be lightly dismissed as 'high spirits', 'energetic' or merely 'active'.

The hyperactive child is like the proverbial elephant: difficult to define, but, by golly, we know one when we see one — or live with one! His nomadic wilful style in the sitting room or the classroom is his hallmark. His behaviour at times can be so disruptive and frenetic that he may be referred to a psychologist by his parents who, not infrequently, feel demoralized by their inability to help him or manage him. The hyperactive child is the cause of significant and frequent complaints at school.

Take the case of Nicola, an over-active, incredibly potent, and wilful three-year-old. She commanded an inordinate amount of individual attention, monopolizing her mother's time wherever she was and whatever she was doing. She clung to her and followed her everywhere (even to the toilet) refusing to let her out of her sight, even for a few moments. Her favourite coercive tactics were screaming, whining and nagging. Nicola would not play with other children, including her siblings — who had no real problems. By the time she was referred to our University Child Treatment Unit, her behaviour problems (including restlessness, defiance, aggression and self-centredness of an extreme kind) were rampant,

the problem at home

and having serious implciations for herself and her family.

It is important to show reluctance to apply labels to any child, and particularly the 'hyperactivity' one; nevertheless certain features in Nicola's case, apart from her sex — it is mainly boys who are over-active — are fairly typical. What stands out in the 'shell-shocked' mind of any mother or father is a child who is a sheer 'mobile disaster area'. With his short attention span, rapidly changing goals and insatiable touching, combined with a rather 'muscular' ham-fisted approach to the environment, he leaves in his wake broken toys, smashed ornaments and upset grocery shelves — if his mother is foolhardy enough to take him into a supermarket. The apparently incessant motion of the seriously over-active child gives the impression that he is driven by a motor, and to continue the metaphor, by a motor which is tuned to turn over too quickly, even when it is idling. A closer look at the supposedly fast tempo in the activity suggests that it is really the fragmented, disorganized nature and frequent direction changes of his actions, which give the impression of speeded up behaviour. Where he does differ from other children who are also often naughty and exuberant is in the extent of his unwillingness or inability to inhibit his antisocial and frenetic activities, in the home or classroom.

His inability to brook *any* thwarting or delay in the gratification of his desires is indicative of a more general problem of low frustration tolerance — a sign of immaturity. The hyperactive child has an uncanny gift for choosing to do things which compel his parents to intervene either to prevent injury to himself (he is often impulsive and fearless) or to others. His attention-seeking succeeds to a degree that is so all-embracing that his parents feel themselves to be on a twenty-hour-a-day duty rota. From their point of view the child seems out of control! They report that they very rarely praise him — it is difficult to find things to praise. The parents and child get involved in endless nagging sessions and tearful disputations which end up with smackings and only the briefest respite before the child is up to the same misdemeanour as before, or a new one. The all-round despair and misery generated in these situations means that even by the tender ages of three, four or five (in the home) and at older ages (in the classroom, too), these children can have potentially serious behaviour problems. In their wake comes social isolation (for parents and child), learning difficulties at school, and much unhappiness.

Teachers find that not only does the 'hyperactive' child fail to learn efficiently but he disrupts his classmates' concentration. Parents try to deny, even to themselves, the sometimes murderous feelings they harbour toward a child who is ruining their marriage, their enjoyment of life. It should be said that this is an 'averaged' thumb-nail sketch. Not all over-active children are alike; not all are as extreme as the picture painted above.

What do we know about this daunting problem? A majority of studies of hyperactivity have failed to establish it as a specific medical entity; rather the so-called 'symptoms' emerge as part of a behavioural disorder. A hyperactive child is a child with a variety of conduct problems, but with the added complication of being overactive. The activity problems may improve as the child matures toward adolescence, but the poor, antisocial conduct tends to persist if not treated, and, indeed, may get worse. No single invariable cause has been identified. It may be that minimal damage to the brain and central nervous system is present in some children — the consequence perhaps, of a difficult birth or lead poisoning or some other obscure agent. Deficits in the ability to attend may be biochemical in origin. Poor concentration makes learning — at home and at school — extremely difficult for some hyperactive children. The repercussions are devastating! A fashionable view is that hyperactive children suffer from a vitamin deficiency allergy to certain food additives. Triumphant reports have appeared, proclaiming the results of vitamin therapy and allergy-free diets. The more all-embracing claims have not been satisfactorily confirmed by carefully controlled studies; certainly these causes do occur in some cases, but certainly not in all hyperactive children. Some aspects of hyperactivity — the uncontrolled, impulsive, antisocial behaviour — may be due to emotional disturbance arising from social and psychological causes.

why hyperactivity?

a case-history   In many cases, poor self-control is clearly associated with a constitutional factor interacting with faulty social training. Looking at Nicola's history, we see the volatile chemistry brought about by a child with a difficult temperament, brought up by parents unsure of themselves. Nicola was, by turns, withdrawn and highly active from birth. What makes the issue of 'activity level' so interesting is that it is one of a few temperamental (constitutional) attributes which can be identified reliably, soon after birth. Furthermore it is a characteristic which tends to be stable over time and — with certain other temperamental attributes with which it is commonly associated — makes for a combination which is highly off-putting to parents. Understandably, as the various tasks of maternal care-giving and social training require a degree of stillness, attention and co-operation from her infant, overactivity is particularly irksome and sometimes disturbing. These circumstances become particularly fraught in single-parent families or in situations which the mother is socially isolated or overburdened with work.

Nicola started life on the wrong foot. From the day of her birth, she would cry day and night. The nights were particularly difficult. Her mother spend most of them nursing her to allow the rest of the family to have some sleep. There were also serious feeding problems. Her parents were worried that Nicola would starve herself, so forced feeding was necessary for several months. It could take up to three hours to feed the baby. Her mother and father found it impossible to plan family outings — she hated any change in routine and was predictable only in her unpredictability. Being of such a commanding temperament she learned from early on how to gain attention from her mother and the rest of the family. The parents always intervened when she was crying, shouting, screaming; when she was frustrated, disobedient and aggressive they would most often obey her commands, for the sake of peace, to save time, or to avoid embarrassment. A variety of situations became cues for verbal disputations and other forms of attention (needless to say, Nicola usually got her own way). Essentially, Nicola was being reinforced for her anti-social, defiant behaviour — albeit unwittingly — by the family.

What treatments are available for hyperactivity? Medication has been of some benefit. Sadly, the discovery that certain stimulant drugs brought about dramatic and rapid improvements in the behaviour of some children, also led to abuses. Apart from ignoring unfortunate side-effects of the medication itself, these powerful drugs were prescribed, particularly in the USA, with abandon, until a series of court cases brought back discretion and common sense. This concentration on the chemical control of hyperactivity diverted attention from psychological and social factors, and the issues of prevention and proper long-term management of their obstreperous, out-of-control behaviour. Although medication does facilitate the *short-term* management of hyperactive children in about 75 per cent of cases, it is not a panacea; it has little or no impact on the social, academic or psychological adjustment of these youngsters in the long run. If used, these drugs are probably most effective when prescribed by the doctor for very serious cases, and then alongside counselling and/or behaviour modification.

A behavioural approach to treatment may render the use of drugs unnecessary, or (in combination with medication) make less likely any prolonged drug dependence or the abdication from personal parental responsibility. Another risk which can be reduced, is a psychological one. The child is less likely to attribute change to an outside agent (the pill) rather than to himself and his *own* efforts, when he participates fully in a programme of behaviour modification.

In my experience, behaviour modification techniques will bring about improvement for between six and eight out of every ten children treated. Nicola was trained and encouraged to develop and enjoy the fruits of more effective bodily and self-control; her parents were helped to be more consistent and confident in their management of the child's behaviour. Her therapeutic programme using positive reinforcement and time-out (see Appendix I), brought about a marked improvement. Her mother's own words best summarize what, with hard work on the part of the family, was achieved:

Nicola's treatment programme

Since the treatment programme Nicola's screaming fits have dwindled to almost nil now. We understand her needs and frustrations and are able largely to cope with them. In responding to her intellectual needs and continually keeping her stimulated, she is rapidly developing as a normal four-year-old. Trips out are now taken without fear, although we are still slightly nervous. Supermarkets are visited with few qualms. She still has a rather low frustration tolerance level, but this is very much improved on the situation at the beginning of the treatment programme, and occasionally, she even laughs at her own mistakes and misunderstandings. Best of all though, is the way she now responds to affection, although she has to make the first move. She will both give and receive cuddles and kisses. Mealtimes are no longer a battle and the dining table no longer a battlefield. Her aggressive fits are diminishing, although she can still be verbally aggressive, and is no respecter of persons if something is done that is deemed silly or stupid.

hyperactivity at school The basic need of hyperactive children is for *success* — success in something in which adults and adult society genuinely believe. All children have this need, but unlike most children, hyperactive youngsters seldom enjoy even a modicum of success. Unfortunately, such children are likely to have experienced a sort of 'built-in' failure. Their unacceptable behaviour increasingly excludes them from the circle of acceptance in the family, the neighbourhood, the school and the community at large. They tend to be strangers to the usual range of social reinforcers which regulate appropriate behaviour, for example, encouragement and esteem.

help for teachers Here are some guidelines for evaluating when a hyperactive (or any other) child requires special attention:

1 if his social behaviour interferes significantly with his academic work;
2 if he interferes with the other children's academic work or social behaviour;
3 if he interferes with the teacher's ability to function effectively.

Planning more effective classroom management of hyperactive children requires careful 'target assessment'. First, it is vital for the teacher to find a *level* of social or academic performance at which the child has already experienced success. This provides a realistic basis on which to begin whatever educational programme is planned; this programme must directly reflect the *problems* which the child is presenting. The programme is presented to the child within a setting and *time span* which permit learning to take place. Finally, the educational programme is highly *structured* in terms of the methods used and the environment created for the child.

One of the most useful behaviour modification procedures for classroom management is the systematic application and/or withdrawal of reinforcement, the aim being to increase desirable behaviour, such as academic performance, and reduce disruptive activities. Perhaps the most obvious and natural reinforcement available to the classroom teacher is the attention she can give to her pupils, in the form of a smile, word of encouragement or even mere proximity. The teacher's attention will tend to increase those behaviours which attracted it in the first place. Thus, if a teacher pays attention to a child who is working well ('on-task') she will tend to increase this behaviour. However, if she pays attention to disruptive ('off-task') behaviour *that* behaviour will also tend to increase.

uses of behaviour modification

As we saw, there can be a disability in attending, in the hyperactive child. Attention is a basic skill, underlying or preceding classroom learning. Attention involves the length of time that the pupil (say) can spend at a given task (concentration span), his ability to respond correctly (focus), and his ability to make discriminations (selectivity). The hyperactive child may fall short in all of these aspects. Attending behaviour obviously becomes a crucial and desirable alternative to hyperactivity. Without it academic success becomes increasingly elusive.

The use of rewards for gradually increasing attention to a task can markedly improve a child's concentration. There is evidence that it is possible to modify even such deep-seated aspects of the hyperactivity problem as poor motivation and compliance by the use of social reinforcement.

Psychologists have successfully employed modelling

and self-instruction to modify the aggressiveness of impulsive boys. This is done by providing a model of a young boy who copes with verbal aggression by means of self-instruction. Boys view a videotape which shows a nine-year-old being taunted by other children. In addition to remaining ostensibly calm looking at his taunters and remaining in the centre of the circle, the model is portrayed as coping with verbal assaults through a series of self-instructions. These thoughts, which are dubbed on the tape, consist of statements such as 'I'm not going to let them get me down', and 'I won't get mad.' Nervous children who are less capable of this kind of self control under stress would possibly be given relaxation training as well.

12

Children's fears

There is no doubt about the power of fear to alter and disrupt thought and behaviour. Anxiety (which has been called fear spread thin) can erode our capacity to enjoy life. The problem caseloads of psychologists and social workers are pervaded by the themes of transition and change, and their associated stresses. Not surprisingly this period of history is referred to as the 'age of anxiety'. The transitions for children might include dependency to independence, home to school, school to work, place to place, friend to friend, father to step-father, and attachment to bereavement. All of these bring insecurity in their wake.

Fear is a natural enough response to events which are threatening to a child's personal security; in fact it is a vital *adaptive reaction,* which every mother makes use of in training her child to avoid dangers. It can also be adaptive in preparing him to cope with emergency situations. In such crises, the child experiences a variety of physical sensations such as a pounding heart, shivering and trembling, butterflies in the stomach, dry mouth and perspiring hands. These reactions are due to physiological mechanisms built into the body, and processed by the autonomic nervous system. The physical sensations are by-products of the changes in body chemistry which take place as adrenalin is released into the blood-stream. This outpouring of adrenalin keeps the system toned up until the crisis has passed.

normal fear

Studies of the fears of childhood indicate that they are so common that it might be said to be quite 'normal' for children to be fearful about one thing or another at different ages. Ninety per cent of normal children (in one study) reported having fears. Obviously if a degree of fearfulness is widespread during childhood, the seriousness of particular anxieties can only be judged by the consequences they have for the child's day-to-day existence.

becoming fearful The development of fears is, of course, influenced by the child's history, and by the setting in which the fear-provoking situations occur. The tendency of a child to over-react with fear is closely related to the inherited sensitivity of his autonomic nervous system. There does seem to be a biological potential for learning. All creatures appear to show a great readiness ('preparedness') to acquire certain associations, while other connections are made only with difficulty, if at all. Why, for example, are children so ready to fear snakes or spiders? The chance of being bitten in European countries is, after all, very remote. Perhaps in our evolutionary past, the species developed an apprehension of snakes because of the 'survival value' of such a built-in preparedness. Very early environmental influences, even those going back to the child's first environment — the mother's womb — are thought to sensitize the child to over-react. It has been suggested that, if the mother is under considerable stress during pregnancy, this may make her baby more jumpy and highly strung than he would otherwise be.

Occasional experiences of a very frightening kind can condition a child to feel acute wariness and apprehension in similar situations later, and this conditioning can persist. In other words, anxiety is 'learned' by the child linking an unpleasant experience with a particular situation. More important, all children — especially those who start life by being naturally rather prone to anxiety — are very susceptible to the contagious effect of the emotions their parents express. They are adept at picking up the smallest cues which betray their parents' feelings. Some fears are transmitted unconsciously, not always by words, but by attitude or gesture.

It is important to remember that much of human learning involves complex conceptual processes, aided by symbols conveyed in language. Therefore, the child can learn to fear from what he hears of other people's fears, particularly those of the mother. Parents are rightly concerned to prevent their children from coming to harm. Children must be taught to be wary of the dangers of life, but some are taught to search out every imaginable lurking catastrophe. Thus we move from adaptive to maladaptive anxiety — it is very easy for what started as a reasonable concern to become an unnecessary fuss. If a mother is continually expressing fear in front of her child (as distinct from taking necessary precautions in a matter-of-fact way), then she unwittingly conditions him to see the world as a dangerous place. For example, a divorced and extremely anxious father who lived with his only daughter was obsessed by the idea that a man would come and kidnap or molest the child. The father alerted his daughter to this 'ever-present' danger, and taught her to lock all doors at home, to keep the curtains drawn, to stay indoors as much as possible, and to be especially careful on her way to and from school. It is little wonder that this young girl became terrified of being out alone and obsessional about checking that all the doors were locked — time and time again!

It is helpful for parents to know that childish fears wax and wane, and that most fears prove to be unsettling rather than disabling, transitory rather than permanent.

childish fears

Let us trace their development. We know that some fear is innate or, to put it another way, unlearned. For example, fear is produced in an infant when he hears a loud noise behind him or feels the motions of dropping.

Some children are simply afraid
of the dark

Others are more scared of
missing something

© Norman Thelwell *Brat Race*, 1977, published by Methuen, London.

Until he is about six or seven months, a baby will probably show no concern about being with strangers, but from then on it is quite common for this to change. Babies gradually learn to discriminate between familiar people, like mother, and the other — unknown — people in the world. In many infants, the first fear of separation from mother is quickly followed by a fear of people who are strange or new to them. This fear may generalize, becoming a temporary but widespread fear of the unfamiliar and unknown.

Later, the situations that the pre-school child fears are still mainly those linked to his sense of security and his apprehensions over strangeness and suddenness. Things beyond control — like darkness, large barking dogs, noises, storms, the ocean, the doctor or strange people — are typically feared by youngsters. As the child gets older, his fears change from the tangible to the intangible. There is an increase in the number of fears of the occult, the dark, being alone, accidents and injuries, bad people, the loss or death of relatives, medical treatment, high places, ridicule and personal failure, and dying or ill health. These are 'outgrown' in the natural way that the youngster outgrows toys and childish enthusiasms.

separation anxiety

Children's fears show a clear pattern as they grow up — each age would seem to have its own set of 'adjustment' crises or anxieties. For example, studies of the behaviour of healthy children separated from their parents in the second and third years of life, tend to show a fairly predictable sequence of behaviour. In the first or 'protest' stage the child reacts to the separation — brought about, say, by his mother's hospitalization — with tears and anger. He demands his mother's return and seems hopeful that he will succeed in getting her back; this stage may last several days. Later he becomes quieter; but it is clear that he is just as preoccupied with his absent mother and still yearns for her return. However, his hopes may have faded; this is called the phase of 'despair'. Often the stages alternate: hope turns to despair, and despair to renewed hope. Eventually a greater change occurs; the child *seems* to forget his mother so that, when he sees her again, he remains curiously uninterested in her, and may seem not to recognize her (the so-called stage of 'detachment').

In each of these phases the child is prone to tantrums and episodes of destructive behaviour. After reunion with his parents, he may be unresponsive and undemanding — to what degree and for how long, depends on the length of the separation and whether or not he received frequent visits during that period. For example, if he has been deprived of visits for a good few weeks and has reached the early stages of detachment, it is likely that unresponsiveness will persist for varying periods, ranging from a few hours to several days. When at last this unresponsiveness subsides, the intense ambivalence of the child's feelings for his mother is made manifest. There is a storm of feeling, intense clinging and whenever his mother leaves him, even for a moment, acute anxiety and rage. Here is the mother of a four-year-old speaking:

> Ever since I left her that time I had to go into hospital [two periods, 17 days each, child aged two years], she doesn't trust me any more. I can't go anywhere — over to the neighbours' or to the shops — I've always got to take her. She wouldn't leave me. She went down to the school gates at dinner time today. She ran like mad home. She said, 'Oh Mam, I thought you was gone!' She can't forget it. She's still round me all the time. I just sit down and put her on my knee and love her. Definitely. If I don't do it, she says 'Mam, you don't love me any more'; I've *got* to sit down.

Childhood is notable for fears of many remote and improbable circumstances. Much later — at adolescence — the fears which arise are more immediate and personal, such as those concerning relationships with the opposite sex. The age of eleven tends to bring about an increase in the fearfulness of children. This may be due, in part, to separation from old friends, familiar routines, with the move to secondary school. Among eleven- and twelve-year-olds, worries connected with *school* are nearly half as many again as worries about home matters.

phobias

It is necessary to be cautious in applying the term 'phobia' to some of the anxieties and fears of childhood. Many of these appear, to adult eyes, to be irrational or disproportionate, but (as we have seen) are so common in children at certain ages, that they must be regarded as normal developmental fears. Where the child's fear of really dangerous situations is adaptive, a case of school phobia — the child's avoidance — is clearly not so. It leads to his missing school work, handicaps him when he eventually returns, and so on. Whether or not a child requires treatment depends on whether the phobia itself is crippling in some way, preventing peace of mind and a reasonably productive life.

A child who I once treated had a fear of heights; this might have presented no particular embarrassment to many people but, in his case, visits to relatives and friends took him to many high flats. He became overwhelmed with anxiety when he found himself near a low railing or even when walking along the first-floor balcony corridor of a block of flats. Obviously his social life was adversely affected.

The intense fear provoked by exposure to the phobic object makes the sufferer go to great lengths to avoid the particular situation in which he may encounter it. Some phobias have an obsessive-compulsive quality — for example, fear of a compulsive impulse to jump from a high balcony when near the railings.

The best known (or most notorious) phobias are claustrophobia (fear of confined spaces) and agoraphobia (fear of open spaces). A statistical analysis suggests that many of these fears tend to be interrelated, and can be accounted for by a general factor of fearfulness. In other words, many children will manifest a wide range of phobias. A second factor is a social phobia — a fear of mixing with people; a third, covers fears of separation, and a fourth, those relating to fears of injury, hurt or pain.

learning to be neurotic

Learning is not always benign in its effects, and sadly, the example of 'maladaptive' (i.e. abnormal) learning to be described next was engineered by distasteful experimenting, back in the 1920s, with a one-year-old child. Albert was the child in question. Having first ascertained that the child was not afraid of a pet white rat, Doctors John Watson and Rosalie Rayner gave him the rat to play with. Whenever the child reached for the animal the experimenters made a loud noise behind him — something that they knew made him fearful. After only five associations Albert began showing signs of fear in the presence of the white rat on its own. This fear spread itself to objects which resembled the rat, such as furry objects, cotton wool and a white rabbit — a phenomenon called 'stimulus generalization'. These phobic reactions (or irrational fears) were still present when Albert was tested four months later.

This particular demonstration has proved to be theoretically as well as ethically controversial. Nevertheless, it is often quoted as an example of how a person can learn to be phobic. In Albert's case, the previously acceptable rat acquired the fear-evoking properties of the loud noise. (Fortunately, it is *not* possible to condition human fear to anything and everything.)

The point about these conditioned emotional responses is that they are largely under the control of the autonomic nervous system, not under conscious control. It is no use saying that such and such an anxiety in my child 'is silly and irrational' and that she must 'take hold of herself and stop it'. It is not under her control to switch the fear on and off. It is as involuntary as an eyeblink to a puff of air.

he can't help himself!

The contagious effect of calmness and lack of fear has been used in extinguishing fears. In other words, we see the process (described above) used in reverse, to *good* effect. Nursery school children who were afraid of dogs were treated successfully during eight brief sessions by observing unafraid children playing happily with a dog.

overcoming fear

The most effective methods used by adults to help their offspring are those which:

1 Help the child develop skills with which he can cope with the feared object or situation;
2 take the child by degrees into active contact and participation with the feared object or situation;
3 give the child an opportunity gradually to become acquainted with the feared object or situation under circumstances that at the same time allow him the opportunity either to inspect or ignore it.

Methods that are sometimes helpful in enabling the child to overcome his fears include:

1 verbal explanation and reassurance;

2   verbal explanation, plus a practical demonstration
    that the feared object or situation is not dangerous;
3   giving the child examples of fearlessness regarding
    the feared object or situation (parents frequently
    quote the example of other children who were not
    afraid.);
4   conditioning the child to believe that the feared object
    is not dangerous but pleasurable.

self-help   It has been found that, even without help, children can
overcome fears, either as part of the general process of
growing up or by using the following techniques:

1   practising overcoming their fear by enlisting the help
    of adults or favourite toys;
2   talking with other people about the things they fear;
3   arguing with themselves about the reality or unreality
    of dreaded imaginary creatures or fantasized events
    — say death — that they fear.

fear of the dark   Many youngsters learn to fear the dark and this causes
bedtime problems. To be left in the dark is not initially
an unpleasant experience for a young child. Sooner or
later, however, when he is in pain with a tummy ache,
frightened by a dream, hungry, cold or miserably wet, he
will cry for his mother. She comes hot foot to his rescue,
putting on the light as she enters the room, and soon
comforts him out of his distress. What better
conditioning model could there be for unwittingly
associating darkness with distress, and light with positive
reinforcement in the form of a consoling mother? What
she might do is to enter the room without putting on the
light, chatting to him and reassuring him until she has
ascertained the trouble and then, if essential, switching
on the light to remedy the situation. This sequence of
events ensures that there is no direct and recurrent
relationship between the arrival or presence of mother
and the light. If the child has learned to fear the dark
because of terrifying tales from peers about ghosts and
burglars, punishment is obviously quite inappropriate.

what to do   Your child has a fear of the dark (say) and comes to your
bedroom during the night. First of all you might leave
the light on for him to get to sleep, switching it off when

he is asleep, and leaving the door open with a light on outside so that he will not wake up in total darkness. Move the light gradually towards the door and out of the room, a little further each night. (If you have one, use a dimmer switch to achieve this gradual process.) To avoid sudden distress on the child's part you could explain it to him as ' a game'. Make sure that he knows how to switch on the light for himself should he wake up and want it on. When sleep supervenes you can again turn the light off. Because the situation is under the child's control there will be no call for panic. Given sufficient patience on your side, your child will eventually get tired of leaving the comfort of his bed in order to switch on the light, and will decide (hopefully) that there is more profit and sense in going back to sleep with the light off.

bad dreams

We mentioned dreams earlier on. Aggressive children tend to have more hostility in their dreams (which can be frightening) than gentle youngsters; anxious children have more unhappy, worrying dreams. Children who have been separated from their mother by a long stay in hospital, are more likely to be prone to nightmares subsequently — though there is no noticeable effect on the dreams of children who are separated from their mothers *but* remain in their own home. Unpleasant dreams tend to increase when a child is in poor health, with vivid nightmares about death, illness and other morbid topics.

Nightmares often set in for short periods when a child, particularly a sensitive child, is unsettled or worried by a change of school, a move to a new town or the trial of examinations. If he has emotional problems — if, for instance, he cannot come to terms with his parents' separation, or a new stepfather — he may have recurrent nightmares, often on the same theme. Disturbing dreams tend to become a problem for children around the ages of ten to eleven; one third or more experience them. For a girl, nightmares peak in their incidence at six or seven years of age. They become less frequent as she gets older.

Another form of sleep disturbance is the 'night terror' which can frighten parents almost as much as their child. If you find your child crouched on his bed, rigid with fear, or rushing about in a frenzy, screaming and crying, his eyes wide open and staring, with dilated pupils, then he is suffering a night terror. He is not fully awake, does not seem to recognize you and is thoroughly disorientated, not sure where he is or what he is doing, though he answers your questions and gradually responds to soothing reassurance. In the morning he remembers nothing about it. Night terrors may indicate that the child is going through a period of worry and tension. You may be able to pinpoint the cause — perhaps he is being bullied, maybe a beloved pet has died — but if there is no obvious reason and the night terrors persist, then take your child to the doctor.

first aid The best way of handling a nightmare or night terror is simply to sit with your child until he has calmed down, preferably until he is nearly asleep. Do not try to talk about the dream or the anxieties which may, or may not, lie behind it. Next day encourage him to talk about it, when he is feeling relaxed. Do not force the issue if he is able to describe the dream in any detail to you. Simply sharing the fear may help, but you may detect clues in repetitive dreams, to what is troubling him. If the child is too young to articulate his fears make as little fuss as possible when you comfort him. If he feels you are upset and worried, you only aggravate the problem. Try to make sure that going to bed is a peaceful, happy business, without too many excitable games last thing at night and no stories or (for the impressionable child) television about the supernatural.

coming to mother's bed For a variety of reasons, including those just described, children fall into the *habit* of getting into their parents' bed. Even when fear is no longer present it can be a difficult habit to 'break'. It may seem obvious that a simple, structured and persistent strategy will get the child to stay in her room, and yet many resourceful parents tell us that they get defeated by this problem. It certainly requires an investment of dogged persistence and imperviousness to 'wheedling'; it means a few broken nights. But then your nights are being broken anyway by the invasion of your rest by an importunate child.

Teaching your small daughter to go to sleep on her own in her own bed will require considerable effort. The first few nights may well be exhausting, but with determination on your part the retraining process should work. The following points are important:

a step-by-step strategy

1 *Preparing for bed* This should be made a pleasant, reassuring time for your child, with a well-established time and routine.
2 *Preparing for sleep* This should occur with the child in bed. A story or two can be read together and you will probably wish to chat a little. Explanations of the new routine should be given at this time. The final part of this stage includes tucking her in, and a kiss, saying calmly but firmly: 'Goodnight, have a good sleep, see you in the morning.'
3 *During sleeping hours* If she cries or calls out ignore it — unless there is a note of urgency or panic — until she gets out of bed. If she does get out of bed (and you have assured yourself she is all right) take her back, without fuss, to her room and put her to bed in a matter-of-fact way. She should then be told 'You *must* stay in bed: if you come out, I will take you right back.'
4 This action needs to be repeated consistently *throughout the night,* whenever she gets out of bed. As *little* reinforcing attention (e.g. chats, cuddles) as possible should be given to her for these activities during the night.
5 Pin up a 'bedtime chart' which is marked out in squares for every night of the week. If she does not come to your bedroom, tick the appropriate square and put a star on a star chart or let her colour in one section of a picture. In the one below (members of the family can think up their own symbolic reward chart) the child would be colouring in her 'own' face, one for each successful night. Every success receives a lot of praise. Promise a special treat at the end of the week — having a friend to tea or an extra trip to the park — when all of the heads are coloured in. The rest of the picture is then coloured in and moved from her bedroom and pinned up in a place of honour in the sitting room. If she does get up on any night,

THE GOOD BED

Sue's Chart. Let Sue colour in a head the morning after she has successfully remained in her own bed. Explain that each head represents herself on a particular night of the week.

you must repeat (3) and (4) with *unremitting* persistence. (It is helpful if you have someone to take turns in executing the programme!)

tension and stress   Anxiety takes its toll, not only in the psychological sense of dread, apprehension and feelings of tension, but also in the form of physical illness. The term 'stress' is often used in this context; it has become widely used to describe any state of overload where the human being is pushed to his limits. Stress reactions may manifest themselves as an increase of asthmatic attacks in an asthmatic child, headaches, tummy aches or other physical symptoms; they may take the form of 'bad' habits so-called (by parents) — a display of somewhat bizarre behaviours referred to as 'tension' or 'comfort' habits by psychologists. These are the hair-pulling, picking, sucking and biting that children openly enjoy. Adults learn to conceal them, or find socially acceptable ones like smoking or chewing sweets.

When tension habits appear in isolation, and are not particularly dramatic, they may simply be signalling mild and fleeting problems — the common stresses and strains of development. It is important to remember that most of the tension symptoms described here occur in normal children.

When tension habits are part of a serious problem, there tend to be other signs of disturbance. One of the marks of an anxious person is that he tends to 'overdo' or to 'understate'. A slight affront or criticism may send him over the top and into a rage; or he may have what seems like an excess of calm when there really is something to get emotional about, as though he were under duress to batten down the lid on his feelings.

There are many sources of stress in both animals and humans, overcrowding and noise produce emotional and physiological effects, including aggression, anxiety and fear. So do the stresses of a psychological kind which arise from living in a competitive society, in particular the emphasis on success. A degree of tension seems to be an inescapable feature of living — even for infants.

thumbsucking

This is sometimes interpreted as a mild tension-reducing or comfort-providing behaviour. Occasional thumb-sucking is a common developmental phenomenon of early childhood. About 40 per cent of children between two and seven years indulge in thumb-sucking. If it occurs in isolation — with no sign of other anxiety symptoms — there is no need for parental concern. Sucking can be modified by using the principle of negative reinforcement. A television programme — Nigel's favourite one — was switched off temporarily each time his thumb went into his mouth. As each such action produced the 'shutting-down' of the entertainment, the youngster's tendency to suck declined dramatically. Thumb-sucking is *not* important enough to merit such 'way-out' methods — especially if they are applied at the cost of good parent-child relationships. Such methods, referred to as 'aversive training' have other limitations. By focusing too obviously on the thumb-sucking habit, parents' attention may reinforce the very behaviour they wished to eliminate. When you see your child with his thumb in his mouth, use the classic distraction method: send him on a small errand or give him something else to do. If a child's hands are occupied with some interesting activity, he cannot suck them at the same time. In the case of Nigel's hands, which had stopped straying to his mouth when he was denied the television, they showed no such restraint outside the laboratory. The child's training had no effect upon his thumb-sucking in general!

an important digression

This highlights a technical problem in child training or therapy. You cannot take it on trust that what you teach a child in one situation will generalize to *other* situations. You may have to steel yourself for the hard slog of training him specifically for those other situations or circumstances.

twitches (tics)

These are rather unsightly (automatic) involuntary movements. Twitchings, which are not under the child's control, are called tics, and include blinking the eyes, jerking the head, twitching the hands, grimacing, and clearing the throat. Although tics may have a physical cause, and therefore must be medically checked, in most instances they are of psychological origin.

When this is so, the tics may be indicative of inner tension or inappropriate habit formation. Children with tics tend to be restless, self-conscious and sensitive, and commonly have parents who are too demanding — perfectionist, over-controlling and inclined to punish. Big adjustments in life, such as starting school, may trigger off tic habits. To plead with the child to stop the habit, or to scold or punish him, only intensifies the pattern. Focusing the child's attention on his tic, so as to make him self-conscious, simply exaggerates it. Much of the time, a sensitive appreciation by parents of the fears, frustrations and insecurities which maintain the tic, together with reassurance and understanding, should be sufficient to facilitate its imminent departure. Tics are usually transient, so wait them out. There are special means of modifying more resistant habits, but these are best left to the specialists (see Appendix II).

nail-biting

Nail-biting is an example of the kind of 'bad habit' commonly cited as a characteristic of the nervous or anxious child. Indeed it may appear as part of a general emotional disturbance, but it usually does not necessarily imply any psychological problems at all. Of boys in the eight- to eleven-year age group, at least two-thirds are nail-biters; the proportion for girls is only slightly less. In other words, nail-biting is a 'normal' if unsightly practice — one which is still commonly seen in teenagers, and not a few adults. Like thumbsucking, this habit is best ignored.

PART IV

Issues that worry parents

Parents often seek advice about day-to-day issues like parenting and child-care; sex education; jealousy in the family; discipline; and the pros and cons of using physical punishment. They also wish to know how to change their child's behaviour for the better. Sometimes they ask advice on major crises such as an impending separation or a serious delinquent action by their child. Having sought advice it is often difficult to actually take it. It is even more difficult (or should be, as it may be so presumptuous) to give it! How do you give reliable advice when knowledge about children and their ways is still so hedged in with so many ifs and buts. After all, what is the truth about 'good' parenting or the 'right' kind of discipline to use? Many of the issues concern *values* rather than facts. In that sense we really do find that 'truth is never pure, and rarely simple'. Oscar Wilde said this in *The Importance of Being Earnest;* and Bernard Shaw went even further. He maintained that 'the golden rule is that there are no golden rules.'

Because each child, parent, and family is unique, it is inconceivable that there could be hard and fast rules or advice on parenting and child-care, even if we knew, broadly, the manner in which to approach such goals. Parents, anxious and concerned about their child, and deeply in need of reassurance, hope, nevertheless, for explicit advice and firm prognostications. 'What must I do to put things right?'; 'When will he be right again?' These questions arise from real anguish. Listen to the voice of a mother (and distinguished writer) Jill Tweedie:

> There are few things other than stark tragedy that can cause so much general disarray in the parental bosom as the sort of letter I received a short while ago. It came from my son's school and it conveyed a message to the effect that the headmaster thought him disturbed and withdrawn.

The alarm and despondency starts in the stomach, and spreads through the body and spills over into every aspect of thought and feeling so that the immediate physical reaction is to find a dark broom cupboard and retire into it for good. What other way of coping with the news, that you, your love, your deeds, your principles, indeed your entire way of life is somehow mis-shapen and actively damaging to the human being you love best in the world? . . . Children are everyone's Achilles' heel and when something is wrong with them then everything is wrong, an acid smog descends and erodes your resilience at exactly the time both you and your child need it most.

There is a particular problem which besets the would-be counsellor. When a child is physically ill the doctor can give his mother or father quite explicit instructions based upon a painstaking diagnosis — for instance to keep him in bed for one week; give him four tablets a day at regular intervals. The child psychologist faced with a mother complaining of her child's temper tantrums or jealous outlook, cannot be anything like as explicit. At best he can suggest a general change in policy on the parents' part — for instance, that they stop being so punitive — or plan a programme of treatment (see chapter 16) which bears some comparison with the doctor's prescription.

But the real difference appears when the parents put the advice into practice. As far as the psychological advice is concerned, what is crucial is *how* the parents carry it out; indeed the advice consists precisely of the suggestion that the parents themselves should change.

What the psychologist can do is to provide parents with a new awareness of how their actions, attitudes and relationships affect the child, which, hopefully, generates changes in behaviour, attitude and understanding. This surely means sharing his knowledge with them. Parents have the right to be spoken to as equals, and to be given the facts about their children. There is nothing more demoralizing to parents than the bland uncommunicativeness which some professionals adopt towards their clients.

Of course, we all have our pet theories and prejudices about the particular and significant consequences of early childhood experience. We 'know' deep down, because of our contact as parents, teachers, or professional workers both with individual children and groups of youngsters, that children's lives and adjustment do vary according to their families' treatment of them. These variations may be temporary — a result of some family crisis or improvement of family conditions — or they may be long enduring. The trouble is that this 'knowledge' is more often intuitive rather than factual, which is not to decry intuition, but simply to suggest the need for caution. Much of the present-day insecurity about the parental role arises from the diversity of advice available on child care. There are radical changes taking place in our concepts of parenthood and childhood, and indeed, in the status of the family itself. This is our cue for a consideration of these issues in the following chapter.

13

Being a parent

The birth of a first child to a couple makes parents of them and transforms their relationship into a family. The family is not only crucial for the care and protection it offers the young during their relatively prolonged period of dependence; it plays a major role in the introduction of infants into the ways of their social environment — their culture. This social role, as we saw in chapter 1, includes teaching the child the attitudes, norms, and other attributes of his culture. In addition to these matters, the family circle is the most vital social unit in which both the child's and adult's personality are rooted and nourished. Although society delegates its most crucial functions to the family, there is little formal education or training offered to would-be parents; even the informal learning and experience once offered to older children caring for younger siblings in large families, or the help from the experienced members of the extended family or from relatives living nearby, may not be available to the relatively isolated modern family.

the changing role of the family

The idea of privacy in the family household is relatively modern, as indeed is our concept of childhood itself. Such privacy dilutes somewhat the pressures on parents to conform; in turn this flexibility results in a greater range of individualism in the children produced by the society. There is a greater 'danger' that many parents and their children will be out of step with their society. Or so it is claimed. The very freedom which families and individuals have won for themselves — the loosening of the social fabric — may have brought in its wake the problems of non-conformist, idiosyncratic, even alienated youth.

The family is part of a social network which is linked with outside social institutions. One of its functions is to provide parents themselves with a variety of supports.

Parents depend on a variety of sources of social, emotional and economic support — the extended family, the community and the work place. There have been several investigations showing that parents who abuse their children have fewer associations outside the home, receive less help in caring for their offspring, and perceive their neighbours more negatively than other parents.

In many families there is an element of conflict which sometimes flares up into fighting and feuding. Much of it has its source in envy, resentment, rivalry, and plain jealousy. Jealousy is a powerful and painful emotion which shows itself in various ways: quarrelling, bitchiness, complaining and hostility. Families have finite (sometimes limited) resources — material, affectional and so on. There is only so much to go around. Mother's attention and energy can only go so far. Her husband sulks because he does not get so much of her attention any more. The new baby takes up every minute — or so it seems, in his jealous frame of mind. John, now a toddler, is also jealous. He throws temper tantrums and generally makes himself as big a nuisance as possible. He has regressed (there is not much in it, between him and his father) to old baby ways, refusing to eat unless his mother feeds him spoonful by spoonful, yelling his way along the street until she picks him up. The mother bides her time, lovingly, and waits stoically for all to blow over — as these things usually do. Heroic 'inaction' is her motto. The lesson she has learned is that like so many other family dramas, there is more sound than substance to these rows. Still, they take their toll! Perhaps another woman will reject such stoicism and would perceive inaction as anything but heroic. Unlike times gone by — as best we can judge such attitudes — there is a pervasive insecurity about the mother's functions, duties and obligations.

'Mothering' is regarded in our society as the most **motherhood** appropriate term to describe the tender loving care of children. Significantly it is a feminine word and reflects the mother-centred connotations of child care, namely the stereotype that the woman is a housewife and that her role is minding home, husband and children. Biology and social convention have 'foisted' these duties on her. For many women these roles are embraced without misgiving; they do, in fact, fulfil them. For others they are *not* enough. Women have been made to feel guilty if they feel this way. The clinical and social work literature on child problems over many years was replete with 'bad mothers': schizophrenogenic mothers, asthmagenic mothers, mothers accused of suffocating their offspring with 'smother' love, or in some other way overprotecting, rejecting or double-binding them into abnormality. The eminent child psychiatrist, Stella Chess, refers to this scapegoating as 'mal de mere', and she is very critical of the injustice of it, not to mention its unscientific bias.

The rhetoric about motherhood, the myths and erroneous beliefs which have attained wide acceptance, the fads and fashions of 'good mothering' which have come and gone, have collectively delivered a body blow to the confidence and spontaneity of many women. It is frequently claimed that the malaise of today's housewives is loneliness; a new condition with the attendant symptoms of nagging boredom and an acute sense of wasting oneself, of lack of fulfilment. The woman who is today's housewife may find herself on her own for hours on end, day after day, month after month, especially as one or more of her children reach the age when they go away to school. Lack of a feeling of belonging and community can do great harm to a mother's sense of purpose and well-being.

Without suitable outlets, these vague feelings sometimes build up into a strong sense of alienation, of not being in charge of their own lives and destinies. The contemporary mother is quite likely to be a woman who is educated, and perhaps highly trained in some skill. She has usually been employed for a number of years. Marrying in her twenties she will have her children before she is thirty, and during this time will usually remain at home with them. Many young women making the first adjustment to motherhood find their economic dependence on husbands frustrating. They may also find that one important loss, caused by the initial move from a working environment to full-time housework at home, is that of social contacts enjoyed at work.

Of course, this is an extremely one-sided picture. Mothering is a great joy to most women. It is sad that society places extra ideological burdens on the hard-pressed woman, which are not backed up by adequate practical, supportive resources. She is made aware by the books she reads and the experts she consults that the child's growth, contentment, and even survival depend to a significant extent on her skill at being a stimulating and tender parent. The father is often out at work so that a child may spend the first crucial years of his life almost exclusively in the company of his mother.

The contemporary young husband, as he fulfils his paternal role, is quite likely to be discovered feeding or bathing the baby. A few stay home to be the main caregiver. Indeed there is no reason why a father cannot be a good 'mother' — in the sense of being the main caregiver — and do an adequate job. Notions of fathering like these are alien to earlier times and other species. Throughout the animal kingdom, males play little or no part in the care and nurture of their offspring. The human male and female establish a family unit, whereas most male and female animals come together for mating purposes and then part. In fact, humanity took a long time to discover what fatherhood was. The 40 weeks of pregnancy dividing the moment of conception from the birth of a baby prevented our ancestors from connecting the two events.

fatherhood

Given the undoubted changes in social attitudes, researchers have been eager to see whether such changes are 'skin deep'. For example, do babies 'trigger' the same kind of responsiveness in males and females? They usually show men and women films of babies crying and at the same time measure their psychophysiological responsiveness, for example, their heart rate and blood pressure. In general men and women appear to react in similar ways. Second, researchers have examined the ways in which parents greet their newborns, since in many species parental behaviour is programmed to protect newborns and enhance responsive behaviour toward the young. Again, the similarities outweigh any differences. Most studies find that children do not distinguish between their parents — either can serve as an emotional haven — although there is some evidence to suggest that under severe stress children tend to show a preference for their mothers.

In present-day society some men do become highly involved with their children. But most make what is really a token effort to keep up with the practical skills of child rearing, concentrating more on becoming 'super pals' to their youngsters. Nevertheless, many have an underlying feeling that their fatherly relationships are not on as sound a footing as their wives' maternal 'bonds'. These patterns continue long after infancy.

Researchers who have studied the father's contribution to family life conclude that any new father should be encouraged to spend as much time as possible with his wife and child. The earlier he can feel involved with the child, the more likely is a strong relationship to develop between them. Having a child deserves a careful decision by both father and mother; and ideally, the prospective parents ought to feel a joint commitment to their future family before the child is conceived. Although this mutual interest should carry on through pregnancy, it is only too easy for the father to begin feeling left out at this stage.

The most frequent barrier between father and child is the father's work schedule. Many fathers, because of long-term goals, sacrifice time with their families only to find that they have 'lost' their children, at least psychologically, in the process. In some cases, modifications in the daily work routine ensure his fuller participation in family life, but all too often work is used as an excuse for avoiding family responsibilities. Many fathers who are competent and active at work feel totally inexperienced and ineffectual when at home with their children.

the pursuit of happiness for children

Parents tend to talk in fairly general terms when you ask about their offspring — their aims and objectives as parents. For example, they all hope that their children will grow up to be happy and contented. William James, the eminent American psychologist, wrote as follows:

If we were to ask the question: 'What is human life's chief concern?' one of the answers we should receive would be: 'It is happiness.' How to gain, how to keep, how to recover happiness is in fact for most men at all times the secret motive of all they do, and of all they are willing to endure.

It has been said that if the child is provided with the conditions which allow for his or her happiness, all else will follow. Presumably this means that, if the child is happy in some general sense, then the details of child-rearing are not too important, as the child is bound to turn out all right.

Generally speaking, there *is* an association between intense and prolonged feelings of unhappiness and other evidence of emotional disorder. It is a characteristic of certain psychological problems in adults and children, that the individual feels a loss of his sense of well-being. Whether the attainment of fairly consistent happiness is a sign of positive mental health is much more debatable.

The trouble with happiness is its elusiveness. It is difficult to recognize it, even when we have it. The conscious search for happiness for children, is like the search for gold at the end of the rainbow; if it is interpreted superficially and equated with fun, it may prove treacherous as a goal in life. Some critics comment on the pervasiveness of 'fun morality' — the pleasure-seeking principle — in our culture. The implicit motto is 'what is fun is good; what is good is fun.' They claim to see the worship of fun and play in our daily activities, at home and at school. If taken too far, these play strategies can lead to a chaotic alienated existence, lacking long-term purpose and meaning. Some parents encourage a fun morality in their children by the apologetic attitude they adopt in training them in the traditional 'virtues' of altruism, duty, mutual obligation, work and self-sacrifice. Critics of Western child-centred values in child-rearing maintain that so much is done for children, so little asked of them, that egotistical ('me-first') attitudes are encouraged. Haim Ginott cautions parents thus:

> Happiness . . . is not a destination; it is a manner of travelling. Happiness is not an end in itself. It is a by-product of working, playing, loving, and living. Living, by necessity involves delay between desire and fulfilment, between plan and realization. In other words, it involves frustration and the endurance of frustration.

The psychologist, Carl Rogers, believes that adjectives such as 'happy', 'contented', 'blissful', and 'enjoyable' are not appropriate to any general description of what he calls 'the good life'. This is especially so for the idealistic young adult who is emerging at the end of the period of life that we have been considering. The adjectives which he finds more fitting generally are those such as 'enriching', 'exciting', 'rewarding', 'challenging', and 'meaningful'. Rogers is convinced that 'the good life' is not a life for the faint-hearted, because it involves stretching and growing, *becoming* more and more of one's potentialities, and having the courage to *be*. Rogers says that 'the good life' means launching oneself fully into the stream of life. One of the most impressive features about human beings is that, when the individual is inwardly free, he chooses as the good life this process of 'becoming'.

Parents who work too hard at attaining happiness for their children often seem to come to grief. It is only immature children and emotionally immature adults who expect or try to live in a utopian rose-tinted world, or for purposes of happiness and enjoyment alone. If the task of parents is to prepare their child for life, then to shelter him from its realities in the compulsive pursuit of a permanent state of happiness is an illusion, and to search for it on his behalf is to invite the opposite of what is desired for him. Some parents strive to avoid all possible frustration. But as we have seen, frustration is endemic to social life, thus frustration-tolerance becomes an important index of the individual's maturity. Such tolerance is truly tested within the family, with its jealousies and quarrels.

is there a 'problem position' in the family? Can family jealousies arise out of the ordinal position of the child among his brothers and sisters? Psychologists and the public at large have long been intrigued by the possible consequences of being an only child, or the first born, the last born, or a middle child, in various sizes of family.

What evidence there is suggests that there is in fact no 'ideal' position. There is no niche in the family hierarchy which does not involve, as a consequence of its particular nature, certain special problems of adjustment. But each child thinks his position is uniquely disadvantageous. The eldest child complains that she has to do all the chores and look after the baby; the second child complains that her older sister is allowed to stay up late and has all the privileges. The middle one says she's always getting the cast-off clothes and, furthermore, no one loves her or bothers about her. The youngest — a boy — complains that his sisters are always making a fuss of him, and that everyone treats him like a baby when he's already nearly four. Parents can't win!

Being first to arrive on the family scene has advantages and drawbacks. It has been established that first children tend to be slightly more at risk than others in developing emotional problems; they tend to appear (proportionately) more often on the files of child guidance clinics than later children. The eldest child's emotional vulnerability may be due to the inconsistency of the parents, and the related fact that parental inexperience and anxiety often gives rise to over-protection.

the eldest child

    The first-born child presumably gets his advantages because parents expect a lot from him and he usually has first call on family resources. He has an edge over later-born children, not only because he is achievement-orientated and rather successfully so, but also because he tends — and this is particularly so with only children — to be very verbal. This is understandable given his consistent and, for a time, more or less unadulterated exposure to adult speech and company.

Later-born children are more independent and flexible than their predecessors. For example, the second-born child escapes much parental uncertainty and intensity. The mother tends to be more relaxed; in many ways she 'enjoys' this child's babyhood more, and is prepared to 'let him be' to a much greater extent. Consequently, this child is less dependent than the first child. The mother is likely to be less weighed down by her sense of responsibility, and if she was originally resentful about losing freedom as a result of becoming a mother, she may by now have resolved these tensions. The younger child's difficulties may arise from the older one 'lording it' over him, and perhaps bullying him. But there is often an admiring and very affectionate, if at times turbulent, relationship between the pace-making older sibling and the 'catching-up' younger one. The second child often resents the privileges of the older child. (These

later children

advantages may seem to the elder more apparent than real, and far outweighed by his responsibilities. This is particularly so if the child is saddled with looking after small brothers and sisters.) The second child tends to do well on mental tests, particularly if he has a brother for an older sibling. For some reason, an older brother, more than an older sister, stimulates and alerts the younger ones so that some aspects of their developmental timetable are accelerated.

It is one thing being the second child in a sequence of children; it is sometimes a rather different matter when a child is sandwiched between two others in a permanent pattern of three. Although the middle child does not necessarily follow a definite and invariable pattern of emotional development, parents frequently recognize him as very different from the first and the third child. Practically all the evidence we have concerning middle-borns, has a somewhat negative connotation.

The last — the youngest child — is quite likely to be pampered and spoiled, especially if there are lots of sisters around. In families of three or more, parents often refer to the youngest child as the 'baby' of the family. And they may continue to treat him as such, long after it ceases to be the appropriate thing to do. He may get enjoyable attention from this but, because he is much younger than the others, he may be left out of certain family activities, and treated as if he did not quite fit into the bigger 'scheme of things'. The two extreme possibilities — spoiling and exclusion — may well colour his entire outlook, and make for self-centred and 'chip-on-the-shoulder' attitudes respectively.

The age difference between children is an important influence on how the mother treats them. When they are closely spaced, she tends to treat them more rationally, more democratically and with more understanding. If the age differences are great, parental expectations of the older and younger children tend to be more rigid, and may contribute to poor sibling relationships.

only children   All first children are 'only children' for a while, and a few remain so during all their formative years. The potential problem for the only child is that the parents may not learn to relax and eventually to relinquish their over-anxious, over-attentive attitude towards him —

especially as there tends to be such a highly-charged emotional investment in him, as the 'only' one. Some children are only ones because of the conscious choice of their parents; but others are in this position because their parents have no choice in the matter. There may be some physical problem which prevents the mother from giving birth to another child, or the parents may be relatively elderly people who had difficulty in conceiving one baby. This tends to make the child a particularly precious object to the parents. He is irreplaceable, in the absolute, as well as metaphorical sense of the word. Such circumstances predispose the mother, and sometimes the father as well (which makes the situation doubly difficult), to be overly nurturant.

Mothers tend to favour the only boy to a much greater extent than the only girl. There is some evidence that, while the close relationship of only children to their parents facilitates their need for achievement, it carries a risk, also, of too strong an identification with the parent of the opposite sex. Thus, there is a tendency for the only boy to be slightly more feminine than other males, and the only girl slightly more masculine than other females. In keeping with these tendencies, only children are somewhat more susceptible to sexual deviations than other children. There is no need to panic about such a finding. A majority of only children are sexually normal; this is simply a statistical trend indicating a slightly increased problem of sexual adjustment. Although the evidence is far from consistent, there is a tendency for 'only' children to contribute disproportionate numbers to the ranks of the generally 'maladjusted'. But the problems of being an only child were overstated in the early days of child psychology.

14

Fighting and feuding

Out of the blue, small children will horrify their parents by their outspoken jealousy, asking hopefully: 'When is *it* going away?' (the 'it' being the new baby). My small nephew told his mother (on being told that she was expecting a baby): 'But isn't our family of six big enough already?' The six included himself, his mother and father, his brother, the dog and the hamster.

Because of the great emphasis on emotional intimacy, success and materialism in society and in family life, sibling rivalry can be a potent force for jealousy, anxiety, but also — it must be admitted — for constructive striving, among children. Sibling rivalry is the name psychologists give to the often rancorous competition between brothers and sisters. Some individuals continue this sibling rivalry into adult life, and their competition with colleagues and opponents has all the intensity and fierceness of half-forgotten rivalries from childhood. Almost every child has some feelings of envy and rejection when they have to compete with a new baby who demands so much of his mother's attention. Finding that her day no longer revolves round him is a set-back for his confidence and self-esteem. He may feel unloved or 'cast off' in favour of his brother or sister, however unjustified his feelings may be. His jealousy is often accompanied by attention-seeking infantile behaviour as if he can only compete for his previous monopoly position by becoming a baby again.

attacks on the baby   If you notice signs of regression in your child, it may be necessary to give him a generous helping of attention and affection — but *not* in such a way and at such a time that it seems to be rewarding immature actions. Let him see the advantage and privilege of being older. However, there may be a rather more worrying problem to deal with — open or sneaky attacks on the baby. Of course, you have to protect the baby from a toddler who pinches it, or tries to tip it out of the pram when your back is turned; but punishing the child, telling him how wicked he is will not resolve anything. It is more likely to increase his anger and vulnerability, just when he needs reassurance that you still love him. Encourage him to 'help' you with the baby, talking to him, and praising him, while he is doing it. Once the baby is settled, make sure he has some time to himself when he gets your undivided attention. The trouble with stressing the advantages of being, not a baby, but a big boy, is the tendency of visitors to subvert this line, clustering around and clucking over the baby — unmindful of the 'big boy' hovering around.

All of this applies to older children as well. A certain amount of rivalry and competition is natural. Do not try obsessively to treat all your children *exactly* the same. It is impossible! But do not play favourites. Make sure each one has a part of your time, however short, to himself. Sometimes rivalry spills over into continual bickering.

they're always fighting

Try to keep out of your children's fights as much as possible, so long as they do not get too gory and gruesome. Holding inquests to find out who is in the wrong will only increase any jealousy or resentment which is already there; you only encourage more squabbles if you take too much notice. If you do have to intervene, concentrate on treating their self-righteous anger with equal disdain while putting a stop to the fight. Then try to suggest a compromise, or point out something interesting to distract their attention.

Brothers and sisters have to live side by side, but they need to develop their own personalities. Even if there is little room to spare in your house, make sure each child has his own private place to keep his toys or his school things, and let the children take turns in choosing treats, bedtime stories or television programmes. The elder child has to learn that her younger brother is weaker and less capable, but at the same time the younger child must realize that the elder needs some time 'to do her own thing'.

competition
and self-
esteem

Rivalry between children can be useful in spurring them on to greater efforts, so long as the competition does not become too intense. It is important not to compare their achievements directly, but to show that each is an individual with her own special talents — one may be good at sport, be good at fixing things, one may sing well and also have a way with animals. If parents set their levels of aspiration too high — beyond the child's capacity — it will affect his self-esteem adversely. If he suffers from low self-esteem, he will be vulnerable to failure and then may withdraw, if he is able, from the challenging activity. To some youngsters, failure acts as an incentive to try harder; to others, it merely confirms an existing conclusion that they are 'no good'. Their fear of failure becomes so pervasive that they throw in the sponge before meeting the challenge.

This matter of the child's own *expectation* of success or failure is important in determining his performance. Each child learns what expectations to have, based on previous experiences and also on the information he has, or imagines he has, about a given situation. The effectiveness of a reward depends partly on the child's prediction of success in a particular undertaking. If he has a low expectation of passing an arithmetic test, yet is successful, the value of the reinforcement occasioned by the triumph may be great.

The youngster's general sense of his competence — his ability to master challenges — may begin from infancy itself. Martin Seligman, a psychologist, puts it this way: 'the infant begins a dance with his environment that will last throughout childhood . . . it is the outcome of this dance that determines his helplessness or mastery.' Being able to control one's impulses requires a sense of *self*, a belief in one's own agency (or mastery) over inner and outer events in one's life.

making
things
happen

When the child behaves in a certain way his action can either produce a change in the environment (he cries and mother comes to his aid) or his action could be independent of what happens (when he cries his mother usually takes no notice). At some primitive level, the infant calculates the link (or association) between his action and the outcome. If the association is highly positive this means that his behaviour actually works, his action is effective, and the infant learns either to perform that action more frequently or to refrain from performing it, depending on whether the outcome is good or bad. But over and above this, he learns that responding actually works, that by and large, there is synchrony (matching) between his responses and their outcomes. When there is little or no link (as in a neglectful home, where his cries bring no relief, his smiles, no answering smile) he gradually begins to feel and *is*, helpless. He stops performing the action. Furthermore, he learns that, in general, responding doesn't matter, that it is pretty futile. Such learning has the same consequences that helplessness has in adults: lack of any desire to initiate actions, adoption of a pessimistic view of life ('it is all so hopeless!') and anxiety and depression. But this may be more disastrous for the infant since it is foundational; it occurs at the beginning of his efforts to build up a sense of confidence! What would also be calamitous is the endless praise of his successful brother at home and at school, and the invidious comparisons of his hopeless attempts to emulate his achievements.

According to Martin Seligman what enhances self-esteem and a sense of competence in the child — thus immunizing him against fatalism, depression and help-lessness — is not only the quality of his experience, but the sense that it is his own actions which *controlled* the experience.

competence

While some children gain from new experiences, others seem to discount such experiences by attributing them to chance or to other 'agencies' and not to their own behaviour or characteristics. Such observations led to the idea of what is called an external as opposed to internal 'locus of control' — an attribute of personality in the adult and child. Children who have the attributes of 'internals' perceive events, whether positive or negative, as being a consequence of their *own* actions and therefore potentially under personal control. 'Externals' (by contrast) perceive events, whether positive or negative, as being *unrelated* to their own actions and thereby beyond personal control. They tend to be fatalistic; their lives, as they see it, are controlled by others, destiny, fate, chance, call it what you will.

I wish he was more like his brother

The child who is a bit slow and who has a very bright brother may suffer from invidious comparisons. Criticism or failure *can* be motivating for the older, bright and able child, yet it will discourage and handicap the one who is already doing poorly. Whereas a reward may not do very much 'extra' for the successful youngster it can be highly motivating for the unsuccessful child. This is *not* to suggest that you should cease encouraging and praising your bright child, but simply to mix in some judicious critical comment when it is appropriate.

The bright sibling expects to succeed, hence success and praise do not surprise him or raise him to new levels of performance. He does not expect to fail or be criticized; hence when such things happen to him, the effect is salutary. The sanction, as it were, is so telling that he redoubles his efforts to avoid encountering it again. The failing child expects failure and criticism, hence it has little effect on him except to confirm his worst expectations and reduce his effort. But an experience of praise or reward is so striking and sweet that he works doubly hard to encounter such a state of affairs again. The moral is provide as much encouragement as you can. There is no need to be entirely uncritical of the less bright child, but you should be moderate with criticism — and generous with praise.

teasing and bullying

These are relatively commonplace problems in and out of the home. But, as indulged in by certain children, teasing can take on a worryingly sadistic flavour. It is usually a form of verbal aggression which tends to 'get on the nerves' of the child who is being victimized, thus leading to quarrelling. It can be a form of bullying, a mental rather than physical assault. Parents and teachers may be unsure whether to let teasing take its course or nip it in the bud. Boys tease and bully more, on average, than girls; and it has been found that children who have feelings of inadequacy, inferiority and insecurity, tend to be the most likely candidates to engage in this sort of harassment.

Teasing may involve pointing out and jeering at a real or supposed disability, using a nickname which arouses anger, or accusing a brother of an interest in some girl. A sister may be taunted with some critical remark about her appearance or her performance in class. Possibilities for teasing are almost infinite, and some boys and girls refine the 'art' to an exquisite degree of cruelty. Quite often it is parents who enjoy getting a rise out of their children. Parents who indulge in this teasing would probably be horrified to know that the practice has bad effects; in their minds they are 'only kidding' and mean no harm.

The child who is a butt of bullying may innocently put his mother in a difficult position. Here is a subtle example of the ambiguities and verbal squeamishness which the well-meaning mother shows when she comes up against the fundamental practical dilemma: Should I, or should I not, encourage violence in my small child, even in self-defence?

> I don't know if you can draw a distinction here between telling a child to stand his ground over something, and hitting back. I dislike this idea of telling a child to hit, you know, because I don't believe in hitting: *in theory*, anyway. I think it would be a wrong thing to tell a child to hit another child; but on the other hand one might say, 'well, you hang on to it if it's yours, and you want it, don't let him get it all the time.' Encourage him to stand up for himself, but not use the word 'hit'.

Given that fighting and feuding are endemic in the life of many families and a phase most children go through — nothing to get too excited about — how do you detect that there is a serious problem in the making? Ask yourself whether it fits into a general pattern of verbal and physical hostility. Is your child *always* fighting and quarrelling? Is he generally abusive? Does he over-react to provocations? Is his anger triggered by small frustrations or by no apparent external event at all? In other words, is it out of all proportion? If you have to answer 'yes' to such questions you need to trace the source of the child's antisocial actions.

A lot of children go around with a chip on their shoulder — prickly, hypersensitive and on a short fuse. Their unhappy backgrounds (often) provide an explanation for their jaundiced view of life. These children not only act impulsively and 'hatefully' but they have a contagious effect, instigating 'out-of-control' behaviour in others.

a chip on his shoulder

There is a higher, more disturbing, notch to all of this.

The child with paranoid tendencies — an extreme sense of persecution — perceives others as being hostile towards him. This may sometimes amount almost to a delusion of persecution, and suspicious, spiteful ways. Such paranoid attitudes, and other negative feelings, can lead some children to an overwhelming desire to maim and hurt living creatures. The child who tortures other children and torments animals is usually a desperately unhappy child and needs expert attention.

controlling aggression

We saw in chapter 2 how a combination of lax discipline and hostile attitudes on the part of both parents encourages very aggressive and poorly controlled behaviour in the offspring. The pattern of child-rearing that produces the most hostile children is one where the parents disapprove of aggression and, when it occurs, punish it with physical aggression of their own or threaten the child. This 'counter-attack' on the part of the parents, though it may work (suppress) for the moment, appears to generate still more hostility in the child, which eventually breaks out. Highly aggressive children are also produced by homes in which the mother is permissive of the child's outbursts, whether or not they are directed against her. Where mothers are both permissive and physically punishing, they are particularly prone to foster aggressiveness in their offspring. Parents who disapprove of aggression and who stop it — but by means other than physical punishment — are least likely to encourage further aggressive actions. Ultimately, an affectionate and tolerant home atmosphere in which the child knows that aggression is an inappropriate strategy for getting his way, is firmly but gently restrained from lashing out ('passive inhibition'), and is able to discriminate the limits beyond which he definitely cannot go, provides the best long-term antidote to an aggressive style of life. Teaching the child alternative means to ends — where the ends are acceptable ones — will also subvert the need to resort to fighting.

your own attitudes

But what if you feel that, while your child does seem to be more than normally aggressive towards others, you and your partner *have* been able to avoid the long-range disciplinary pitfalls of both over-permissiveness and punitiveness. It may help to re-examine the immediate restraints you are imposing on your child. Are they reasonable ones? Or are the 'dos' and 'don'ts' excessive — leading to nagging and an oppressive atmosphere?

It may also be a good idea to ask yourself what your own attitude is towards aggression. Are you a tease or even a bit of a bully yourself? Some parents are more aggressive than they realize, showing hostile behaviour which the child all too readily imitates. There is strong evidence that children model their behaviour on that of their parents, so it is not surprising to find that hostile parents tend to have aggressive children. And sometimes parents — consciously or unconsciously — will encourage aggressive behaviour ('Can't you be more manly?'; 'You get in first!').

Some mothers find it difficult to tolerate their children's hostility, and suppress all signs of it strongly. This may make for over-submissiveness — the fear of anger. Others set *no* limits to the child's impulses — something as disturbing to the child as the other extreme. Children are afraid of their more primitive impulses, especially if there are no guidelines to enable them to judge how far they can go.

Parents can do a lot, without expert help, in tracing sources of frustration, and alleviating them. Threats to self-esteem (for example, failure at school) can make a child 'hit back'. Or perhaps the child is himself the target of another child's aggression. He could be suffering from jealousy of a brother or sister, or there may be some other conflict that is frustrating him. Sometimes, however, the causes of extreme aggression may be too complex or obscure for parents to discover, and then it may be wise to get professional advice.

Remember that even temporary states (general tension, frustration, moodiness, emotional conflict) can affect learning and performance — in parents, as well as children. Symptoms of distress — an inability to meet others without feeling anxious or angry, a reluctance to go out of the house — may be preceded by a period of general tension and stress, as if such states prepare the ground for certain kinds of (maladaptive) learning to take place, as if they put us on a defensive footing, ready to react adversely to relatively minor provocations.

that jaundiced mood

The kind of tension commonly experienced by women during the few days prior to menstruation, make this time (potentially) an occasion of heightened irritability and vulnerability. It is a time to monitor one's handling of the children, as it may be brusque and inconsistent.

second nature — that the child will behave responsibly when there is no one to tell him what to do or check up on him. This does not happen overnight. His parents are the most significant people in his world; therefore he models himself on them and identifies with them. When they criticize his bad behaviour, he begins to criticize himself. Teachers, too, become very significant people in the lives of young children and *their* words carry great weight.

Children whose parents set firm limits for them, grow up with more self-esteem and confidence, than those who are allowed to get away with behaving in any way they like. It is important, however, to give the youngster some freedom of choice within reasonable limits. Naturally enough he is likely to complain and compare his lot with other children when the limits are set down and insisted on, but there is clear evidence to show that children realize their parents are firm *because they care.* They know, deep down, that they cannot cope alone. They need to know someone has charge of their lives so that they can learn about and experiment with life, from a safe base. Children who get their own way all the time interpret such *laissez-faire* permissiveness as indifference; they feel nothing they do is important enough for their parents to bother about. So, if you have to cope with tantrums, recriminations and sulks, grit your teeth, take heart and take the long view. Remain solid and secure; it may cost you a grey hair or two, but it will pay off in the long term.

set limits

Any limits set should be for the child's safety, well-being and development; do not make up rules for the sake of having rules. Keep them to essentials. It is crucial to ensure that the child knows exactly what they are and what is expected of him. Here is a checklist:

1 Are the rules simple?
2 Are the rules fair?
3 Does the child understand them?
4 Does the child know what will happen if he breaks them?
5 Are the rules applied fairly and consistently?

No one can advise parents as to the essential rules. Each family has different values, different interpretations of what is right and wrong. Your standards of behaviour will accord with those of your community or religion, as well as your own values, life-style and personality.

be consistent   When teaching your child to distinguish between appropriate and inappropriate actions, it is important to be consistent. It is confusing if she is punished for the way she behaves today and gets away with the same thing tomorrow, merely because your reasoning or mood has changed. Parents are indignant if asked whether they ever break a promise (say) to give their child a treat. Of course not! It would undermine the child's trust and debase the currency of their words. Yet they may be quite prepared to make idle threats. There is no point in telling a child 'You won't go out to play again if you keep running off', when the mother knows she has no choice but to let her play outside.

Parents often stand out against troublesome behaviour for some time, only to give in eventually. The child asks for a toy every time mother takes her shopping. She is told she cannot have it so she goes on pleading and whining. In the end her mother, exhausted and irritable, gives in for the sake of peace. The child has learned that if she makes a nuisance of herself for long enough she will be rewarded. No doubt she will try again, and the scenes will become longer and more arduous.

It pays (obviously not in the heat of the moment) to think your disciplinary strategies through to their logical conclusions: 'How does Sandy interpret the fact that I am unmovable about certain issues but tend to take the line of least resistance on other matters?' If you are inconsistent, you are, in a sense, only half-trying to get your child to behave in the way you desire; a clear, unchanging policy tells her about what is the right course of action. If you have been forced to resort to repetitious shouting, whining appeals and querulous nagging, your child can be said to have learned — learned to ignore what is being said. Eventually she pushes you to the point of exasperation where you are tempted to lash out at her.

The busy housewife may say that she has so little time to check on the child, that she cannot always follow through her threats to discipline her. But in the long run, the time wasted in nagging exceeds the initial

'Corporal punishment? That's the fifth floor, madam.'
© Reproduced by courtesy of *Punch*

investment in time and effort involved in training the child that mother means what she says. If you have your ground rules — that the child is spoken to once, and perhaps, because she is young, warned a second time, but that *then*, effective disciplinary action will *unfailingly* follow — you establish certainty in the child's mind about the significance of your words.

This guideline on consistency is *not* meant to be a recipe for rigidity or inflexibility. Situations change, children mature and flexible parents are able (*following discussion*) to adapt and modify their rules to meet new circumstances. It is one thing to be consistent in your insistence on important principles of conduct, it is another to be unbending in your response to every contingency (e.g. giving your child permission to stay up late occasionally; allowing her to go away on a camping expedition; admitting you've made a mistake and apologizing for it; letting her explode (just as you have to let off steam) now and then; and so on.

attend to 'good' behaviour

In some households, parents tend to ignore their child unless he is naughty and needs punishment. Always try to 'catch' him out in good behaviour; not only in bad behaviour. This is a worthwhile slogan for parents *and* teachers. His need for attention is often stronger than his fear of a scolding — and the scolding turns paradoxically into a type of 'reward'. So punishment will not necessarily stop undesirable behaviour; in some circumstances it may even increase it. The answer is to give the child adequate attention, but only in appropriate circumstances. (You will know if you are unwittingly rewarding an action when you thought you were punishing it; it will persist at its present level, or even become more frequent.)

explain discipline by giving reasons

Giving explanations is vital to a child's development. It facilitates learning if parents point out the effects of her behaviour, and give reasons for the restrictions or prohibitions they insist on. A child might be told off for being a 'dirty boy' without being told exactly what he has done or why it was wrong. Rather say: 'Don't pick up things from the gutter because they are dirty and might make you ill. Remember how nasty it was the last time you were sick?'

Nowadays, many parents tend not to demand absolute obedience all the time, and do not think they are demeaning themselves by giving reasons for 'dos' and 'don'ts'. In fact, many parents would regard the giving of explanations as a vital part of the exercise. ('I wouldn't automatically obey a regulation myself unless I thought there was a good reason for it. So why not try to explain why we have to have rules in a complicated world, and what would happen if everyone went their own way?') Children are more likely to internalize standards if they are justified in terms of their *intrinsic* value, rather than in terms of the punishments and odium that follow from their violation.

They do need to know! When small, they cannot comprehend unaided the reasons for training. Later on, when in a position to understand explanations, they may be sidetracked; worse still, there may be no possible meaning to the demands made upon them, because what is being asked is unreasonable. In the former category we might get the following exchange:

Parent: You mustn't do that!
Child: Why not?
Parent: Because you musn't.
Child: But why mustn't I?
Parent: Because it's wrong.
Child: But why is it wrong?
Parent: Because I say so! Now that's enough. Be quiet!

When children are expected to be seen and not heard, their parents suppress undesirable behaviour without paying attention to the needs and 'messages' that lie behind it. Children's communications are often in code. This is done unwittingly as they wish (as all of us do) to be understood. So we need to be empathic, looking at what they are saying with an ear tuned to the hidden messages. The child who shows off in front of strangers may really be communicating his uncertainty, even (paradoxically) his shyness. For parents, and professional people who work with children, it is vital to be able to communicate understanding. Haim Ginott is concerned that the *two-way* nature of good communication between adults should also form the basis of conversations with children. A dialogue with your child requires respect and skill. He advises you to listen carefully to what your child says. Messages should preserve his and your self-respect, and statements of understanding should precede statements of advice or instruction. Dr. Ginott says that in this way parents provide a mirror to their children's personality; they learn about their emotional likeness (as they get to know their physical likeness) by having their feelings reflected back to them. The child who comes home saying 'I hate school' learns that it is not *everything* about school that he dislikes when his mother says 'Poor old Peter, it's PE on Monday isn't it? Do you still feel a bit embarrassed changing in front of the others?'. Or when Tom says 'My teacher made me stay in today', you resist the temptation to answer: 'Now what have you done?' or 'I suppose you deserved it', both of which would have inflamed his feelings. Instead, you might acknowledge them by saying: 'You must have felt awful . . . would you like to tell me what happened?'

listen carefully to what your child says

Not all disciplinary abuses in the home are the severe deprivations or punishments that deform the lives of some children. Some arise simply from an insensitivity to the child's curiosity, his intelligence and his feelings. Often there is no intention to frustrate the child; the rejections — such as not listening to him, or fobbing him off with excuses that you are busy — are the consequences of *being* busy, perhaps with other chores, or being tired and irritable after a day's work.

Children have a knack of choosing the most inconvenient or embarrassing time for their Socratic dialogues. However, questioning is a legitimate and necessary part of their adaptation to life. Questioning is by way of being a bargain: 'You are asking me to give something up; well then, give me a good reason for doing so.' It is part of the vital learning process, especially for the development of a value system and conscience. It is not that parents occasionally, and doubtless understandably, have to switch off the unending stream of 'whys'. The point is that some parents do it habitually.

explain clearly Make sure that your child understands what is required of her — what she should do, not only what she can't do. Nagging means that the mother is not getting through to her child. Observe the typical scene of a mother nagging her son not to pinch his baby sister, or to wash his hands before sitting down to a meal. The mother's voice is strained, resigned, hectoring, shouting, or even hysterical with frustration; and it is like the sound of a record stuck in a groove, with the same repetitious, monotonous, senseless quality. The child may be answering 'Yes, mummy', or nodding his head, or more likely, not even bothering to answer at all. It is perfectly plain, from his unfocused look, that he is not paying attention to what is being said, and has no intention of carrying out the instructions given to him. He is 'habituated' to the message; it is simply 'noise' buzzing around in the background. What is being said does not convey an urgent communication which implies action of some sort or another. This nagging situation is the epitome of non-communication. It is words — sound and (perhaps) fury — but without meaning. The mother has not managed to convey to the child what she wants him to *do*, instead she has given him a list of dont's.

Another aspect is the actual issue involved. So often do the naggings concern trivialities, that the tension and unhappiness that permeate the mother—child or father—child relationship seem a high price to pay. So choose your priorities of obedience, and explain them in terms of appropriate actions. These you insist on — in a voice that is matter-of-fact, and calm, but firm and decisive.

Praise and encouragement make behaviour worthwhile, in other words, rewarding. Reward desirable behaviour, at reasonably frequent intervals, with praise and attention — and the child will want to repeat it. So if you want your young child to be kind, let her know how pleased you are when she shares her sweets or comforts a younger child who is crying.

use praise and encouragement

You reward *every* observed occasion of correct behaviour while a child is acquiring a new habit or a new skill, but only on odd occasions when the habit or skill has been mastered. Unfortunately, parents sometimes get themselves into a philosophical or technical muddle over rewards. Here is a typical dilemma: Clive's parents promised him a big present if he did well in his school exams, but he did not, even though he tried very hard. Should they still buy him that expensive remote-control car that he wanted so much? Here is an ethical question — a value judgement — and a technical issue. The ethical question is this: 'Is it appropriate, or merely invidious, to offer children rewards for passing exams? Whatever one's answer to that may be, there is also a technical problem which arises because the parents did not think through their aims and objectives; they promised to reward him for results rather than 'effort' when it was the latter they had meant to encourage. As it is a good rule to stick to their word, they might give him a modest consolation prize for *trying*. In future, they would do well to work out fairly precisely what their incentives are for — achievement or striving — and how the attainment of particular goals can be unambiguously agreed upon. A reward is not necessarily a present. You help a parcel-laden mother and child onto the bus, and her smile of gratitude and relief is highly rewarding.

What about the philosophical, or ethical, issue? Some parents are concerned that giving rewards for good behaviour is a form of bribery. 'Surely my child should do the right thing as a matter of course, simply because it is right?' But a *bribe* is actually a reward for some corrupt practice. An occasional treat or privilege for a child who has made a big effort to master a new skill or managed to give up a bad habit hardly comes into that category. We all like to award ourselves a little extra something if we give up smoking or lose half a stone, so why not the child? As adults, the idea of doing our duty is deeply entrenched, and we tend to forget that a child has to learn it the hard way.

Modest rewards can ease her path. Most of the time she will not need a tangible reward, like a trip to the park. A little praise, a word of thanks or a kiss will be enough. An extra incentive can be useful. If you want her to leave her friends and their absorbing game and follow you quietly around the supermarket, then the promise of an ice lolly makes for a reasonable bargain. It will only undermine your discipline strategy if you wait until she is lying on the floor, kicking and screaming and refusing to go to the shops, and *then* begin handing out ice lollies. That is how you encourage her to play up next time. Timing is of the essence! Remember grandma's rule: 'when you . . . then you . . . !' (chapter 3). The lolly is promised but the reward is only delivered *after* the child delivers up her side of the bargain — accompanying mum in a civilized fashion around the shop. 'When you've come shopping with me in a sensible way, then you'll have an ice lolly.' You should also bear in mind that a child's actions are influenced by much more than the particular *nature* of rewards and pay-offs. Do make sure that there is a clear connection: the child must understand the relationship between her own behaviour and the reward.

prepare your child for life by developing family routines

Most routines are useful short-cuts to living. For example, routines help a child to master and carry out automatically such daily tasks as feeding, washing, dressing, going to bed — thus helping her to achieve more with less effort.

Habit is taught by repetition of routine. A child feels secure if the main events of her day are as regular and familiar as the sunrise. If going to bed, eating and washing always happen in more or less the same way, she accepts them with little or no fuss. The morning ritual of preparation is a potent 'push' factor in getting a child off to school. The bedtime ritual is a particularly powerful habit; a regular routine of supper, bath and then a story before bed makes the child's world seem well-ordered, safe and comfortable. It is not trivializing to set up these routines. Psychologists and social workers who visit chaotic homes — strangers to certainty, regularity and routine — know how disturbing this is to young children, and not helpful to older ones who enter the relatively orderly life demanded at school.

The ultimate aim is to give your child the ability to discipline herself, to compromise between what she wants and what society demands of her. Once she can do this, her dealings with other people will be easier. It is easy to lose sight of the purpose of discipline. A disciple is one who learns from or voluntarily follows a leader. Probably everyone would agree that some discipline is necessary. The change in attitude of modern theorists concerns the questions of *how* to discipline, and the reasons for requiring obedience to certain rules.

teach the child to discipline herself

Everyone needs some self-discipline (rules of conduct) in order to adjust her needs and desires to those of others, and this is necessary (paradoxically) in order to be a free and happy person. The child *needs* the affection and approval of people around her; being self-centred and egotistical will not win this approval. Nowadays it is not rules for rules' sake, or obedience for its own sake. The change in the 'hows' of discipline has been most evident in the gradual erosion of absolutist, authoritarian and punitive methods of discipline.

16

How can I change my child?

When a new behaviour problem occurs, it is possible to work out a practical campaign to deal with it. The following steps provide a guide to action.

Step 1   Ask yourself, what *precisely* is it that he/she is doing wrong?

If your answer is woolly and vague (e.g. 'Tony is always disobedient'), it is impossible to plan your strategy and tactics to bring about change. If, however, your answer is specific (e.g. 'Sally has a temper tantrum when I insist that she obeys me, for example when I tell her to eat up her breakfast') then an effective procedure can be worked out.

Before you can change your child's behaviour you have to look at that behaviour very closely. Let's take temper tantrums as an example, and work through the remaining steps.

Step 2   Observe the tantrums carefully.

The undesirable behaviours you wish to change are called (in psychologists' jargon) 'target behaviours'. Remember the ABC of behaviour (chapter 3). The 'B' term stands for *behaviour*, and the 'B' is (in this instance) to do with temper tantrums. Temper tantrums are our target behaviours.

Step 3   Describe to yourself *precisely* what it is that you are going to observe.

Q. 'What is it your child *does* and *says* that makes you refer to his actions/words as a "temper tantrum"?'

A. 'He stamps his foot, clenches his fists, kicks the chairs, etc., he also screams and swears.'

Stamping, fist-clenching, kicking, screaming and swearing are — more precisely — our target behaviours.

Observe how frequently he loses his temper.   *Step 4*

Count the number of tantrums (defined by those actions you described) that he has per day, i.e. the number of episodes. (You could also time how long each episode lasts.)

Do this for three or four days.

What is the average per day? (Divide the total number of tantrums by the number of days observed)

Keep a brief diary record of each episode, with particular   *Step 5* emphasis on that ABC sequence.

A: What led up to the

B: tantrum?

C: What happened immediately afterwards?

Here is an example:

A: 'I was waiting my turn at the check-out counter at the supermarket. Wayne kept putting chocolates in the basket. I kept taking them out. He said, "I want a sweet!" I said, "No, love, you can have a biscuit when we get home." He said loudly, "Give me a bloody sweet!" I asked him not to make a fuss please.'

B: 'He began to scream and kick the counter; then he lay down on the floor blocking the counter so other people couldn't get to it.'

C: 'Everyone was looking at me and I felt so embarrassed I gave him a chocolate and said, "Wait till we get home . . . !" He quietened down immediately and began to eat it. I felt very angry, resentful and humiliated.'

Q. 'And then?'

A. 'I said no more at home, to keep the peace.'

Analyse your information, first the antecedents.   *Step 6*

Q. When you look at your diary after a few days, and your tally of tantrums, are they part of *a more general pattern*? (Are the As, the antecedents, rather similar?)'

A. 'Yes, they seem to form a pattern of defiance. They follow two lines; either Wayne commands me to do something. If I don't, he insists, and eventually has a tantrum. Or I ask Wayne to do something . . . He ignores me, or says "I won't!" If I insist he has a tantrum.'

Step 7   Find out how specific the tantrums are.
Q. 'When you look at your tally do the tantrums seem more *frequent*:

1   at certain times?
2   in certain places?
3   with certain people?
4   in particular situations?'

A. 'The answer in this case is *yes* to all those questions. They are most frequent in the morning and at night; in the bedroom, at dinner table; with me; when I try to dress him; get him to eat up his meal; or put away his toys.'

Step 8   Analyse the consequences.
For example: Have you slipped into the habit of simply repeating your commands parrot-like — over and over again — without really expecting any result? Do you always give way, perhaps because it's the easiest thing to do? (Anything for a quiet life!)
Q. 'Looking at your diary again, can you see any kind of pattern in the Cs, the consequences or outcomes, to these trying confrontations?'
A. 'Yes. Wayne usually gets his own way . . . not always, but nearly always. He *also* gets me going. I sometimes end up in tears. He *always* gets me into an argument and I have to devote a lot of time to the dispute.'

Step 9   Ask yourself: 'Who was I really observing?'
The answer inevitably will be *not only* your 'problematic' child. You are observing, as part of your analysis of As and Cs — in the ABC sequences — yourself *and* others. It is not possible to understand a child's behaviour without looking at the influence of other people on him, and his influence on them.

Step 10   Identify the reinforcers.
In this case, *you* (and others) have unwittingly reinforced (strengthened) the very behaviours (tantrums) that you wished to weaken, and reduce in frequency.

Reinforcer 1 = he gets his own way; reinforcer 2 = he riles you and enjoys getting a rise out of you; reinforcer 3 = he has monopolized your attention; even if it is scolding it is rewarding (after all the behaviour is as *persistent* as ever).

Be quite clear in your mind how he must change in order for the situation to improve. Also be specific.

Step 11

For example, 'I expect him to obey me when I make a reasonable request or command, so that if (say) I ask him to put his toys away he does so without endless arguments or fits of temper.')

Retrain your child.

Step 12

There are two general principles involved in putting right the unsatisfactory situation we have gradually disentangled and thus clarified. In retraining your child you will have to:

1 *weaken* the undesirable actions;
   2 *strengthen* a desirable action that is incompatible (i.e. competes) with, the undesirable one.

Your child tantrums too easily, so you will attempt to weaken tantruming while (at the same time) you strengthen a competing behaviour such as 'co-operating with mother'.

Choose your method (see Appendix I).

Step 13

Think of a desired alternative action — one that cannot be performed at the same time as the 'problem' behaviour. (He cannot help you pack your box at the supermarket and tantrum at the same time.)

Step 14

Remember to reinforce (words of praise, cuddles, a star for a star chart) the actions — and you may have to prompt him at first — that compete with tantruming, i.e. acts of compliance and co-operation. If he goes through the check-out counter without a tantrum praise his behaviour ('You're a big boy, behaving so well'). Give him a reward when he gets home (a symbolic one — a star on his chart) and a tangible one (a biscuit) *as* you leave the shop. Repeat your *reasons* for this acknowledgement. Gradually you should be able to phase out the tangible reinforcers when tantrums are no longer a major part of his repertoire.

Step 15   Make sure that *No* instance of his tantrums receives any
              reinforcement!

              In other words, you weaken the tantrums by not
              reinforcing (rewarding) them. This method is called
              'extinction': you extinguish the *behaviour*. You might
              ignore the tantrum, turn your back on it, or you might
              use what is called 'time-out' (TO). The technical term is
              'time-out from positive reinforcement'. When Wayne
              has a temper tantrum he is told that he will have to spend
              three minutes on his own (in the hall, a spare room, or
              simply at the far end of the same room, in isolation). If
              he ceases his temper tantrum, take him out of TO after
              three minutes; if he continues, give him another three
              minutes, and so on. Use a kitchen timer. (See figure 1.)

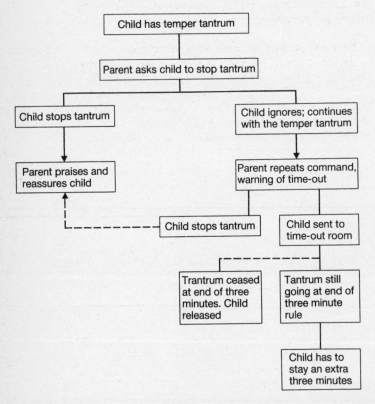

Figure 1   Dealing with temper tantrums

If you do decide to use TO, explain *once* why you are going to use it; give *one* warning only of the imminence of TO, each time he begins a tantrum. But having begun TO, use it on *every* occasion that he tantrums — unless he desists. *Do not scold or dispute on the way to, or during TO.* Be gentle, but matter of fact and very firm. *Never use a frightening place for time-out!* But do use a place that is unrewarding (unstimulating) like the hallway. The main thing is to be *consistent* and *persistent*; then you should get results.

Do persevere!   *Step 16*
    Some behaviours change only slowly. If you take the line of least resistance, 'giving-in' on the odd occasion ('just this once') you won't be back to square one; it will be square minus one! You will actually make things worse for yourself.

Check out whether you are getting anywhere.   *Step 17*
    Go on counting the tantrums. If you go on keeping a record, you can observe the changes taking place, gradually, day-by-day. Do not be discouraged if things get worse before they get better. If you remove the old reinforcers, the child may well work harder (escalate the screaming, say) to get them back.

17

This hurts me more than it hurts you . . .

What a hollow sound that statement has! However, it does highlight our mixed feelings about punishing children. But what *is* punishment? You know from experience that what is punishing for one child may not necessarily be punitive for another. A slap works wonders for Jill, but makes Andrew even worse. Psychologists have a conveniently circular definition of punishment: it is punishment when a behaviour is *weakened* by an unpleasant event which immediately follows it. Thus scoldings are punishments only if they produce a reduction in the behaviour they follow. They are rewarding if their net effect is to increase them. But parents and teachers are not so much interested in academic definitions of punishment as in guidelines or general principles concerning its effectiveness or adverse side-effects.

It is so often the case that it is the painful, extreme, and perhaps rare effects of punishment that are worried over in debates about punishment, while the smaller 'shocks' and 'pressures' that occur day in and day out, and which may ceaselessly, slowly and effectively change our habits, are ignored. What about the evidence?

effects of punishment It is almost certain that a child learns faster if he receives *both* positive and negative reinforcement. Negative reinforcers come in many guises and must not be equated always with *physical* punishment. Positive reinforcement tells a child what he may and should do. Negative reinforcement tells him what he may not and should not do — what he should desist from doing to avoid punishment. Thus he is more fully informed if he receives both types of reinforcement than if he receives only the one.

The effects of punishment (negative reinforcers such as blame, reproof, experience of failure, the word 'wrong' and the removal of positive reinforcers, but *not* physical punishment) on children, tends to improve learning and performance in various school tasks. Boys trained in this manner are more realistic, are neither uncontrolled or too constricted. There is no simple, clearcut relationship between negative reinforcement and performance. Among other factors found to be influential in determining outcomes are the youngster's intellectual and achievement level, the complexity of the task, delay of reinforcement, the nature of the instructions, the child's and experimenter's personality, and even the atmosphere in the home or classroom.

The fact that so many factors interact in a complex fashion, explains the inconsistent results of research on punishment. Now, in the 1980s, the view seems to be that, under certain conditions, penalties and sanctions may be extremely effective. But what parents and professional people really want to know is not whether punishment is effective in stamping out altogether (or suppressing temporarily) particular antisocial behaviours, but what it does to a child as a *person*. And the issue that arouses passionate debate is the one of physical punishment.

Drs Sears, Maccoby and Levin, quote a mother who was much below average in her use of physical punishment. She said:

physical punishment

> I don't spank my children. I can't recall really spanking them. I have had occasion where, when I have wanted — felt the urge — to strike, and oh, sometimes when I've seen her temper and Jill is stamping around, and I'll say, 'All right, upstairs you go.' And she doesn't go right away, I'll just give her a little motion on her rear and that's about all. But you wouldn't call that a spanking. That's well, it kind of lets my steam off a bit; it doesn't hurt, but she knows I mean business. And she doesn't recognize it through the pat on her bottom; she recognizes it in my tone.

Once again, the attitudes of people (including experts) are polarized. Some say that spanking a child is a policy of defeatism.

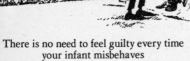

There is no need to feel guilty every time
your infant misbehaves

But do not base your disciplinary
methods on your own childhood
experiences

© Norman Thelwell *Brat Race*, 1977, published by Methuen, London.

We also get an old friend of mothers, Dr Benjamin
Spock, pointing out that in the olden days children were
spanked a good deal, and nobody thought much about it.
Then a reaction set in, and many parents decided that it
was shameful. But there were still problems. The trouble,
as Spock sees it, is that if any angry mother keeps herself
from spanking, she may show her irritation in other
ways, for instance, by nagging the child for half the day,
or trying to make him feel deeply guilty.

Spock hastens to add that he is not particularly
advocating spanking, but he thinks it is less poisonous
than lengthy disapproval, because it clears the air for
both parent and child. This is how he qualifies his
advice:

The right punishment is the one which seems right to
the parent and which works. It all depends on the
parent, on the child, and on the misbehaviour. A slap
on the hand or the behind works like a charm for one
parent—child combination. Another mother only feels
like a brute for hours afterward; and another child is
made furiously resentful by this indignity. A brief
isolation in his room sweetens up one child in five
minutes. Another child makes the family wretched
with his crying for the better part of an hour. Fines

and withdrawal of privileges are more appropriate for the school-aged child, and when they are fair and not run into the ground they even appeal to his sense of justice. In another case, though, they lose all moral value and lead only to bookkeeping and arguing.

So there is no system of punishment that is neat or that will work the same in any two families or that will function automatically. Punishment *alone* has never made a bad character into a good, or even insured temporary good behaviour. Good discipline is mainly based on mutual love and respect. In childhood it has to be reinforced with teaching, firmness, reminders. Punishment is only one form of reminder, a particularly vigorous one for emergencies — usually with strong feelings involved — to get a child back into the groove.

'Spanking', of course, is a euphemism. It is meant to denote a less-than-brutal form of hitting, a carefully measured and controlled response to provocation. It doesn't sound quite so *physical* as a beating or a hiding. And certainly the smacks administered by most human mothers have the 'short, sharp, shock' quality to be seen in the warnings (nips and cuffs) offered by mothers of many animal species to their offspring. They constitute a mild form of aversive conditioning.

Sadly, there are parents who make regular use of extreme force and it is displayed in many forms. Yet, if there is one principle that has been established by scientific investigation, time and again, it is that *physical* punishment — and this amounts to violence in some cases — is the least effective method when it comes to *moulding a child's behaviour.* All the evidence to date — and there is a considerable body of it by now, shows that physical methods of punishment, against a background of parental hostility and rejection, lead to hostility and delinquency in many of the children on the receiving end.

If you hit/punish the child regularly/excessively: **cautions!**

1 You are teaching him to fear and dislike you. Any   *for parents* stimulus associated with punishment tends to become aversive itself.

2 You are building up his arbitrary obedience instead of his understanding and acceptance of ethical standards.

3 You are offering a bad example for him to imitate.

4 You are using less skill and ingenuity than any other technique.

5 You may actually worsen rather than eliminate your child's misbehaviour.

6 You merely change behaviour not motivation (e.g. desire).

7 You teach him to escape and avoid punishment in ways that are not particularly desirable (e.g. by lying, making facile promises, etc.).

for teachers If you punish with regularity, the child comes to associate you with the punishment and may:

1 try to avoid your class. He may think of excuses not to come to school or dawdle in the corridors.

2 He may avoid your presence because the 'atmosphere' you create is threatening.

3 Similarly, he may try to escape when you are around. If you come into the room, he soon leaves.

4 The youngster may show great fear or anxiety in your class. When you ask him a question, he clams up, yet he is a chatterbox with everyone else.

intensity and timing Mild punishment leads to only mild reactions. More severe measures (harsh criticism, hidings) can have consequences that are more devastating than the misdemeanour that the child committed in the first place. Such outcomes can be almost impossible to reverse, therefore only use punishment with caution, and certainly in moderation.

Try not to get into the habit of warning the children that they will have father to face when he gets home, if they do not behave. This is unwise because children do not always understand (especially when young) those sanctions that are far removed in time from the misdemeanour. Not only is such punishment ineffective but it is unfair for the father, in his absence, to be associated with an 'aversive stimulus', that is to say, a threat. Homecoming should be a happy relaxed time, not a time of apprehension and dread of an 'avenging' father, who, for his part, has to adopt an angry and punitive attitude. I am not suggesting that the father should opt out of the disciplinary role, but that parents discuss when and how he can most effectively play his part.

Punishment (the type involving the deliberate infliction of pain on the child) may, for the time being, suppress the behaviour that it is meant to inhibit, but the long-term effects are less impressive. Delinquents have more commonly been the victims of adult assaults — often of a vicious, persistent and even calculated nature — than non-delinquents. Boys who have been caned at school for smoking are more likely to increase their smoking than those not caned.

long-term problems

Dr Sears and his colleagues, are quite clear about this aspect of their research. They say:

> Punitiveness, in contrast with rewardingness, was a quite ineffectual quality for a mother to inject into her child training. The evidence for this conclusion is overwhelming. The unhappy effects of punishment have run like a dismal thread through our findings. Mothers who punished toilet accidents severely ended up with bed-wetting children. Mothers who punished dependency to get rid of it had more dependent children than mothers who did not punish. Mothers who punished aggressive behaviour severely had more aggressive children than mothers who punished lightly. They also had more depressed children. High physical punishment was associated with high childhood aggressiveness and with the development of feeding problems. Our evaluation of punishment is that *it is ineffectual over the long term as a technique for eliminating the kind of behaviour toward which it is directed.*

This particular area of child-rearing is one in which it is only too easy to pontificate from the ivory tower — introducing idealistic values and utopian solutions which the busy mother with several young children must find somewhat ironic. Nevertheless, the trouble with smacking is that it *is* too easy — and therefore it is habit-forming. It does not require much thought, and in the very short term it works. A smack terminates the child's yelling for a few blessed minutes, thus bringing relief to the harassed mother; this reinforces the likelihood that she will smack the child again in similar circumstances. It can become, only too easily, a way of life.

failure of communication?

I have often heard mothers say, as this one did:

> I can see the point of not smacking too often or too severely; and I can see that it certainly isn't constructive. And this rational attitude is fine as an ideal. But sometimes my child will go on and on being impossible. Doing something that is not only naughty but dangerous. Distracting him doesn't work; talking to him nicely doesn't work and, in the end, only a slap on the leg cuts through all the tension and nagging. Sometimes I even get the feeling that he's deliberately working up to a smack; almost testing me out, pushing me to the limit!

How does one answer this sort of parent — more often than not a conscientious and loving mother who is deeply concerned about doing the 'right' thing? What is the cost if she is driven occasionally to lash out with a smack? What one can say is that it is very doubtful whether the occasional smack meted out against a background of a loving, accepting home, does anyone much harm. But this is true only if the punishment is not too severe or overpowering, and if alternative actions are available to the child as substitutes for the punished acts.

Perhaps smacking should be regarded as a last resort and even then as something of a failure in communication between parent and child. Children who are able to understand explanations and who enjoy a relationship of trust and affection with their parents usually listen to firm demands and prohibitions from them — especially if they know why they are necessary.

alternatives to punishment

When a child is doing something which is a 'punishable offence', suggest an acceptable alternative action to him — so that he can avoid punishment. To illustrate: 'Clive, you know you're not allowed to paint on the sitting room carpet. Take the paints through to the kitchen, and you can paint your picture on the table there.'

In this example the parent has specified:

1   the conditions (the kitchen table as a workplace);
2   the action (leaving the sitting room carpet);
3   the reinforcer (permission to go on painting).

Try to recommend actions that compete, or are incompatible with, the behaviour you find reprehensible. For example, children cannot race around the sitting room, endangering ornaments, *and* play a game of Monopoly at the same time.

Ignoring — as we have seen — can be very effective when children are behaving in a disruptive way simply to get attention. There is a problem with this guideline. Some children do not get sufficient parental attention even when they are behaving well. They soon learn that the best way to get mother's attention is to be a pest. Never mind if the attention looks 'negative' to the adult; scolding and nagging and irritated distractings may be 'nectar' to the youngster who feels he does not get enough of his mother's attention. It is rather like the case of the actress who said: 'Rather bad publicity than no publicity at all.' For some children it is better to get a scolding than have no attention at all.

18

Sex and sex education

When parents or teachers complain that a child has a sexual problem, what they usually mean is that *they* have difficulties dealing with a child who is indulging in sex play or masturbation; they are most likely to be the 'problems' of sexual curiosity and ignorance. Children's sexual curiosity and experiments take many forms and include (although it may shock some people to read this) heterosexual, homosexual, transvestite (cross-dressing), voyeuristic, exhibitionistic and masturbatory experiences. Whether these normal (i.e. commonplace, although sometimes secret) manifestations of interest become matters of concern depends largely on parental attitudes and the way parents handle the child's curiosity.

Sex has a far wider meaning and function than is popularly attributed to it. Those who deny that the infant has any sex life commonly do so because they are only conscious of adult sex experience, and consequently imagine, when it is suggested that the infant or very small child is affected by sexual feelings, that this must necessarily be a comparable experience to that of the adult. Aspects of childhood sexual behaviour which we shall look at are sexual curiosity and masturbation, sex education and sexual identity.

The sex drive does not appear fully fledged, as if by magic, at adolescence. There will probably be some parents who will object to the suggestion that children have any sexual interest or sex life at all. To believe this is to shut one's eyes and ears to what they do and say as they grow up. It was commonly believed in the last century, that children were sexually neutral until the time of the maturing of the sex glands at adolescence. In fact, from early on, youngsters enjoy exposing their bodies and looking at others' bodies.

sex play

Sex play with other children often takes the form of undressing or exploring the friend's body while playing 'doctors', or 'mummies and daddies'; it is quite common by the age of four. In a survey of heterosexual play in boys, it was found that the incidence rises from nearly 5 per cent at five years to a third of the boys at eight years. As many as two-thirds had indulged in sex play by the age of thirteen. The amount of sexual activity is lower in girls than in boys, but also shows an increase with age. In these immature youngsters, sexual interest and behaviour are intermittent and casual, in fact rather unintense. Homosexual play — sex play between children of the same sex — also rises in incidence as youngsters get older. It usually takes the form of children handling each other's genitals. This occurs in 30 per cent of thirteen-year-old boys, and the figures for girls are comparable. Homosexual activities are much more common in boys' and girls' boarding schools than in day schools, but there is no convincing evidence that this transient phase of homosexual activity has any bearing on *long-term* adult homosexuality. What can be said is that the child's setting and the presence or absence of opportunities for heterosexual contacts, influence the manifestation of homosexual activities.

What conclusions can be drawn about sexual experimentation in pre-adolescent children? It seems clear that we cannot suppress children's sexual interests and explorations, even if we should wish to do so. The adults who reported their sexual behaviour in the Kinsey studies were brought up in a far less sexually permissive atmosphere than exists today; it was a period when the deeds they recalled were likely to be severely punished. However, repression of their childhood sexuality was singularly unsuccessful in its aim. Fifty per cent of the men and women had sexual contacts with peers before adolescence. It has been argued that the only effect of extreme efforts at suppression is to drive the behaviour underground and to permeate it with a sense of shame and an aura of furtive excitement. For a girl, the harsh suppression of her sexuality during childhood and adolescence is one of the main contributory causes of frigidity in adulthood.

masturbation   Almost all children masturbate at some time; fortunately, despite old wives' tales it does *not* adversely affect the mental or physical development of the child (either in the present or in the future!). If mothers worry excessively, apart from causing *themselves* harm, they may *create* a problem for the child where there need not have been one.

Most industrialized and monotheistic cultures train children not to masturbate. It seems to be a training which almost universally breaks down at adolescence and even before then, particularly in the case of boys. Late in the first year of life, it is possible to observe the infant's increasing awareness of his own body. Inevitably he discovers his 'private parts' and the pleasure associated with playing with them. Pre-school children — during the two- to five-year-old phase — show increasing interest in their genitals. Masturbatory activities occur in more than 55 per cent of boys and 16 per cent of girls. About 80 per cent of boys masturbate by their thirteenth year.

There is considerable emotional reaction to masturbation from mothers. Although most modern mothers have heard, read, or personally experienced the fact that masturbation is harmless, they feel anxious when their children do it. Fewer than one-fifth of mothers interviewed felt that a certain amount of playing was to be expected; while one half considered it wrong or harmful. Some said masturbation might not do anything if it happened just once, but that all the same, they would not like it to happen. Interestingly, they did not back up their strong opinions with strong action, since 45 per cent of them only used mild or indeed, no pressure against masturbation, and only 5 per cent used severe pressure against such behaviour.

For the very young child, a major function of masturbation (like thumbsucking) at bedtime seems to be that of closing off contact with the outside world so that sleep can ensue. *Elaborate* measures to curb infantile masturbation are inappropriate. The desirable course seems to be to give the young child a reasonable amount of freedom to find out about his body, without unintentionally giving masturbation more importance than it deserves.

Like most behavioural patterns — even innocuous

ones — masturbation, if carried to an extreme, becomes a problem — or is symptomatic of an already existing problem. Many children who are deprived, unhappy and poorly-adjusted, masturbate excessively as a source of solace and compensation. It is the compulsive element which is a sign that all is not well with the child's emotional or social development.

What children do about their sexual relationships as they approach sexual maturity will depend upon their education about sex during the years of childhood. And this means education not only about the 'facts of life' but about sexual morality, the obligations human beings have to one another, and ideals and values such as respect, responsibility and love. It is important to remember, in connection with the 'who, what and when' of sex education, that the religious and moral aspects of sex — the sexual value system — vary from home to home.

sex education

For example, our own society's somewhat ambiguous demand for chastity before marriage is by no means universal. A survey of 158 societies showed that 70 per cent of them permit premarital intercourse. Schofield points out that most of the youngsters he questioned disapproved of extra-marital relations, whether or not they were sexually experienced. Despite the social pressures (teenagers want to be like other teenagers) towards sexual intercourse, many teenagers resist these influences.

Where sexual development is concerned, it is only really possible to offer guidelines, and these, in their turn, must be interpreted flexibly.

There is no sexual discrimination when it comes to dealing with general questions, so it seems illogical to have sexual matters discussed only by mother ('ask your mum') or dad ('no, dad's the expert'). As it takes two to make love, the combination of mother and father on these matters would seem to make sense.

who should tell?

The questions about sex which are darted at sometimes harassed parents are likely to be searching ones. Some are metaphysical and have no answer, others are so

telling the truth

complex that Einstein (or Kinsey) would be hard put to provide an answer. It is probably best to admit that there is no answer, or that you do not have one. *Where* you can (and *when* you can) show your child how answers can be obtained from other people or from books ('Let's look at your encyclopaedia'). Most parents give reasonable and truthful answers to the questions a child asks about the world around him — so why teach him lies and distortions about sex?

how not to tell   Whenever you betray confusion or shame over your child's question, you are conveying more to her by the form of your answer (the faltering speech, euphemisms and circumlocutions) than by the content of what you say (i.e. that there is something odd and sinister about sex). Try to avoid being facetious, punitive, hasty or (more difficult) embarrassed. The accuracy with which children perceive the subtle nuances and hidden meanings which are conveyed by adult naivety and awkwardness is impressive. The child who provokes no special attention by saying the words 'leg' or 'arm' notices that the same audience focuses the spotlight on her when she talks about sexual organs — and that she provokes winks and nudges.

Sadly, there is a tendency to abandon simple language and a temptation to become verbose when talking to children about sex. There is also an undesirable tendency to be sentimental. If the child discovers that you can speak *freely*, she becomes less fearful of her curiosity and can vent her thoughts and feelings.

setting an example   However excellent the teaching about sex — formal and informal — at home and at school, the most important aspect of sex education (in its broadest aspect) is the example set for children in the parents' lives. Through the kind of family life they live, youngsters can learn that love and sex are based on respect for other human beings — a respect they can feel only if they first have it for themselves.

when to tell   Sex education starts in intangible ways almost at the beginning of a child's life. The parent is providing sex education simply by being there. Psychologists claim that it is *not* what parents *say* so much as what they *do* that educates the young child in the home. It is at two or three, when the child is talking, and is active enough to take an interest in his own body and the bodies of people around him, that he generally begins to ask specific questions. If parents are too early, the best efforts are wasted, and if they are too late, they risk making themselves faintly ridiculous. As the humorist, James Thurber says in a piece entitled 'What should children tell their parents?', parents hesitate to discuss things calmly and intelligently with their children for two reasons: either they feel a kind of dread of learning something they do not want to know, or, if they must learn anything at all, they would like to be spared the humiliation of learning it from their offspring.

It has been said that when a child asks about intercourse or reproduction, *that* is the time to answer him. But what if the child never asks questions? Behaviour, as well as questions, may indicate whether a child has some curiosity bottled up inside him. It is probably unwise to 'wait him out'. A marriage, a pregnancy or a birth in the family or neighbourhood are all quite natural events which you can raise casually as starting points for a talk.

how much shall I say?

While there is no reason why children's sex questions cannot be answered frankly, the answers need not be a whole course in physiology, sexology or obstetrics. They can be brief, phrased in a sentence or two. But can parents do any harm by saying too much? Children, especially those from reasonably happy and secure homes, are much more robust than is sometimes imagined! Putting things clumsily, saying too much, and so on, are unlikely to have more than, at most, a transitory 'ripple' effect.

The issue of what language to use — vernacular or technical — does not seem overwhelmingly important compared with the development of a healthy attitude to what the words stand for. Do what *you* feel comfortable with.

sexual knowledge

The questions children ask are many, and frequently searching. Here are some examples: 'What is that?'; 'Why doesn't a girl have a penis?'; 'Where does a baby come from?'; 'Where does a baby come out?'; 'Why can't men have babies?'; 'Will I have a baby too?'; 'How does a baby get inside the mother?'; 'When do you and Daddy make babies?'; and countless others. At a later stage, there are other questions which preoccupy teenagers, as shown by the questions asked at sex education meetings: 'Should teenagers go steady?'; 'Should teenagers make love?'; 'How far should one go?'; 'What about contraception for teenagers?'; 'What is a perversion?'; 'Is it wrong to masturbate?'; 'What are venereal diseases?'; 'What is a homosexual?'

The nature of these questions highlights one of the fundamental difficulties of sex education — particularly in schools where the audience is composed of children from different home backgrounds, whose religious, ethical and moral training may differ quite considerably. Some questions can be answered 'scientifically', as matters of biological information. Others involve moral and personal values. Should a teacher (or for that matter a parent) go further and explain not only the biological elements of sex but also the whole complex of love life? Sexuality, after all, is so much part of life as a whole that nothing short of a consistent set of values — indeed a philosophy of life — enables us to formulate principles about sex life as part of this whole. While books, films, special talks and experienced lecturers can be very helpful in the sex education process, only you who know your child very well are able to answer the supplementary questions that are almost always asked (sometimes much later and only after information has been digested). Only you can fit the biological facts into the chosen system of values.

It is in the early teenage years of adolescence that the parents' role in sex education is perhaps most vital. Parental knowledge of the physical and psychological problems of this phase of life can help to give them tolerance and compassionate insight into what (if their own memories of this time are still fresh) they will recognize to be a difficult period of adjustment. Sex education at school can be particularly helpful at this stage because so many children feel too shy and awkward to approach their parents about sexual problems and anxieties. And the anxieties may be quite bizarre, but intensely felt for all their unreasonableness. Even in these supposedly enlightened times, there are girls who think they may become pregnant because a boy had a heavy petting session with them, and boys who think they will harm themselves because they masturbate.

How do differences between the sexes — biological and psychological — arise? Gender is imposed on each individual from the moment when fertilization takes place, when a particular combination of maternal and paternal chromosomes determines the genetic sex of the embryo. Although the issue of physical gender has been decided at conception, it takes several weeks of embryonic life before the first slight signs of sexual differentiation are manifested. The embryo grows without showing any sexual characteristics until the *primordia* of the sex glands (the gonads) show themselves as masculine or feminine. In human embryos, the rudimentary testes and ovaries can be distinguished by microscopic examination at the sixth week of life. The first sexual differences appear in males, and interestingly, the male form derives from the more basic female form — rather than the other way round.

influences on sexual behaviour

Sexual patterns of behaviour — such as identification with a particular gender, sexual arousal and stimulation, choices of partner and styles of sexual gratification — are very complex. Genetic, anatomical, hormonal, environmental, cultural and social factors all play a part in determining them. The precise importance of these factors, relative to each other, is still arguable.

gender identity

The evidence suggests that, from the psychological point of view, the newborn human is not, in any essential sense, sexually differentiated. Gender identity and sexual role are acquired during childhood. From as early as the second year of life, the child begins to distinguish between 'masculine' and 'feminine'. By the age of four, he has divided the world into male and female people and is preoccupied with boy—girl distinctions. Preference for one sex role or the other also begins to emerge early in life, probably by the third year.

By the age of seven, a child is passionately committed to shaping his or her behaviour to the cultural mould of what is 'appropriate' to his or her biological sex. The child manifests anxiety, and even anger, when accused of acting in ways regarded as characteristic of the opposite

sex. Once the standards of 'sex-role behaviour' are
learned, they are not easily altered. Intense conflicts are
generated because of anxieties about deviation from sex-
role standards or 'ideals'. These standards are learned so
well and so early — in other words, they are so deeply
implanted — that they seem eventually to arise from
fundamental biological differences between the sexes.
'Seem' is the operative word. Are the sexes *really* different
in temperament, in a fundamental 'inborn' sense?

Children usually accept the gender in which they are
reared during the first years of life, even where there is
some ambiguity in their anatomy, such as abnormal
external genitalia or true hermaphroditism. Although
biological factors have some influence, it is the gender
identity *assigned* to the child by the parents which is
crucial. The die is cast, pretty well, by the age of six,
after which major realignment of the sex role and sense
of gender identity is very difficult, but not impossible.

19

All the king's horses and
all the king's men . . .

Like Humpty Dumpty, many marriages have a great fall and can not be put together again. In fact so many marriages will falter or fail irreparably, that nearly one-quarter of the babies born in the UK today, are likely to experience a separation of their parents before they reach school-leaving age. People tend to assume that children from broken homes are at a disadvantage in life, and will suffer inevitably from emotional or behavioural problems.

This assumption indicates an awareness of the suffering of the child and that divorce is interpreted by many youngsters as a rejection or desertion of themselves. They cannot comprehend all the adult implications of an unhappy marriage. On the other hand, the assumption of unfavourable consequences of divorce does not allow for the many children who overcome their grief and the disruption of their most intimate relationships and grow up to be normal, contented members of the community.

divorce and after

If all divorces, all broken homes, led to serious psychological difficulties, society would indeed have an appalling problem on its hands. The highest risk or likelihood of a divorce (at present) occurs in the fourth year of marriage. In other words, it is very likely to be *young* children who are involved in the lead-up to, and aftermath of a divorce. Separation — the event that really hits children — is likely to precede divorce by several years.

You may have read that children hold themselves responsible for the break-up of their parents' marriage and feel very guilty about this. In fact such reactions do not seem to be very widespread; much more common is anger towards the parents for separating. Children of all

The Quarrel
Copr. © 1932, 1960 James Thurber. *The Seal in the Bedroom*, published by Harper & Row.

ages frequently express the wish that their parents be re-united, and they blame either, or both of them, for the split; most children do not want their parents to separate and they may feel that their father and mother have not taken *their* interests into account.

A marital separation may result in children reappraising their own relationships with their parents and, indeed questioning the nature of all social relationships. For younger children in particular, there is the painful realization that not all social relationships last forever. If mum and dad can end their marriage, what is safe? Couldn't the same thing happen to their own relationship with either parent? Many childish reactions at such a time are expressions of their fear of being abandoned by one or both parents, and such fears are likely to be most acute if contact has been lost with a parent. If, however, relationships between parents and child can remain intact and supportive, these fears are usually short-lived.

the first shock waves   Pre-school children usually appear to be very sad and frightened when their parents separate, and they become very clinging and demanding. Bedtime fears and a refusal to be left alone, even for a few minutes, are not uncommon. Children attending school or nursery may become very anxious about going there, and may protest strongly when left. Vivid fantasies about abandonment, death of parents, or injury are encountered, and they often express aggression towards other children, and quarrel with brothers and sisters.

With somewhat older children, grief and sadness remain a prominent feature but anger becomes more marked. This is usually directed at the parents, especially the one with whom the child is living — which more often than not means the mother. ('Is there no justice?', she must sometimes ask herself.) Regardless of the actual events leading to the breakdown, she is likely to be blamed by the child for everything that has happened. The absent father is quite likely to be idealized (again, regardless of realities) while the mother is held responsible for driving him away. Children, especially in the age group seven to eight may express very strong yearnings for their father.

Pre-adolescent children tend to demonstrate less of their inner hurt and distress, which is not to say that it does not exist. Covering up is common and they seek distractions in play and other activities, in the way that an adult might seek solace in alcohol or frenetic busyness. It may be difficult to get through to such children; they are loath to talk about what they are feeling because of the pain and embarrassment it causes them. Underneath this apparent detachment is anger; again, they may align themselves very strongly with one parent and even refuse to see the other. Adolescents sometimes show overt depression; they appear to 'opt out' of family life and withdraw into other relationships outside the home. Worries about their own relationships, sex and marriage may surface.

These are the immediate reactions to parental separation. Usually they are seen in an acute form for a matter of months and then (hopefully) begin to subside. Unfortunately, the evidence concerning long-term consequences is very meagre and difficult to evaluate.

One of the questions of concern to parents is the effect of divorce on the child's mental health, later on when adult. Researchers have found that those people who experience

the fall-out

a broken home in childhood have only a slightly higher risk of developing psychiatric problems compared with those from unbroken homes. For those from a comfortable economic background, there is no difference at all in the risk factor. Indeed, children from broken homes may fare better than youngsters from *unhappy*, unbroken homes!

These findings, however, do not allow us to be at all complacent. The relatively reassuring information about the effects of broken homes on psychiatric illness in later life is not repeated in the area of delinquency. Here, the influences are more malign, given certain aggravating circumstances. Delinquency is associated with the break-up of homes where there has been a great deal of parental *disharmony*; the association is not with the disruption of the home, as such. The loss of a parent through a marital separation is much more likely to cause long-term problems than a loss through death. This may be because of the unpleasant events that often precede the break-up or because the child experiences a feeling of betrayal, of some intentional abandonment.

What we do not yet know for certain, is whether the long-term ill-effects are reduced if a child remains in contact with both parents after a break. But indirect evidence indicates that this condition may be important. Among the longer-term problems that have been associated with divorce and separation are depression, low self-esteem, problems in heterosexual relations (especially in girls), difficulties on assuming parenthood, and an increased likelihood of divorce in the youngster's own marriage to come. There are many question marks over the precise significance and extent of these effects but we can be sure that if at all present, the differences between children from a background of divorce and those with no such background, are small. Much depends on influences like the quality of relationship with each parent, and how these change after the separation.

An atmosphere of strife and turmoil in the home — prior to separation — seems to be one of the most corrosive influences. This quarrelling is something that children describe as very damaging — especially episodes of hostility between mother and father. Some divorces are characterized by much sound and fury, not to mention violence. Children who witness fights between the two people they love, are exposed to unresolvable conflicts of loyalty and sheer desolation. They may be forced to take sides. They all too frequently become the battlegrounds for marital warfare and are a tempting target for mutual recriminations about such things as neglect, favouritism or 'bad blood'.

Being powerless, children are ideal scapegoats at a time when the parents feel miserable and frustrated. As the offspring of the disliked (possibly hated) spouse, the child reflects qualities which are annoying in the marriage partner. This brand of unreason arises from the tensions and hostility of an unhappy marriage; the pressure on adults who have to live in close proximity, despite their incompatibility, makes them do and say spiteful and vicious things which they would not permit themselves under normal circumstances.

The number of mothers and fathers bringing up their children in single parent households (for many reasons other than divorce) is on the increase. The problems they face are somewhat similar whether they are separated, divorced, widowed or unmarried: finding enough energy and hours in the day to cope with a thousand and one chores. The lack of emotional support, the occasional morale booster can be sorely missed when one bears the responsibility all alone for rearing children. There is a rather special apprehension for many divorced parents, especially mothers: what harm, they wonder, will come of the traumatic experiences the children have lived through? Will the difficulty of rearing boys unaided be too much for me?

the one left behind

The generalities about the consequences of broken homes do not take into account the individual's suffering. Whatever the long-term statistical trends, we are still left with the intense and immediate (even if temporary) grief, confusion and apprehension affecting many children in the period leading up to and following the divorce. And the parent left behind has to cope with it. Fathers may feel they lack the intuitive touch — the understanding and sensitivity of women; mothers tend to worry over disciplinary problems, especially when the children's upset finds an 'acting out' aggressive outlet.

The adverse effect on the child of a very poor marriage has been found to be dramatically ameliorated if the child has a *good relationship* with at least one of the parents. Economic factors are vitally important. Poverty puts a mother under great strain. A prolonged period of difficulty leading up to the finality of divorce may leave the mother feeling depressed, and mentally and physically drained.

There is a close association between fatherlessness and poverty, and many of the unfavourable consequences of deprivation of a father, are primarily the consequences of poverty. Financial strain may exhaust the last emotional reserves of the mother left alone. For women in this predicament, housing is particularly difficult to find. Children under five years of age need special care and close attention. However, if the mother is short of money, she may be forced to seek employment, without finding satisfactory substitute care; and this sometimes leads to inadequate protection and supervision of the child. Mothers often lose their social life, as well as their emotional and physical support when deprived of their husbands. Given all these factors, it is scarcely surprising that some women question their resourcefulness and adequacy to cope with all the responsibilities of rearing children alone.

Single parent families carry the risk of being somewhat claustrophobic, especially if the parent — out of sheer desolation — clings to the child and makes too many emotional demands of her ('Kim is like a sister; she goes everywhere with me') or him ('Peter is the man of the house now; I have him to lean on'). The continual attempt to compensate the child for her loss ('I feel so guilty, I must make it up to her') is unusually misguided, frequently leads to spoiling and thus a self-centred unappealing youngster.

As so many families have only one parent, it is just as well that children brought up by one adult can be as psychologically 'healthy' as those reared in the more common pattern. Nevertheless mothers are particularly worried about the problem of being mother *and* 'father' to the child. For example, they sometimes get concerned, in the case of a boy, about the normal development of his masculinity.

To reassure mothers, it should be emphasized that a boy will not be effeminate simply because he grows up

'I'm disturbed because I come from a two-parent family.'
© David Austin *Private Eye*

without a man about the house. If he lacks a model of his
own sex within the home he has many in the family
(uncles), the school (teachers), and in the outside world
(peers), to learn from.

All this may sound somewhat academic to those parents
who are teetering on the edge of the abyss of a breakup,
but (quite rightly) considering the best interests of their
children. It *is* so often a 'messy' and miserable outcome
whichever way you choose — staying together or parting.
You cannot escape, by rationalization, the fact that
separation will inflict pain on the children. Every child
would prefer to go on living with two happy parents.
However, if you cannot find a peaceful and viable way of
living together, you are doing your child no service by
staying together for *their* sake. If the sad and often
tawdry aspects of divorce can be mitigated by sensitive
handling from parents who put the children's interests
before their own, the youngsters will at least know that

**for those on
the edge of
the abyss**

mother and father care about what happens to them. You may like to know what children say about divorce; their comments help define their best interests.

Yvette Walczak's study is of great interest here, because, unlike most researchers, she has looked at divorce through the eyes of 100 people (adults and children) who had been at the receiving end. She found that of the factors that were significant to a benign outcome for children — after all the misery of a divorce — three were of the utmost significance:

1   communication about separation;
2   continued good relationship with at least one parent
3   satisfaction with custody and access arrangements.

Children who considered themselves most damaged were:

1   those whose parents were not able to talk to them about divorce (apart from blaming their ex-spouse);
2   those who did not get on well with at least one parent after separation;
3   those who were dissatisfied with custody and access arrangements — whatever these happened to be.

Most children would have liked two happily married parents, but most preferred to live with a single parent than two unhappily married ones.

parenting after marriage ends

Yvette Walczak also sees a need for a change of public attitude and legislation. The roles of mother and wife, and father and husband, are no longer always linked in reality. Parenting *after* the marriage ends, needs to receive as much recognition and attention as parenting *within* marriage has so far received. In marriage both parents are recognized as legal custodians of their children. Following divorce (with few exceptions) one parent is deprived of custody and legal rights. Although successive Acts of Parliament have referred to the welfare of the child as being of paramount importance in divorce, the courts have often paid lip service to this principle, endorsing existing arrangements, conducting superficial enquiries, paying much attention to material circumstances and little to relationships. Yvette Walczak would like to see joint custody being the rule, and custody to one parent an exception, with — whenever possible —

the parents discussing, agreeing and submitting joint proposals of arrangements for their children's future.

The good sense of such an endeavour is illustrated in her thumbnail sketch of Tony, a twenty-year-old salesman. He describes himself as over-anxious: 'I keep looking over my shoulder, making sure there is no one behind me.' He traces this feeling of anxiety to his parents' separation when he was twelve. He did not anticipate his parents' divorce and little was said at the time. Tony has been exposed to his mother's anxiety and over-protectiveness, previously counter-balanced by his father's easy-going disposition. Since his father's departure, Tony had felt that his mother, the house and everything in it had become his responsibility. He resented his mother's boyfriends and hated being alone in the house when she went out in the evenings. He missed his father and felt he did not see him often enough. The first two years following separation were thoroughly depressing. He was dissatisfied with the amount of communication he received concerning the divorce, and also with the access arrangements.

softening the blow

For some children, the disruption may be minimized by parents who somehow arrange that they are protected from the more unpleasant features of the deteriorating marriage. Can they therefore arrange for contact with the departing parent to be frequent, free of the jealousy and competition for affection which beset so many post-divorce arrangements?

In the period both preceding and following a divorce, such factors as the integrity of the child's personality, the resourcefulness of the parent he remains with, the presence of fond grandparents or brothers and sisters who absorb some of the shock, all influence the outcome of the child's tragedy.

A long drawn-out 'trial' period of reconciliation, breakdown, re-reconciliation and further separation, in which the child's hopes rise and fall, rise again and finally are dashed, causes more harm than a decisive resolution of conflict after quiet, private and careful consideration of their marriage by the parents. They may find it helpful to consult a neutral but understanding person — a marriage guidance counsellor, or minister. The trouble with friends as peacemakers is their

reluctance (or too great a willingness) to take sides —
either of which is unacceptable to one of the partners.
Following a decision to separate, the children should be
informed as soon as possible, so there is no risk of them
hearing the news from someone else.

If you do not know how to break the news, there are
some useful books available with suggestions about
answers to awkward questions, and on how to say the
'unsayable' about the breakup of a family. It may be
helpful (but small comfort) to know most families go
through a transition period of two or three years before
they settle down to their new way of life. Wise parents
might adopt the philosophical attitude that although
they have failed as husband and wife to make a success of
their marriage, they can at least try (for the sake of their
children — after all they do *remain* parents) to make a
success of their divorce.

step-parents   When a child's parent remarries — and they usually do
— there may be problems of adjustment. The difficulties
of being a step-child are legendary; so are the problems
of being a step-parent in the growing number of
reconstituted families. Research studies have confirmed
these 'legends'. There is an increased risk of psychological
problems in persons whose parents remarry — especially
where it is the parent of the same sex as the child who
finds a new spouse. These findings are statistical, and
reflect a slightly increased risk only. There are, of course,
many instances of step-parents who have brought great
happiness and solace to the children they adopt. The
friction, jealousy and ambivalence which are a common
feature of step-child—step-parent relationships can be
overcome (as can most psychological problems) with
thoughtful and empathetic handling. This means trying
to see things from the child's point of view — the most
imaginative thing a parent can do. For example, if the
step-child lets herself go, and calls her step-father 'daddy'
and shows him affection, might she not lose the love of
her real father because of her disloyalty? If she *does*
accept the new situation, is she not admitting finally that
her parents are not going to change their minds and have
a reconciliation? These are some of the dilemmas the
child faces, and the step-parent herself (or himself) is not
immune from conflict. To what extent should I try to be

a mother when Carol still has a mother? Am I as the step-father permitted to discipline the child? Again, books have been written by 'insiders' suggesting means of dealing with such issues.

More devastating than the fear and jealousy aroused by remarriage, may be the fear of abandonment felt by a child whose parents allow a succession of romantic attachments to take priority over their relationship with their child.

I have discussed the breakdown of marriage and its effects on children. Childhood security may be shattered temporarily by the death of a loved parent or relative. The trauma can be mitigated for the child, by sensitive caring and explanations. The quality of the relationships — the continuity and reassurance of loving care — matters more than the disruption of bonds as such. Indeed, long-term problems are less associated with the decease of a parent (despite the finality of the break in an emotional attachment) than it is with divorce where attachments may still be retained. There is sometimes what is called a sleeper effect, in which adverse consequences — sometimes depression — appears after the passage of time. Where ill effects do occur, they are more likely if the mother dies when the child is very young; the father's death is more likely to have adverse effects if it occurs when the child is older.

death and bereavement

Children are extraordinarily good at accepting the sad facts of life and getting on with living. A simple, straightforward explanation of the death (say) of a grandparent is usually sufficient, particularly if given in a calm manner. Tell your child that Gran will be remembered by all of you, and in that way will remain with the family. Opinions differ as to whether a child should attend the funeral. There is probably no simple answer to that question. A child who is too young, or too imaginative, may be appalled by the disappearing coffin.

Questions about death, illness and separation are quite likely to issue from the inquiring minds of three- and four-year-olds. 'Are you going to die, Mummy?' 'Where do you go when you die?' Do not fob your child off with lies and circumlocutions. It will not help to ask her to wait for an answer until she is older. Answer as fully as you can (admitting it when you have no answers) at a level your child will understand. Whether or not you say that Gran is in heaven will depend upon your religious convictions.

Epilogue

I ended chapter 4 by suggesting that parents should not be discouraged by their 'mistakes', or by the set-backs and trauma that beset all children (admittedly some more than others) as they grow up. What might be called 'normal' problems — the type which occur so commonly in connection with development — have a high probability of diminishing and disappearing as the child gets older. Even children who were referred to child and family guidance clinics with emotional problems (fears, phobias, social inhibitions and the like) are indistinguishable from other people in terms of their mental health — as adults.

The more enduring traits — those that continue into adult life — become manifest from about six to ten years old. The degree of continuity of behaviours seems to depend upon whether the behaviours are in accord with society's values and norms. If they are, they tend to persist; if not, they slowly change. Even in the case of the exception to the generalization that *most* childhood behaviour problems are transient, namely children with *extreme* antisocial, aggressive tendencies, they may get better if professional help is obtained.

One of the lessons for parents is that it is within their grasp (with or without professional help) to assist their children in their attempts to adapt to the inevitable vicissitudes of life. Children are learners and parents are their teachers; resourceful, imaginative teachers can help the youngster with the step-by-step mastery of developmental tasks essential to his or her long-term well-being.

Infants are born in an incomplete and dependent state into a complicated and sometimes capricious world. What impresses me after many years of having the privilege of working with children, is their essentially robust quality and their remarkable capacity (in most cases) to find a viable and satisfying life-style.

Appendix I
Behavioural methods

strengthening
new
behaviour
patterns
positive
reinforcement

In order to improve or increase your child's performance of certain actions, arrange matters so that an immediate reward follows the correct performance of the desired behaviour. You might indicate your intentions by saying — for example — '*when* you have put your toys away, *then* you can go out.' The 'when . . . then' formula reminds you that you only reward after the desired action is carried out. When the child has learned a behaviour it is no longer necessary to give rewards regularly. Remember that words of praise and encouragement at such a stage can be very reinforcing.

developing
new
behaviour
patterns
encouragement

Secure your child's co-operation by guiding and helping him towards some desirable action or way of thought. Use a combination of suggestion, appreciation of his difficulties, praise for his efforts and pleasure at his success.

shaping
(successive
approxima-
tions)

In order to encourage your child to act in a way in which he has seldom or never before behaved, reward approximations to the correct action. You take your child through mini-steps towards a goal by rewarding any action that approximates the behaviour you want. You continue to reinforce the approximations to the behaviour you wish to elicit. No reinforcement is given to 'wrong' behaviours. Gradually you make your standards (criteria) of your child's approximations to the correct response more and more stringent until, in the end, he is only rewarded for the precise behavioural sequence that is required.

In order to teach your child a new pattern of behaviour, give him the opportunity to observe a person who is significant to him performing the desired behaviour.

modelling

Simulate real-life situations in which skills are to be developed. During rehearsal:

skills training (e.g. behaviour rehearsal)

1 Demonstrate the skill.
2 Ask your child to practise the skill. (Use role play. Provide a model if necessary.)
3 Provide feedback as to the accuracy/inaccuracy of his performance. (If possible, it is advantageous for the youngster — and video equipment is most useful here — to evaluate the effectiveness of his own performance.)
4 Give homework assignments, e.g. real-life planned practice of skills. Not only does behaviour rehearsal provide for acquiring new skills but it also allows their practice at a controlled pace and in a safe environment, and in this way minimizes distress.

In order to train your child to act at a specific time, arrange for him to receive a cue for the correct performance just before the action is expected, rather than after he has performed incorrectly.

cueing

In order to teach your child to act in a particular manner under one set of circumstances but not another, train him to identify the cues that differentiate between the appropriate and inappropriate circumstances. Reward him only when his action is appropriate to the cue (e.g. he is praised for crossing the pedestrian crossing when the signal is given).

discrimination

In order to encourage your child to continue performing an established pattern of behaviour with few or no rewards, decrease the frequency with which the correct behaviour is rewarded — gradually and intermittently.

maintaining new behaviour
intermittent reinforcement

To get your child to desist from acting in a particular way, allow him to (or make him) continue performing the undesired act until he tires of it. Of course this would not be appropriate if the act was dangerous or

stopping inappropriate behaviour
satiation

seriously antisocial. (If he tears up your curtains give
him bundles of newspapers to tear up *ad nauseam.*)
Psychologists have asked older children to 'practise' a tic
energetically for five minutes several times a day. This
makes a child more aware of his bad habit and helps him
to inhibit it.

extinction To stop your child from acting in a particular way,
arrange conditions so that he receives no rewards
following the undesired acts. Ignore (in other words,
pretend not to notice) minor misdemeanours such as
whining, pestering, tantrums. If a child grabs toys or
other goodies from his small brother, try to ensure that
grabbing has no rewarding outcome. Return the toy to
its owner. (You could combine the training that grabbing
is unproductive, with the teaching of *sharing* in the little
one, and saying 'please'/waiting patiently in the older
son. Encourage them to take turns.)

Withhold reinforcements such as approval, attention,
and the like, which have previously and inappropriately
followed inappropriate behaviour. *Remember: your child
may 'work hard' to regain the lost reinforcement and
thus may get 'worse' before he gets 'better'.* If the problem
behaviour has been continuously reinforced in the past
then extinction should be relatively swift; after all it is
much easier for the youngster to recognize that he has
lost reinforcers than it is for the child on intermittent
reinforcement. In the latter case, extinction tends to be
slow. *Planned ignoring* — for behaviours such as temper
tantrums and whining — includes:

1 as soon as the misbehaviour begins turn away or walk
   away from your child;
2 say nothing and try not to show any expression at all;
3 resist getting into any debate, argument or discussion
   with your child while he is misbehaving;
4 if you think he deserves an explanation for whatever
   is upsetting him then say to him 'when you have
   calmed down we will talk about it.'

time-out This procedure is intended to reduce the frequency of an
undesirable behaviour by ensuring that it is followed by a
reduction in the opportunity to acquire reinforcement,

or rewards. In practice one can distinguish three forms
of time-out:

1 *Activity time-out* where your child is simply barred
   from joining in an enjoyable activity, but still allowed
   to observe it — for example, having misbehaved he is
   made to sit out of a game.
2 *Room time-out* where he is removed from an
   enjoyable activity, not allowed to observe this, but
   not totally isolated — for example standing outside a
   classroom having misbehaved.
3 *Seclusion time-out* where he is socially isolated in a
   situation from which he cannot voluntarily escape.

Time-out sometimes leads to tantrums or rebellious
behaviour such as crying, screaming, and physical
assaults, particularly if the child has to be taken by force
to a quiet room. With older, physically resistive children
the method may simply not be feasible. So the procedure
and its choice requires careful consideration.

When the behaviour to be eliminated is an extraordinarily compelling one that all but *demands* attention
(reinforcement) from those present, or when time-out is
difficult to administer because the child is strong and
protesting, an equivalent of time-out may be instituted
by removing the sources of reinforcement from him. So
if the mother is a major source of reinforcement she
could remove herself, together with a magazine, to the
bathroom, locking herself in when her child's temper-
tantrums erupt — coming out only when all is quiet.

The child is warned in advance about those of his
behaviours that are considered inappropriate and the
consequences that will follow from them. Time-out may
last from three to five minutes.

In practice 'activity' or 'room' time-out should always
be preferred before any form of 'seclusion' time-out.

Time-out is a familiar procedure to the teacher; it has   *time-out in*
probably been used by most teachers at one time or   *the classroom*
another. Teachers have long used the procedure of
placing a child at the side of the room, at the back of a
room, or, in days gone by, on a dunce's chair. There is
disagreement as to how far it is effective in changing

unacceptable behaviour. It does have the advantage of providing both the teacher and the pupil with a breathing space in which tempers can cool, thus avoiding the use of harsher methods of control. Time-out has a number of counterproductive effects for the child. He is in the limelight, possibly acting the buffoon and therefore still the centre of attention. Or he is getting out of doing some unwelcome scholastic task or away from a sarcastic, frightening teacher. If this is the case the teacher should have a hard look at his teaching and/or his interactions with this child.

Behaviour modification techniques such as time-out, which are designed to eliminate inappropriate or undesirable behaviour, are unlikely to succeed unless supplemented by the reinforcement of an alternative and more appropriate behaviour pattern.

A critical determinant of the effectiveness of time-out is the extent to which the child actually enjoys the situation from which he/she is removed. If that situation is positively frightening, anxiety-provoking or boring, it is possible that the time-out procedure might involve removing the child to a less aversive situation and thereby actually *increase* rather than decrease, the frequency of the inappropriate behaviour.

overcorrection (restitutional overcorrection) Require your child to correct the consequences of his misbehaviour. Not only must he remedy the situation he has caused, but also 'over-correct' it to an improved or better-than-normal state. In other words, you enforce the performance of a new behaviour in the situation where you want it to become routine.

overcorrection (positive practice) Get the child to practise positive behaviours which are physically incompatible with the inappropriate behaviour. For instance:

1 A child who steals and breaks another youngster's penknife is required to save up enough money not only to replace the knife, but also to buy a small gift betokening regret. He is praised at the completion of the act of restitution. A boy who deliberately punctures another child's bicycle tyre not only has to repair the tyre but also must oil and polish the entire vehicle.

2   A child who indulges in self-stimulatory behaviour is required to do something which is physically incompatible with the action (e.g. walking, to counter rocking). Of course, alternative sources of stimulation would have to be sought.

Positively reinforce a particular class of behaviour which is inconsistent with, or which cannot be performed at the same time as, the undesired act. In other words, to stop a child from acting in a particular way, deliberately reinforce a competing action.

positive reinforcement (promotion of alternative behaviour)

Incentives are considered artificial if the rewarding events would not normally occur as a consequence of the behaviour outside the training or treatment situation (e.g. being given stars for getting dressed). They are considered 'natural' if the rewarding events used to strengthen the behaviour during training or treatment closely resemble what would normally occur as a consequence of that behaviour outside the training situation (e.g. being complimented for being well dressed). Therefore, 'natural' as opposed to 'artificial' incentives, would normally result in more permanent training effects.

'artificial' versus 'natural' incentives

To stop your child from acting in a particular way, arrange for her to terminate a *mildly* unpleasant situation immediately by changing her behaviour in the desired direction. (For example, every time she throws her toys in a dangerous manner the offending toy is locked away in a box for a week. She can avert this by heeding your warning.) This penalty system is called 'response cost'.

negative reinforcement

This procedure achieves a reduction in the frequency of an undesirable response by ensuring that its occurrence results in the removal of things which the youngster is known to value. In practice it usually involves removing rewards or incentives according to a predetermined 'tariff' of fines or sanctions, after the occurrence of an inappropriate behaviour.

response cost, or fining

For example: Peter is always pulling items off the supermarket shelf when he goes shopping with his mum. Prior to entering the supermarket she explains to him that he is not to touch items on the shelves, and he is to hold on to the shopping trolley with one hand, and in the other hand, he can carry around a bar of chocolate. Every time he touches an item on the shelves the chocolate bar has a piece removed. Note: it is necessary to get a child to repeat the instructions to check that he has understood them. At home, a jar of marbles (each one representing a unit of pocket money) can provide a visible reminder of the 'cost' of reprehensible behaviour. Add in some extra marbles so your child can earn a bonus by desisting from (say) offensive remarks. It is important to be precise about what the penalty is for, namely that one marble is removed each time he is rude. No arbitrary changes in the penalty system should be introduced!

Appendix II
Sources of help

In modern Western societies the state has considerable rights in the health and education of children. The school constitutes the most important environment for the child outside the family. Here is an environment of critical importance in helping families to meet children's needs and to shape their thinking and personalities.

The primary aim of the Schools Psychological Service — which is often linked with Child and Family Guidance Centres — is to offer professional support that will promote the social, emotional and intellectual development and educational progress of children in school and elsewhere and help to ensure that they receive learning opportunities appropriate to their individual needs. Children's problems arise from the interaction of a particular child and his setting — home, school and community. In helping to resolve these problems, educational psychologists in the service draw on insights from social and community psychology and skills in consultation and psychological intervention. A knowledge of child development, together with assessment skills, is of central importance and forms the clinical foundation on which a broader contribution is based.

the Schools Psychological Service

The traditional treatment of problem behaviour takes place in a clinic or a hospital. Parents bring the child to the professional (a psychiatrist, psychologist or social worker) who works primarily with the child as the client with 'target' problems to be modified. The setting for the therapy is the consulting room and the expert 'treats' the child. Although the parents and teachers are sometimes advised (say) to be more consistent, warm, loving or

the clinic

understanding, they are often left to their own devices to translate such instructions into action. As a result, many do not know specifically how they should change their handling of the child.

Professionals are turning increasingly to more practical family-orientated methods of intervention such as behaviour modification and family therapy.

behaviour modification in the natural environment

Behaviour modification (see Appendix I) is not only about changing the undesirable behaviour of 'problem children' but also about altering the behaviour of the persons — parents, teachers and others — who form a significant part of the child's social world. Help is directed to the modification of that environment rather than withdrawing the child from it. The parents become the real agents of change, thus contributing to the problem of extending positive changes over time.

family therapy

There is no space to describe in detail the approach called 'family therapy'. However, family therapy is not so much a school or system of therapy as a basic redefinition of the therapeutic task itself. The target for assessment and intervention is far broader than the child himself. Whereas the conventional treatment model tends to identify the 'nominated client' (the child) as the unit of attention, diagnostic thinking has since been considerably influenced by systems theory. Family therapists attempt to conceptualize the problem in a more horizontal (rather than vertical—historical) manner, viewing the client as part of a complex network of interrelating social systems, any aspect of which may have a bearing on the present predicament and which may indeed provide the clue to the 'real' problem — often formulated in terms of unsatisfactory patterns of dominance, blurred roles, poor communication and ineffective decision-making.

the psychologist, psychiatrist and social worker

Very often people ask, 'What is the difference between a psychiatrist and a clinical psychologist?' The essential differences are ones of training and orientation. The would-be psychiatrist completes a medical degree and then goes on to specialize in the study and treatment of mental illnesses. But the student who wishes to embark on the career of clinical psychologist takes an honours or master's degree in academic psychology in a university department before (like the psychiatrist) continuing his training in a hospital or clinic. After obtaining his degree in clinical psychology, he will often aim at obtaining a PhD in psychology.

The clinical psychologist, then, is a non-medical specialist in certain phases of human nature; but because human nature, the mind and body, cannot be rigidly compartmentalized, much of his training, knowledge and day-to-day work overlaps with that of the psychiatrist and other specialists in human problems.

The psychiatrist is a qualified doctor who specializes in his field of psychiatry in the same way that other medical men specialize in surgery, obstetrics or paediatrics. He does his training at a mental hospital or in a teaching hospital for psychiatrists. In most child psychiatric clinics and child guidance clinics, the psychiatrist is one of a team which co-operates on diagnosis, and on the planning of a therapeutic programme for the patient. The team (depending on its setting) may include a psychiatrist, clinical psychologist or educational psychologist (in the case of child guidance clinics), psychiatric nurses, a speech therapist, an occupational therapist and a psychiatric social worker.

The psychiatric social worker obtains a qualification in social work. The student gains experience and specialist training in child guidance clinics and psychiatric hospitals. She will apply her knowledge of the social sciences to the problems of the adult or child with emotional problems — problems which inevitably have social repercussions and very probably, social causes. As part of the team approach she will make home visits, and sometimes school visits, and will interview people important in the child's social milieu. Apart from collecting information, she will give advice and counselling in the hope of modifying attitudes which are contributing to the child's problems. The social worker might be involved in sorting out practical social problems. She may be contacting agencies for the care of children who are without their mother, arranging for financial support of a wife who is at home looking after the children, or arranging for home help, or a child minder.

Further reading

The following works may be of interest to those who wish to pursue the subject of child care and child development, especially in an academic or professional context. The asterisk denotes those more suitable for parents.

Achenbach, T. M. *Developmental Psychopathology,* John Wiley, Chichester, 1982. An excellent source book of references and information on the problems of childhood put into a context of normal development.

*Barber, D. *One Parent Families.* Teach Yourself Books, Hodder & Stoughton, London, 1978. An anthology of experience — conveyed in personal accounts by parents and children — of life in one-parent families (covers bereavement, lone mothers, lone fathers, decisions, politics and other themes).

Beech, J. R. *Learning to Read.* Croom Helm, London, 1985. This book describes a cognitive approach to reading and poor reading.

Damon, W. *Social and Personality Development.* Norton, London, 1983. An innovative introduction to the social world of the child.

Herbert, M. *Emotional Problems of Development in Children.* Academic Press, London, 1974. The problems which most commonly beset children at certain ages and stages are discussed within a framework of normal development. The reader's attention is drawn to the child's stage of cognitive, moral, ego and social development at particular ages, and the developmental tasks and crises with which he/she has to cope.

Herbert, M. *Behavioural Treatment of Problem Children: A Practice Manual.* Academic Press, London, 1981. A 'how-to-do-it' manual (with many caveats) for the helping professions. Illustrated with flow charts and case studies.

*Hinton, J. *Dying.* Penguin Books, Harmondsworth, 1967. A helpful book for dealing with a fraught subject.

*Maddox, Brenda. *Step-Parenting: How to live with other people's children.* Unwin Paperbacks, London, 1980. 'Reconstituted' families are on the increase. Here is a step-parent describing the rights, duties, myths, dilemmas and joys of step-parenting.

*Miles, T. R. *Understanding Dyslexia.* Teach Yourself Books, Hodder & Stoughton, London, 1977. Describes how dyslexic children are recognized and what provisions exist for helping them.

*Newson, E., and Hipgrave, T. *Getting Through to Your Handicapped Child.* Cambridge University Press, Cambridge, 1982. Written for parents and professionals — down-to-earth and practical. Contains a useful bibliography.

Rapoport, R., Rapoport, R. N. and Strelitz, Z. *Fathers, Mothers and Others.* Routledge & Kegan Paul, London, 1977. A comprehensive review of the role, tasks and needs of parents through history and in modern times.

Review of Child Development Research. Russell Sage Foundation, New York, 1964 onwards. An invaluable storehouse of research data on children — normal and abnormal — in a series of volumes.

*Rutter, M. *Helping Troubled Children.* Penguin, Harmondsworth, 1975. A highly readable, simple (but not simplistic) account of the problems of childhood; it includes case histories illustrating diagnosis and treatment.

Rutter, M. and Hersov, L. *Child Psychiatry: Modern Approaches.* Blackwell, Oxford, 1977. A compendium of psychiatric approaches to childhood disorder.

Source material: references

Ainsworth, M. D., et al. *Patterns of Attachment.* Erlbaum, Hillsdale, New Jersey, 1978.

Aries, P. *Centuries of Childhood.* Penguin, Harmondsworth, 1973.

Aronfreed, J. *Conduct and Conscience.* Academic Press, London, 1968.

Baer, D. M. 'Laboratory control of thumbsucking', *Journal of Experimental Analysis of Behaviour,* 5, 525—8, 1962.

Bandura, A. *Aggression: A Social Learning Analysis,* Prentice-Hall, Englewood Cliffs, New Jersey, 1973.

Baumrind, D. Current patterns of parental authority, *Developmental Psychology Monograph,* 4, (1), part 2, 1—103.

Bell, R. and Harper, L. *Child Effects on Adults,* Lawrence Erlbaum, Hillsdale, New Jersey, 1977.

Bowlby, J. *Attachment and Loss,* Vols 1, 2, Penguin Books, Harmondsworth, 1980.

Brackbill, Y. 'Extinction of the smiling response in infants as a function of reinforcement', *Child Development,* 19, 115—24, 1958.

Brockington, I. F. and Kumar, R. (eds) *Motherhood and Mental Illness,* Academic Press, London, 1982.

Bronfenbrenner, U. *Two Worlds of Childhood.* Russell Sage Foundation, New York, 1970.

Brown, G. W. and Harris, T. *Social Origins of Depression: A Study of Psychiatric Disorder in Women.* Tavistock Publications, London, 1978.

Brown, H. and Corcoran, D. W. J. 'Child Socialisation'. In *Socialisation,* The Open University Press, Milton Keynes, 1971.

Bruner, J., et al. (eds) *Play: Its Role in Development & Evolution.* Basic Books, New York, 1976.

Burns, R. R. *The Self Concept.* Longmans, London, 1979.

Chess, S. Editorial in *American Journal of Orthopsychiatry,* 1964.

Clarke, A. D. B. 'Problems of assessing the later effects of early experience', in E. Miller (ed.), *Foundations of Child Psychiatry,* Pergamon Press, Oxford, 1968.

Clyne, M. B. *Absent.* Tavistock Publications, London, 1966.

Erikson, E. H. *Childhood and Society.* Penguin Books, Harmondsworth, 1965 (revised edn).

Ginott, H. *Between Parent and Child.* Staples Press, London, 1969.

Hartshorne, H. and May, M. A. *Studies in the Nature of Character,* Vols 1–3, Macmillan, New York, 1928, 1929, 1930.

Hawkins, R. P., Peterson, R. F., Schweid, E. and Bijou, S. W. 'Behaviour therapy in the home: amelioration of problem parent—child relations with the parent in a therapeutic role', *Journal of Experimental Child Psychology,* 4, 99–107, 1966.

Heinicke, C. and Westheimer, L. *Brief Separations.* Longman, London, 1966.

Herbert, M. *Conduct Disorders of Childhood & Adolescence.* Wiley, Chichester, 1978.

Hersov, L. A. 'Persistent non-attendance at school'/'Refusal to go to school'. *Journal of Child Psychology & Psychiatry,* 1, 130–6, 137–45, 1960.

Hewston, M. (ed.) *Attribution Therapy.* Blackwell, Oxford, 1983.

Hoffman, L. and Nye, F. E. (eds) *Working Mothers.* Jossey-Bass, New York, 1974.

Hoffman, M. L. 'Moral Development', in P. H. Mussen (ed.), *Carmichael's Manual of Child Psychology,* Vol. II, John Wiley, London, 1970 (3rd edn).

Hutt, C. *Males and Females.* Penguin, Harmondsworth, 1972.

James, W. *The Varieties of Religious Experience.* Longmans Green, London, 1952.

Jersild, A. T. and Holmes, F. B., 'Methods of overcoming children's fears', *Journal of Psychology,* 1, 75–104, 1938.

Kanner, L. *Child Psychiatry.* Charles Thomas, Springfield, Illinois, 1953 (2nd edn).

Levy, D. M. *Maternal Overprotection.* Columbia University Press, New York, 1943.

MacFarlane, J. W., Allen, L. and Honzik, M. P. *A Developmental Study of the Behaviour Problems of Normal Children Between Twenty-one Months and Fourteen Years.* University of California Press, Berkeley, 1954.

McClelland, D. C. *The Achievement Motive.* Appleton-Century-Crofts, New York, 1953.

Marshall, H. H. 'The effects of punishment on children: a review of the literature', *Journal of Genetic Psychology,* 106, 23–33, 1965.

Mayle, P. *Divorce: What Shall We Tell the Children?* W. H. Allen, London, 1979.

Money, J. 'Psychosexual differentiation', in J. Money (ed.), *Sex Research: New Developments.* Holt, Rinehart & Winston, London, 1965.

Moore, T. 'Difficulties of the ordinary child in adjusting to primary school', *Journal of Child Psychology & Psychiatry,* 7, 299, 1966.

Mussen, P. H. *The Psychological Development of the Child.* Prentice-Hall, Englewood Cliffs, New Jersey, 1963.

Mussen, P. H., Conger, J. J. and Kagan, J. *Child Development and Personality.* Harper & Row, New York, 1979.

Newson, J. and Newson, E. *Patterns of Infant Care in an Urban Community.* Penguin Books, Harmondsworth, 1965.

Newson, J. and Newson, E. *Four Years Old in an Urban Community.* Penguin, Harmondsworth, 1970.

O'Leary, K. D. 'Skills or pills for hyperactive children', *Journal of Applied Behaviour Analysis,* 13, 191—204, 1980.

Parke, R. D. and Walters, R. H. 'Some factors influencing the efficacy of punishment training for inducing response inhibition', *Society for Research into Child Development Monograph No. 109,* 1967.

Patterson, G. *Families: Application of Social Learning to Family Life.* Research Press Co., Champaign, Illinois, 1971.

Pavlov, I. P. *Conditioned Reflexes.* G. V. Anrep (trans, and ed.), Oxford University Press, London, 1927.

Piaget, J. *The Development of Thought, Equilibration of Cognitive Structures.* Viking Press, New York, 1977.

Rogers, C. R. 'Towards a modern approach to values: the valuing process in the mature person', *Journal of Abnormal and Social Psychology,* 68, 160—7, 1964.

Rutter, M. 'Normal psychosexual development', *Journal of Child Psychology & Psychiatry,* 11, 259—83, 1971.

Rutter, M. *Maternal Deprivation Reassessed.* Penguin, Harmondsworth, 1972.

Rutter, M., Maughn, B., Mortimere, P., Ouston, J. and Smith, A. *Fifteen Thousand Hours: Secondary Schools and their Effects on Children.* Harvard University Press, Cambridge, Mass, 1979.

Schaefer, E. S. 'A circumplex model for maternal behaviour', *Journal of Abnormal & Social Psychology,* 59, 226—35, 1959.

Schaffer, H. R. *The Growth of Sociability.* Penguin, Harmondsworth, 1971.

Schofield, M. *The Sexual Behaviour of Young People.* Longman, London, 1965.

Sears, R. R., Maccoby, E. E. and Levin, H. *Patterns of Child Rearing.* Harper & Row, London, 1957.

Seligman, M. E. P. *Helplessness: On Depression, Development and Death.* Freeman, San Francisco, 1975.

Sluckin, W., Herbert, M. and Sluckin, A. *Maternal Bonding.* Blackwell, Oxford, 1983.

Spock, B. *Problems of Parents.* Crest Books, New York, 1962.

Stendler, C. 'Sixty years of child training practices: revolution in the nursery', *Journal of Paediatrics,* 36, 122—34, 1950.

Stone, J. and Church, J. *Childhood and Adolescence.* Random House, New York, 1968.

Stuart, R. B. (ed.). *Violent Behaviour: Social Learning Approaches to Prediction, Management and Treatment.* Brunner Mazel, New York, 1981.

Sutton, Carol, *Managing Difficult Children.* Centre for Behavioural Work with Families (unpublished booklets), 1984.

Sutton Smith, B. and Rosenberg, B. *The Sibling.* Holt, Rinehart & Winston, London, 1970.

Thomas, A., Chess, S. and Birch, H. G. *Temperament and Behaviour Disorders in Children.* University of London Press, London, 1968.

Tweedie, J. Article in the *Guardian,* 30 Oct. 1972.

Wahler, R. G., Winkel, G. H., Peterson, R. F. and Morrison, D. G. 'Mothers as behaviour therapists for their own children', *Behaviour Research & Therapy,* 3, 113—24, 1965.

Walczak, Y. 'Divorce, the kid's stories', *Social Work Today,* 18 June 1984, pp. 12—13.

Watson, J. B. and Rayner, R. 'Conditioned emotional reactions', *Journal of Experimental Psychology,* 3, 1—4, 1920.

Wetzel, R. 'Use of behavioural techniques in a case of compulsive stealing', *Journal of Consulting Psychology,* 30, 367—74, 1966.

Wolfenstein, M. 'The emergence of fun morality', *Journal of Social Issues,* 7, 15—25, 1951.

Wright, D. *The Psychology of Moral Behaviour.* Penguin, Harmondsworth, 1971.

Yule, M. and Carr, J. *Behaviour Modification for the Mentally Handicapped.* Croom Helm, London, 1980.

Index